The Date Palm And Its Cultivation In The Punjab

D. Milne

THE DATE PALM

AND

ITS CULTIVATION IN THE PUNJAB

BY

D. MILNE

Economic Botanist, Punjab,
Lyallpur

PUBLISHED FOR

THE PUNJAB GOVERNMENT
1918

Price, Rs. 5.

CALCUTTA :

PRINTED BY THACKER, SPINK AND CO.

Curing dates on mats in the sun at Multan in 1915.

FRONTISPIECE.

CHAPTER VI.

DISEASES OF THE DATE PALM.

CHAPTER VII.

IMPORTS AND EXPORTS OF DATE FRUITS AND PROSPECTS OF DATE FARMING IN THE PUNJAB PLAINS.

APPENDIX.

PREFACE TO THE SECOND EDITION.

THIS note was originally written as a circular letter to meet the large number of questions which were showered on me in connection with the scheme of date improvement started some years ago in the Punjab. It was therefore only intended for my staff and a few people who were so kindly assisting the Agricultural Department in carrying out the work in connection with the date scheme. It has now been considerably extended and the circulation has become much wider : I therefore wish to say that in addition to drawing on my own knowledge gained in Egypt and in India I have, when writing this pamphlet, made free use of W. T. Swingle's Bulletin No. 53, Department of Agriculture of the United States of America, Dr. Bonavia's book " The Date Palm in India," and other works. I have also to thank Mr. Gaskin, Assistant for Commerce and Trade, Baghdad, and other friends, for their kindness in giving me information. My most grateful thanks are due to Agha Yusaf Ali Khan, my Teaching and Research Assistant, and to other members of my staff, for assistance in the collection of materials from the date plantations laid down by the Agricultural Department in the Punjab, from the experiments which have been carried on, and from the various pieces of information which have been picked up during tours and at demonstrations on date culture. Mr. W. H. H. Young, Lyallpur, of the North-Western Railway, has very kindly made figs. A, B, C, and D of illustrations Nos. 17 and 18, pages 12c and 12d for me.

March, 1913.

D. MILNE,
Economic Botanist, Punjab, Lyallpur.

PREFACE TO THE THIRD EDITION.

In continuation of the object aimed at in the previous editions, the present note is intended to provide readily available information on date culture to those who have so kindly helped the Agricultural Department in the improvement of date culture since I began this work in 1909.

It also aims at interesting farmers in date cultivation in suitable localities in the Punjab and, what seems equally necessary since people have seen the comparatively fine date fruits grown in the Punjab on imported trees, warning intending planters against laying out large date plantations in unsuitable situations. The questions dealt with in the note are those which have been put to me by, or are likely to arise in the minds of, date-growers. They have been dealt with briefly, and of necessity in language as non-technical as possible.

The chief additions made in this issue are as follows :—

(a) Glossaries of scientific, English and vernacular terms in common use in the Punjab in connection with date cultivation.

Practically the whole of the vernacular terms and their definitions are the result of discussions with date-growers in the districts concerned. The glossary of the Multani language by E. O'Brien, I.C.S., and the Dictionary of the Economic Products of India by Sir Geo. Watt have also been consulted.

(b) A few notes on the structure of the palm which may help people to better understand the conditions in which the plant is fitted to grow and give its best returns.

(c) Notes on some diseases of the date palm in the Punjab.

The whole note has been brought more abreast with our work, and endeavours have been made to make it more suitable for its purpose.   Where other workers have helped me as regards material for the note, acknowledgments have been made in the text.

It will be seen there that I have been greatly indebted to Dr. G. T. Walker, c.s.i., Director of the Indian Meteorological Department, for meteorological information regarding the Punjab and the principal date-growing countries of the world, to Mr. H. E. Annett, Agricultural Chemist, Bengal, for certain notes regarding date-toddy and sugar-making from the sap of *Phœnix Sylvestris*, to Mr. Bainbrigge Fletcher, Imperial Entomologist, for the use of illustrations Nos. 45 and 46, to Professor H. M. Lefroy, late Imperial Entomologist, to Mr. C. C. Ghosh of the Entomological Section, Pusa, to L. Madan Mohan Lal, Assistant Professor of Entomology, Lyallpur, and others for most of the material for the notes on the insect pests, and to Mr. Ley, late Director-General of Commercial Intelligence, Calcutta, for information regarding exports and imports of dates, etc.

Mr. J. H. Barnes, Agricultural Chemist, Punjab, kindly allowed the departmental photographer working in his section to develop for me all the photographs which have been used as illustrations, and to take many of these photographs under my directions.

Mr. T. Miller Brownlie, Agricultural Engineer, at considerable inconvenience to himself, was kind enough to allow me the use of his draftsman to make illustrations Nos. 22, 24, 26, 27, 32, and 35.

When the date work referred to in this note was started, our greatest difficulty was to get our instructions regarding the care of young plantations carried out, and the Agricultural Department is specially indebted to Mr. F. W. Skemp, i.c.s., then Deputy Commissioner, Muzaffargarh, for having the plantations there most carefully attended to and for the great personal interest which he took in the work.   The department is also much indebted to his successors for so willingly continuing the work.   It is indebted to Lieut.-Col. Lowis and successive Deputy Commissioners of Dera Ghazi Khan district for help in the work undertaken in that district, to the Jail Department in connection with the plantation in the garden of the Central Jail, Multan, and to the officers of the Canal Department for the experimental plantations which they have put down in their own lands, and for their ever readiness to assist as regards water-supply, or by any other means in their power. A number of other officers and private friends have also given valuable assistance in one way or another less easy to specify concisely. Among these I may mention Mr. A. E. Jeffries, Executive Engineer, Canal Department, who has for years helped greatly with special date experiments and in many other ways. Mr. Paul B. Popenoe, Altadena, California, author of " Date Growing in the Old and New Worlds " and of a large number of other interesting writings on the date industry, has very kindly sent copies of his writings to me from time to time. There are many others.

I wish again to acknowledge my great indebtedness to my staff who have one and all, at various times, done much to clear up points showing how far date cultivation might be made profitable to the people of the Punjab.

It is pleasing to be able to say that all results of investigations made up to date tend to show most decidedly that the people may derive great benefits from date cultivation if it is properly conducted in suitable situations. Major Buck, I.A., Deputy Commissioner, Muzaffargarh, has just acquired a further 19 acres of good land for the District Board to lay out in a date plantation, and we have more orders from local farmers for young date plants than we can hope to supply for several years.

A vernacular translation of this edition is practically ready for publication, and it is hoped that it will be out soon.

D. MILNE,

Economic Botanist, Punjab, Lyallpur.

CONTENTS.

GLOSSARY.

CHAPTER I.

GENERAL REQUIREMENTS OF THE DATE PALM ; A FEW NOTES ON ITS ADAPTATIONS TO ITS HABITAT, AND THE DIFFERENCES BETWEEN THE SEXES.

CHAPTER II.

SOIL AND CLIMATE.

———

CHAPTER III.

PROPAGATION OF DATE PLANTS FROM SEEDS AND SUCKERS
(OFF-SHOOTS), CARE OF YOUNG PLANTATIONS. MANURING,
INTERCULTURE, PRUNING AND WATER REQUIREMENTS OF
ESTABLISHED PLANTATIONS.

CHAPTER IV.

POLLINATION TO FRUIT PRESERVATION.

CHAPTER V.

EXTENT OF DATE GROWING IN THE PRINCIPAL DATE GROWING LOCALITIES OF THE PROVINCE, DATE FRUITS FROM LOCAL AND IMPORTED TREES, AND PROFITS TO BE EXPECTED FROM DATE FARMING.

GLOSSARY.

A FEW COMMON ENGLISH AND SCIENTIFIC TERMS USED IN DATE CULTIVATION WITH THEIR MEANINGS; ALSO VERNACULAR EQUIVALENTS WHERE SUCH ARE COMMONLY USED.

CARPEL .. .. (See para. 8 page 12 and *f.h.k.*, Illustration No. 18, Sketch C, page 12*d*.) The central part of the female flower is formed of 3 carpels closely applied together. The basal oval part of each carpel is called the ovary; the pointed apical portion is called the stigma.

CURING YARD .. *Ver.* "Piri" پڑي (see *Frontispiece*). Sometimes called "Khori." کهوري. Khori is more properly applied to a corner of the curing yard in which the cured fruits are temporarily stored immediately after removal from the curing mats. The floor of the khori is usually a foot or so higher than the rest of the curing yard in order to facilitate drainage in case of rain.

DATE GROVE .. *Ver.* "Khajion ka bāgh :" کهجیون کا باغ "Nakhlistan" نخلستان. A small group of date plants arising from a common stool is in vernacular called a "Thadda." تهڈّا

DATE PALM .. *Ver.* "Khajji." کهجي

FEMALE TREE .. Fruit bearing tree. *Ver.* "Mâdah." مادہ

FERTILISATION .. The fusion of certain of the contents of the pollen grain with certain of those of the ovule of the female flower, and which results in the conversion of the ovule into a seed; in this case containing an embryo or baby plant and a food store around it. I have found no local vernacular equivalent. In Arabic it is called "Talqih." تلقیح

FIBRE AT THE BASE OF
LEAF STALK .. *Ver.* "Kabál." کبال

FLOWER .. *Ver.* "Phūl." پهول
Sometimes a collection of the flowers is called "Būr." بور

FRUIT .. .. The ripened ovary (*see* ovary, page xiv).

Ver. "Mewa" میوه or "Phal." پهل

Ver. "Khajji" کهجي usually applied to the date palm, but sometimes applied to the fruit only.

Ver. "Pind" پنڊ a ripe date fruit.

Ver. "Bhugriān" بهوگڙيان. Date fruits, especially inferior ones, are sometimes plucked from the trees before they begin to soften, are boiled in water to which has been added some oil or "ghi" (boiled butter) or milk and sometimes a little salt. They can be kept for years in this state and are used at festivals. Such fruits are called "Bhugriān." In other cases the fruits are boiled in water, dried and smeared with oil or "ghi." Sometimes they are not boiled but simply dried hard and smeared with oil or "ghi." Rape or mustard oil is preferred. The term is also applied to the dried fruits of the "Ber" (*Zizyphus Jujuba*).

Ver. "Bogh." بوکهه Fruits from polygamous trees: also sometimes applied to any date fruit with little flesh on it.

Ver. "Chirvi" چروي or "Shingastan" شنگستان Date fruits which have been cut open and dried. The seeds may or may not be removed in the process.

Ver. "Dang." ڏنگ A fruit which in the process of ripening has begun to soften.

Ver. "Doka." ڏوکا A date fruit after it has changed from green to its distinctive colour (yellow or purple) but is still quite hard.

Ver. "Gandōra." گنڊورا. Dates which are yet hard and green.

Ver. "Khassi" خصي seedless fruits.

Ver. "Kukk." ڪُڪ A fruit which has shrivelled up prematurely on the tree; usually fed to goats: sometimes made into bread by poor people.

HERMAPHRODITE
FLOWERS .. Both sexes in the same flower.

IMAGO .. .. The form taken in the mature stage in the life history of an insect.

INFLORESCENCE .. In common language, the flower-cluster. It issues from the spathe (*see* Illustrations Nos. 15 and 16, pages 12*a* and 12*b*). *Ver.* "Phulon ka khosha."

پھولوں کا خوشہ An individual branch of the inflorescence is in vernacular called "Lām" لام or "Māla." مالا When the flowers have gone from it, ver. "Bohāra." بوھارا

LARVA ... ... The form taken in the worm-like stage in the life history of an insect.

LEAF ... ... *Ver.* "Patta" پتا or "Pattar." پتر The entire leaf is composed of a strong main axis (*ver.* "Chharrì" چهڑي or "Lakra" لاکڑا) which arises from the tree trunk and bears a row of leaflets (*ver.* Bhūtra بهوترا) along either side, which stand out from it more or less like the pinnæ of a feather. The vernacular term "Chharrì" is sometimes applied to the leaf including both main axis and leaflets. The opening leaves on the head of the tree. *Ver.* "Gācha." گاچا The term Gacha is sometimes applied to the whole leaf system on the tree top. The whole collection of leaves on the tree may also be referred to in vernacular as "Chharion ka majmūa" چهڑيوں کا مجموعہ or "Patton ki chhatri." پتوں کی چهتري The white edible unopened leaves in the centre of the gācha. *Ver.* "Gari" گري (growing point).

LEAF BASE ... The flattened part of the leaf stalk which attaches the leaf to the stem of the tree. *Ver.* "Chhauda." چهودا. Fibre at the leaf base. *Ver.* "Kabāl." کبال

LEAF STALK ... Part of the leaf from where it joins the tree stem to where the leaflets begin to be given off the main axis. *Ver.* "Dhàmbra" دهامبرا or "Dàngra." دانگرا

MALE TREE ... Pollen bearing tree. *Ver.* "Nar." نر

MAT, SMALL ... *Ver.* "Taddi" تدي used for spreading fruits on

MAT, LARGER ... *Ver.* "Parchha" پرچها during curing operations.

MONŒCIOUS TREE Where the sexes are in separate flowers but on the same tree. (Jack) *ver.* "Bogh" بوگهہ

OFF-SHOOT ... A young date plant arising from a bud. These buds are usually given off from near the base of the stem of a date tree (*see* page 10, para. 5). *Ver.* "Bacha" بچہ A tree raised from off-shoot. *Ver.* "Lāgwin." لاگوين

OVARY ... ... *Ver.* "Bij Dān." بيج دان portion of the carpel containing the ovule (*see* para. 8, page 12).

OVULE ... ... A body contained in the ovary and which after fertilisation becomes the seed (*see* also Fertilisation).

GLOSSARY.

PERIANTH ... In this case it is composed of the whorls of scales at the base of the flower (*see* Illustrations Nos. 17 and 18, pages 12*c* and 12*d*).

POLLEN .. ... The fine yellowish powder-like material which is shed from the ripe male flower and which must be conveyed to the female flower in order to fertilise it. *Ver.* " Būr " نور or " Phul ka ghubār." پهول کا غبار Sometimes called " Būr ka ata." بور کا آٹا

POLYGAMOUS TREES With hermaphrodite and unisexual flowers on the same, or on different individuals of the same species (Jacks).

POLLINATION .. The conveying of the pollen from the male to the receptive part of the female flower.

PUPA .. ... The form taken in the dormant stage in the life history of an insect.

ROOT .. ... *Ver.* " Jar." جر " Pār." پاڑ

ROPE USED IN CLIMBING A DATE TREE .. Kamand. کمند

SEED .. ... The hard structure inside the date fruit. *Ver.* " Gakkar." گکر

SEEDLING .. Plant grown from a seed. *Ver.* " Tukhmi " تخمي " Gakkar ka bacha " گکر کا بچه or " Biji." بيجي

SPATHE .. ... The leathery or hard case which encloses the flower-cluster until ready for pollination. Usually three to five inches across and a foot or more in length when it bursts to expose the flowers. *Ver.* " Sippi " سپي (*see* para. 6, also Illustrations Nos. 15 and 16, pages 12*a* and 12*b*).

STEM .. ... *Ver.* " Tanah." تنه " Dud " دد or " Lara." لڑا Stem-stump—*Ver.* " Mundh." منڈهه Upper portion of stem—*Ver.* " Pānd." پاند

STIGMA .. ... The part of the carpel which in pollination receives the pollen grains (*see* also Carpel).

SUCKER .. ... *See* off-shoot. *Ver.* " Bacha." بچه

THORN .. ... *Ver.* " Thua," تهوا " Kānta " کانٹا or " Kanda." کنڈا

TREE, MALE .. *Ver.* " Nar." نر

  ,,   FEMALE .. *Ver* " Mādah " ماده or " Mādi." مادي

  ,,   RAISED FROM A SEED .. *Ver.* " Biji " بيجي or " Tukhmi." تخمي

TREE, RAISED FROM A SUCKER (OFF-SHOOT) .. *Ver.* " Lāgwin." لاگوين

A FEW VERNACULAR TERMS CONNECTED WITH DATE CULTIVATION IN THE PUNJAB, WITH THEIR ENGLISH MEANINGS.

ANNA آنه .. One penny approximately.

BACHA بچه .. Off-shoot, sucker.

BAIKAR بیکر .. The lessee of the date trees. The lease is usually taken before the time the fruits are fully formed. The baikar protects the fruits from enemies, harvests, and disposes of them making what profit he can over the sum which he has agreed (in the lease) to pay to the owner of the trees.

BIJI بیجی .. Seedling : a tree grown from a seed.

BHUGRIAN بهگریان .. Date fruits—especially inferior ones—are plucked from the tree before they begin to soften ; are boiled in water, to which has been added some oil or " ghi " (boiled butter) or milk and sometimes a little salt. They are then dried hard and stored. They can be kept for years in this state and are used at festivals. Such fruits are called " Bhugriān." بهگریان

In other cases the fruits are boiled in water, dried and smeared with oil or " ghi." Sometimes they are not boiled but simply dried hard and smeared with oil or " ghi." Rape or mustard oil is preferred for this purpose. The term Bhugri is also applied to the dried ripe fruit of the " beri " plant (*Zizyphus jujuba*).

BHUTRA بهوترا .. Leaflet : *see* also Leaf.

BOGH بوگهه .. Fruits from polygamous trees. Also sometimes applied to any date fruit with little flesh on it. Polygamous trees are also called Bogh.

BOKAR بوکر
BUHARA بوهارا
BUHARI بوهاري
(A broom) Applied to the male or female inflorescence of a date tree after the flowers or fruits have gone from it. *See* Illustrations Nos. 15 and 16 pages 12*a* and 12*b*.

BUR بور .. .. Pollen ; sometimes flowers.

CHHARI چهري .. (A stick) the main axis of the date leaf (*see* page 7). Sometimes applied to the whole leaf.

CHHAUDA چهوڑا .. Leaf base, *i.e.*, the part of the leaf stalk left attached to the tree stem when the leaf is pruned away.

CHIRVI چروی   OR

CHIRAN چیران   .. From "chīrna"—to cut. Date fruits which have been cut open and dried. The seeds may or may not be removed in the process. Chirvi or Chīran is also applied to beaten date leaves that are used for making ropes.

CHHOHĀRA چهوهارا   .. In the Persian Gulf unripe date fruits are boiled and dried. Large quantities of these are exported to India and are known here as Chhohāras. As these dates are generally of better quality than the ordinary local Indian dates, the best local varieties are now generally known as Chhohāras.

DANG دنگ   .. A date fruit which (in the process of ripening) has begun to soften. This softening usually begins near the distal end of the fruit and is accompanied by a change of colour. Date fruits in the Punjab are usually plucked from the trees at this stage.

DĀNGRA دانگره   OR

DHĀMBRA دهانبرا   .. Leaf stalk.

DOKA دوکا   .. A date fruit after it has changed from green to its distinctive colour (yellow or purple), but is still quite hard.

DUD دد ..   .. Stem.

GĀCHA گاچا   .. The opening leaves on the head of the tree. Sometimes applied to the whole leaf system on the top of the palm.

GAKAR گکر   .. Seed.

GANDORA گندورا   .. Dates which are yet hard and green.

GARI گري   .. (Kernel) the white edible unopened leaves in the centre of the "Gācha." The same term is commonly applied to the white edible internal part of a cocoanut.

HIK SALI هکسالي   .. *See* " Vareli khajji."

JAR جڙ ..   .. Root.

JHUTT جهت   .. The thicket of suckers, seedlings, etc., which grows up at the base of badly attended trees.

KABĀL کبال   .. The thin but conspicuous network of fibre which appears at the base of each petiole (leaf stalk) where it joins the tree stem.

KAMAND کمند .. A rope used in ascending a date tree.

KAMB کامب .. Leaf stalk.

KANTA کانٹا .. Thorn.

KHAJJI کهجي .. Usually applied to the date palm, but sometimes to the fruit only. "Khajion ka bāgh." کهجیون کا باغ A date grove.

KHAR-KHARA کهرکهرا .. A cluster of fine roots.

KHARAK کهرک .. *See* Bhugrian.

KHAS KHAJJI خص کهجي

OR KHASSI خصی .. From khassi—castrated. A date tree which habitually bears seedless dates.

KHASSI PIND خصی پنڈ Seedless fruits. They are developed from unfertilised carpels.

KHORI کهوزي .. Portion of curing yard used for storing cured dates temporarily. It is usually raised a few inches higher than the rest of the curing yard.

KUKK کک .. Date fruits which have shrivelled up prematurely on the tree. They are usually fed to goats, etc., and sometimes made into bread by poor people.

LAGWIN لاگوین .. A tree grown from an off-shoot.

LAKRA لکڑا .. The main axis of the leaf.

LARAH لڑا .. Stem.

MADAH مادہ .. A female tree.

MAUND OR MAN من .. 82 lbs.

MUNDH منڈهہ .. Basal portion of the tree left in the ground when the stem is cut away, *i.e.*, the tree stump.

NAKHLISTAN نغلستان .. A date grove.

NAR نر .. Male tree.

PAND پانڈ .. Upper portion of the stem.

PAR پاڑ .. Root.

PARCHA پرچا .. Large mat used for spreading dates on during the curing process.

PATTA پتا OR PATTAR

پتر .. Leaflet.

PATTON KI CHHATRI

پتون کي چهتري .. The whole collection of leaves on the tree top.

PHARA پهڑا .. *See* Bhutra.

M, DP

B

PHUL پهول .. Flower.
"Phul ka ghubār" پهول کا غبار—pollen. "Phulon ka khosha" پهولوں کا خوشه—inflorescence.

PIND پِنڈ .. Ripe date fruit.

PIRI پڑي .. See Khori.

RUPEE روپيه .. 16 pence approximately.

SAKAR سکر .. See Gandora.

SEER OR SĒR سير .. $\frac{1}{40}$th maund or $2\frac{1}{20}$th lbs.

SHINGASTAN شنگستان See Chirvi.

SOK سوک .. Date fruits which dry well and the skin does not come off in curing. Also applied to the plant which bears such dates.

SIPP سپ ⎫
SIPPI سپي ⎭ .. (Oyster shell.) Applied to the spathe from which the date inflorescence issues (see Illustrations Nos. 15 and 16, pages 12a and 12b).

TADI تڈي .. A small mat on which date fruits are spread in the sun during the process of curing (see Frontispiece).

TALQIH تلقيح (ARABIC) Fertilisation.

TANAH تنه .. Stem.

THADDA تهڈا .. Small group of date plants arising from a common stool.

THUA تهوا .. A thorn. Large thorns are found on the main axis or petiole of the leaf (see Illustration No. 8, page 6c).

TUKHMI تخمي .. Seedling. A tree grown from a seed.

VARELI KHAJJI وريلي کهجي .. From "Vari"—a turn, and "Wali" signifying possession or relation. A palm believed to bear fruit in alternate years.

ILLUSTRATION No. 1.

Arabian date tree planted 5 years previously at Lyallpur—earth dug away from
one side to expose root system.

(*See para.* 2, *page* 1.)

СУГЬОВННЧ
ПРИЛ ОЬ.

ILLUSTRATION No. 2.

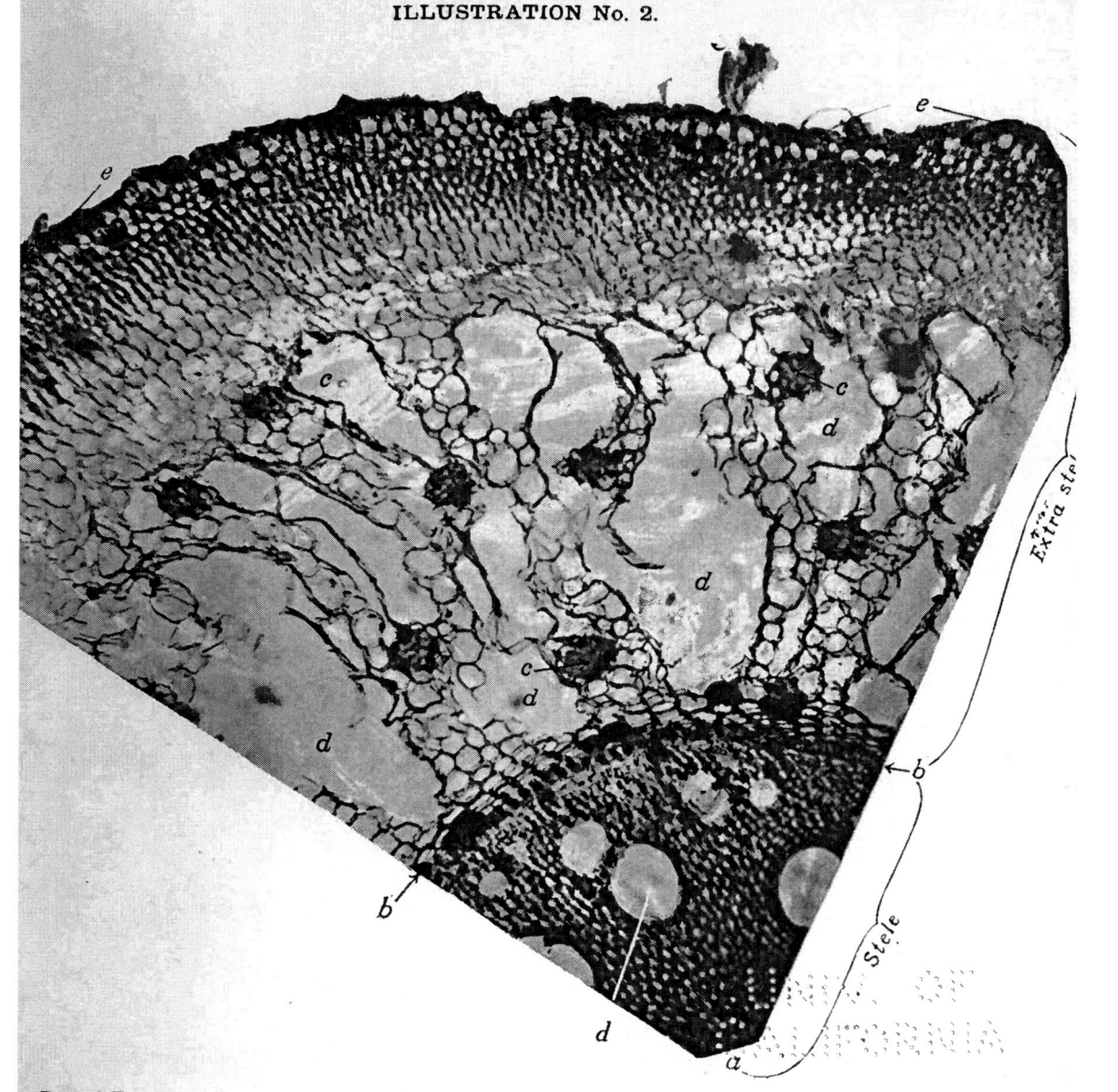

Part of Transverse Section of Secondary root of date palm (Phœnix dactylifera) × 116 diameters.

    (*a*) Centre of the root.

    (*b*) Outer boundary of central portion (stele).

    (*c*) Bands of tough sclerenchymatous tissue.

    (*d*) Large air passages.

    (*e*) Outer wall of root.

The extra-stelar tissues include all those between (*b*) and (*e*).

The stelar tissues are chiefly sclerenchymatous.

(*See para.* 2, *page* 1.)

CHAPTER I.

THE DATE PALM. (*Phœnix dactylifera.*)

*General requirements of the date palm; a few notes on its adaptations
to its habitat, and the differences between the sexes.*

1. The natural home of the date palm is close to a well
or spring or other water-supply, in a dry
parched desert with scorching summer heat.

*General require-
ments of the plant.*

ERRATA.

Page 123, fifth line from top—
For fungoid pest *read* fungal pest.

Page 124, twelfth line from bottom—
For fungoid diseases *read* fungal diseases.

2. Like other plants of its class, the date palm possesses
no large tap root, but has what is known

The root.

as a fibrous root-system, *i.e.*, it has a large
number of secondary roots more or less equal in thickness,
arising in a dense cluster from the base of the stem (*see*
illustration No. 1, page XIX). In this case the secondary roots
are usually about $\frac{1}{4}$ to $\frac{5}{8}$ inch in diameter. These roots give
off a number of smaller lateral roots, and, after decreasing to
a diameter of about $\frac{1}{4}$ inch or rather less, end abruptly.

In transverse sections of the secondary roots (*see* illustration
No. 2, page XX) outside the relatively well-marked central

M, DP   1

CHAPTER I.

THE DATE PALM. (*Phœnix dactylifera.*)

General requirements of the date palm; a few notes on its adaptations to its habitat, and the differences between the sexes.

1. The natural home of the date palm is close to a well or spring or other water-supply, in a dry parched desert with scorching summer heat.

General requirements of the plant.

Such places are often quite cold in winter, but the palms there seem well able to withstand the cold. The fruits mature in summer or autumn, and will not ripen properly unless under excessive heat. Without an unstinted water-supply readily available to the roots, the fruits do not develop properly, while a moist atmosphere adversely affects both pollination (*see* page 45, para. 22), and the proper maturing of the fruit (*see* page 52, para. 24). For the most successful cultivation of dates, an extremely dry atmosphere, a very high temperature, and a plentiful supply of water are, therefore, essential during the flowering and fruiting period. The Arabic saying "the date palm likes its feet in water and its head in fire" is roughly expressive of the requirements of the plant.

2. Like other plants of its class, the date palm possesses no large tap root, but has what is known

The root.

as a fibrous root-system, *i.e.*, it has a large number of secondary roots more or less equal in thickness, arising in a dense cluster from the base of the stem (*see* illustration No. 1, page XIX). In this case the secondary roots are usually about $\frac{1}{4}$ to $\frac{5}{8}$ inch in diameter. These roots give off a number of smaller lateral roots, and, after decreasing to a diameter of about $\frac{1}{4}$ inch or rather less, end abruptly.

In transverse sections of the secondary roots (*see* illustration No. 2, page XX) outside the relatively well-marked central portion (stele) which contains the main sap-conducting tissues, we find a peripheral (extrastelar) region in which even to the naked eye, or under a pocket lens, a great number of large air passages are visible.

Such passages are common in the roots of plants adapted for growth in soils which habitually contain excessive amounts of water, and which are usually less well aerated than ordinary soils. They are not found in common plants which habitually grow on well-drained soils. The older parts of the roots of the rice plant (*Oryza sativa*), for example, show very large air passages in that region, while none are found in that part of the root of a wheat plant (*see* illustrations Nos. 3 and 4, page 2*a*).

The huge air passages in the date root structure indicate that the plant should have a plentiful water-supply available to it, and that the dangers of over-watering are not nearly as great as in the case of other common fruit trees. In the light of the above, we cease to be astonished that the date palm can yield good crops of fruits when the soil is under water for some months every year, as, for example, on the banks of the Nile in Egypt and near other large rivers.

It is not, however, adapted for living permanently in stagnant water-logged soils. We find that date palms growing on land which has been submerged in more or less stagnant water for a period of several years are not in good health; their roots are more or less decayed, and the crops of fruits are miserable (*see* illustration No. 23, page 72*a*).

The best crops of dates are obtained where the soil water is always fresh as well as plentiful.

On the roots of common flowering plants which habitually grow on ordinary well-drained soils and from the leaves of which a good deal of water is transpired, hair-like outgrowths known as root-hairs are found. These root-hairs are only developed on a limited region a short distance behind the root tip. Their special function is to absorb the water and dissolved salts from the soil

ILLUSTRATION No. 3.

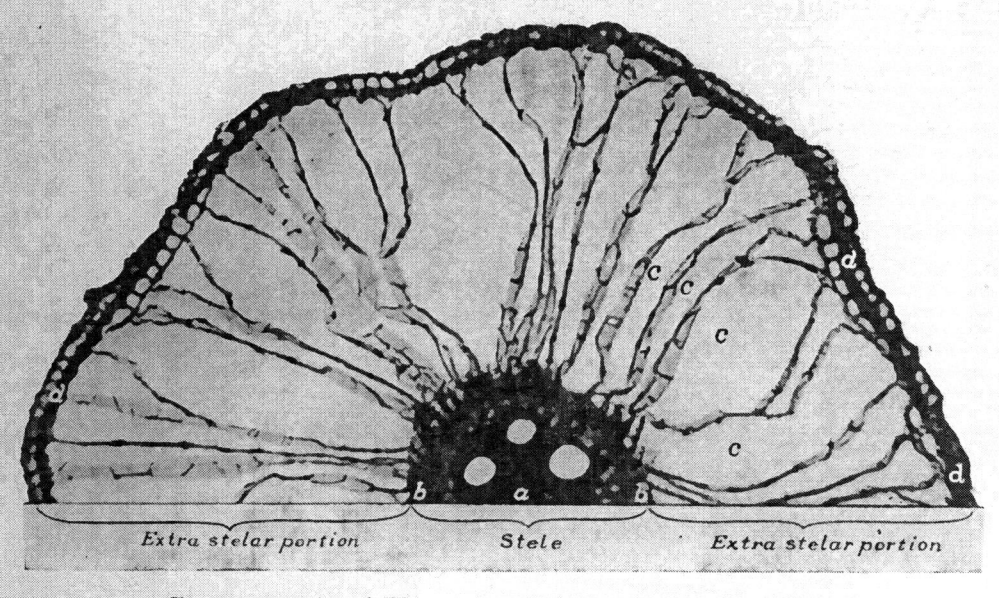

Transverse section of old root of Rice (oryza sativa) × 116 diameters.
  (a) Centre of root.
  (b) Outer boundary of central portion (stele).
  (c) Large air passages.
  (d) Outer wall of root.
The extra stelar tissues include all those between (b) and (d).

(See para. 2, page 1.)

ILLUSTRATION No. 4.

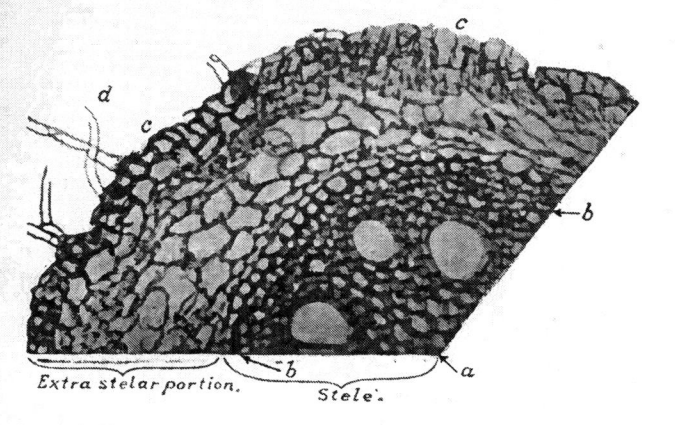

Transverse section of root of wheat (Triticum Vulgare) × 116 diameters.
  (a) Centre of root.
  (b) Outer boundary of central portion (stele).
  (c) Outer wall of root.
  (d) Root hairs.
Note the comparatively poor development of the extra stelar area and the absence of
  huge air passages in it.

(See para. 2, page 1.)

which are necessary to carry on the vital functions of the plant. Plants which develop no root-hairs seem to absorb sufficient water and salts for their needs through cells non-protuberant from the main surface of the roots. Root-hairs greatly increase the root's absorbing surface. Some writers (*see* Kerner and Oliver "Natural History of Plants," Volume I, page 91 and others) lead us to understand that root-hairs are absent in the case of the date-palm. I may, therefore, mention that root-hairs have been found on the roots of date palms in the case of plants growing in well drained soil at Lyallpur where the permanent water-level is at about 80 feet depth ; at Mazuffargarh at a depth of 8½ feet where the subsoil water-level during most of the year is 7 feet or less from the soil surface but which at the time of examination was at 9 feet depth ; and elsewhere.

Root-hairs are also found on the rice plant.

In the peripheral (extrastelar) region of the root of the date palm numerous bands of sclerenchyma (fibrous tissue strengthened and toughened by the deposit of a substance called lignin) are developed, which together with the sclerenchymatous tissue in the central portion of the root give to that organ great tensile strength—a character most important when the date tree has to hold itself erect against the force of the fierce winds that sometimes sweep through desert regions.

A date tree planted as a sucker at Lyallpur five years previously was found to possess approximately 350 secondary roots. The longest of these roots was about 18 feet in length and was one of those which started from the stem most near the surface of the soil. It left the stem at an angle of less than 20 degrees to the horizon, and bent sharply down into the soil when about 9 feet away, so that its tip was only about 13 feet from the tree.

Several other roots near the soil surface described a similar course. The great mass of the roots, however, when they started from the tree descended at a very sharp angle (*see* illustration No. 1, page XIX) and ended within a radius of 6 feet from the stem. The tips of the deepest of these penetrated to a depth of 7 to 9½ feet. The permanent water-level in the locality is at a depth of about 80 feet. The tree was irrigated when necessary from a small water channel which passes within 4 yards of it and flows about once a week. One root followed up in another tree planted as a sucker in the Taleri Bagh, Muzaffargarh, five years previously, was 25 feet in length, and ended at a distance of 18 feet from the parent tree.

With the exception of a comparatively few roots which spread out more or less horizontally, the root-system of the five years old date trees examined in the Taleri Bagh were contained within a radius of 6 feet from the parent stems. The roots ended at depths between 2 and 6½ feet. The subsoil water-level at the time of examination was 7 feet below the surface. In the case of older trees in the same vicinity date roots were followed up to 1½ feet under the permanent water-level. In view of the special internal structure of the root (see above, same paragraph) this was to be expected.

The root-system of a date tree planted near Lyallpur 21 years previously was examined. The soil was a medium loam. The permanent water-level was 80 feet deep, but there is a large perennial canal 50 feet wide running at a distance of 160 yards from it. About 26 feet from the tree a small channel about 3 feet wide runs almost continually.

The following data were got :—

Age of the tree.	Total number of secondary roots on the tree.	Percentage of the total number of secondary roots which reached the following radial distances from the tree.				REMARKS.
		4 ft.	6¾ ft.	8½ ft.	10½ ft.	
21 years..	7000	34%	25%	23%	12%	On the side of the tree facing the small water channel.
		29%	20%	14%	8%	On the side of the tree facing parallel to the small water channel.

ILLUSTRATION No. 5

Sections taken across a line running from the tree parallel to the small water channel.

SCALE = ½ inch per foot.

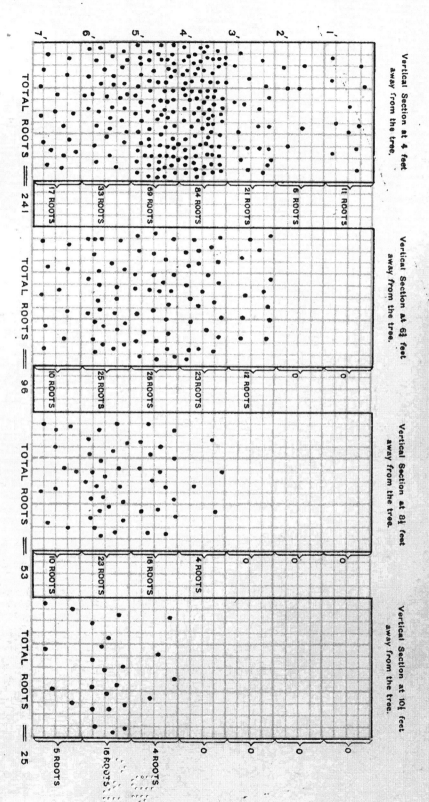

Vertical Section at 4 feet away from the tree.

Vertical Section at 6½ feet away from the tree.

Vertical Section at 8½ feet away from the tree.

Vertical Section at 10½ feet away from the tree.

TOTAL ROOTS = 241

TOTAL ROOTS = 96

TOTAL ROOTS = 53

TOTAL ROOTS = 25

ILLUSTRATION No. 6.

Sections taken across a line running directly from the tree to the small water channel.

SCALE = ¼ inch per foot.

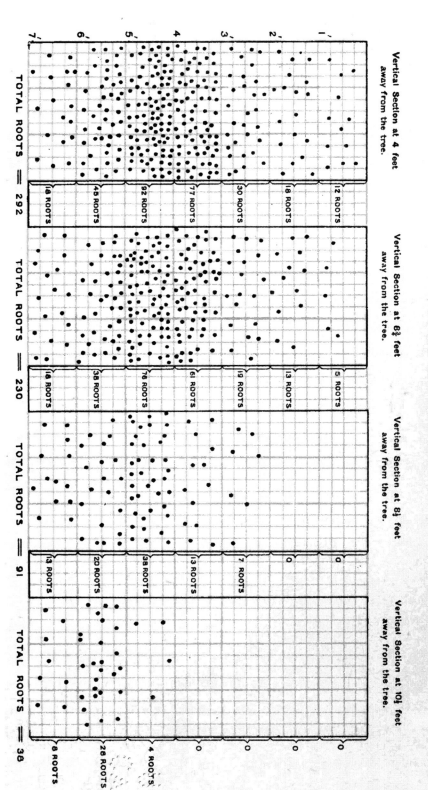

Vertical Section at 4 feet away from the tree.

TOTAL ROOTS = 292

12 ROOTS
18 ROOTS
30 ROOTS
77 ROOTS
92 ROOTS
45 ROOTS
18 ROOTS

Vertical Section at 6¾ feet away from the tree.

TOTAL ROOTS = 230

5 ROOTS
13 ROOTS
19 ROOTS
61 ROOTS
76 ROOTS
38 ROOTS
18 ROOTS

Vertical Section at 8½ feet away from the tree.

TOTAL ROOTS = 91

0
0
7 ROOTS
13 ROOTS
38 ROOTS
20 ROOTS
13 ROOTS

Vertical Section at 10½ feet away from the tree.

TOTAL ROOTS = 38

0
0
0
0
4 ROOTS
28 ROOTS
8 ROOTS

The diagrams on pages 4a and 4b show numbers and positions of secondary roots of the above tree in 3 feet wide and 7 feet deep sections of the soil at the undernoted distances away from the tree.

About 75 to 80 per cent. of the roots of this tree descended from the stem at an angle of 55 degrees or over from the horizontal, and, as will be seen from the above table and diagrams, did not extend beyond a radius of 6. feet from the tree trunk. They ended at depths from 4 to $8\frac{1}{2}$ feet. The uppermost of the 20 to 25 per cent. approximately which extended to greater distances from the tree started from the stem at angles less than 20 degrees from the horizontal and usually bent sharply down near their extremities. The spreading roots rapidly decreased in number as the distance from the tree increased, and on the side of the tree facing parallel to the water channel there were only 8 per cent. of the whole at a distance of $10\frac{1}{2}$ feet away from the parent stem.

On the side facing the water channel 12 per cent. were found at $10\frac{1}{2}$ feet distance from the tree. Apparently the roots were attracted by the soakage water from the channel. The deepest of the roots descended to 7 feet, but the majority of them ended at depths of 2 to 6 feet.

The same general arrangement of roots was found in other date trees examined. Obviously the roots which spread more or less horizontally are of very great use in preventing the trees from being overturned by winds. Some of these were traced to over 30 feet from the parent tree. The fact that a very large proportion of the roots only spread to a distance of a few feet from the stems explains why considerable crops of fruits can be got even when the trees are grown very close together, as they usually are in date-growing regions, and as far as the root-system is concerned, it seems to indicate that if only dates were grown a full return would not be got from the land, if the trees were planted further apart than 20 feet.

3. The stem of the tree is cylindrical. Unlike the stems
of most trees which increase in thickness prac-

Stem.

tically throughout their whole life, the stem of
the date palm does not increase in thickness after it has developed
a full crown of functional leaves. This is attained by the time
that a distinct stem covered with withered leaves or—where
these have been pruned away—their bases can be distinguished
above the level of the ground. The age of an adult date palm,
therefore, cannot be told from the thickness of its stem. Even
the length of the stem and the number of old leaf bases on it are
not very accurate indications of age, as a palm in good conditions
of soil and climate grows very much faster and matures more
leaves per year than those in adverse conditions.

The stem when opened and examined by the naked eye
(*see* illustration No. 7 opposite) is seen to be composed of a vast
number of tough string-like fibres commonly over $\frac{1}{2}$ millimeter
in thickness lying apparently close together and mostly running
lengthwise in the stem. The string-like fibres are the vascular
bundles (sap-conducting tissues) of the plant (*see* illustration
No. 7a, page 6b) surrounded by a good deal of hard tissue
(sclerenchyma). The vascular bundles are connected with the
sap-conducting tissues of the root. In the stem they give off
branch bundles occasionally which can be traced across the
vertical ones in an upward slanting direction into the leaf
bases. This mass of tough strings is held together by a
matrix of cellular tissue which near the periphery of the stem
becomes so much lignified (thickened and toughened by a deposit
of lignin) that it is almost as tough and hard as the fibres
themselves, the whole making a stem far exceeding those of
ordinary trees in strength and resilience. When the palm is
cultivated, the leaves are pruned off near their bases after they
begin to lose their vigour, but in the wild state these leaves simply
bend downwards when they wither, and remain attached to the
tree for many years later. Whether the old leaves have been
left on the tree or pruned away, the stem proper remains closely
and permanently covered with the hard old leaf bases. This

ILLUSTRATION No. 7.

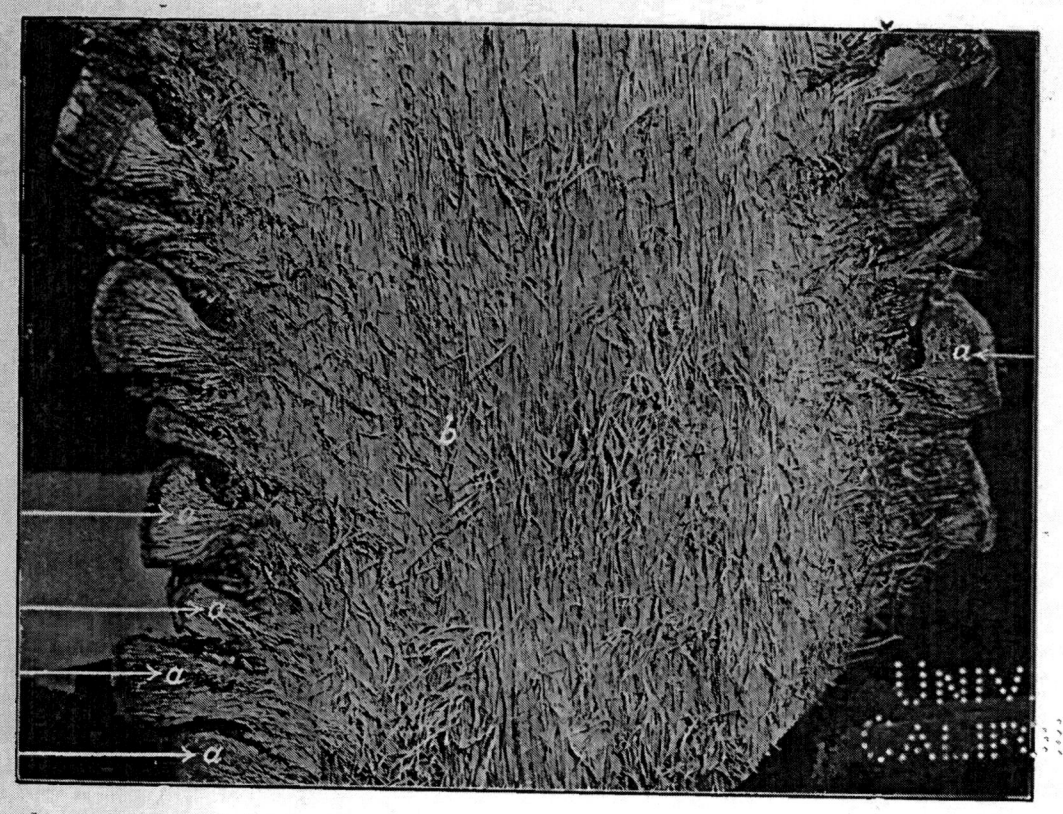

Longitudinal section of date stem——

(*a*) Old leaf bases.

In the region of (*b*) and elsewhere in the photo, the cut ends of the branch, fibre-like bundles, can be seen leading in an upward slanting direction towards the leaf bases.

(*See page* 6.)

ILLUSTRATION No. 7a.

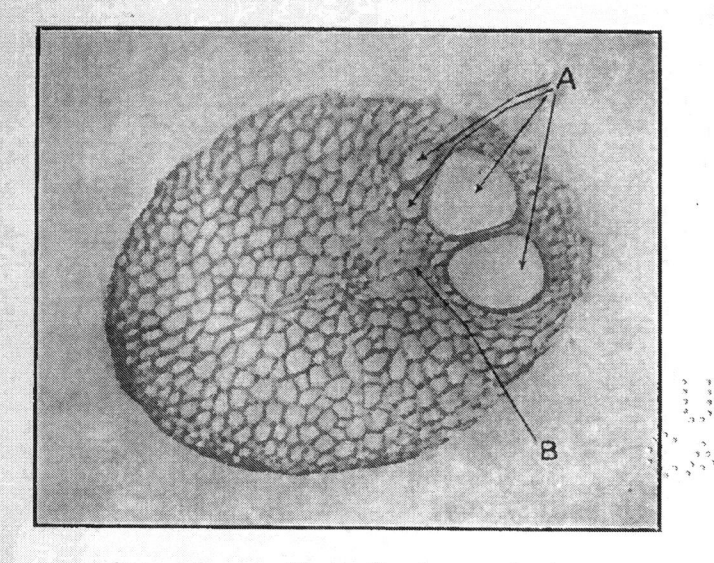

Transverse section of one of the string-like bundles of sap conducting tissues of the stem
× 116 diameters.

A=Xylem vessels. These conduct salt solutions absorbed from the soil by the roots to the leaves.

B=Phloem tissue. This tissue conducts the foods elaborated by the leaves back to the various parts of the plant. There is only a small patch of phloem tissue. In the illustration it is about one centimetre in diameter. The arrow points to the centre of it. Its comparatively thin walls give it a distinctive appearance here.

The remainder of the bundle consists of sclerenchymatous tissue which gives great strength to it.

ILLUSTRATION No. 8.

Leaf of date palm showing Pinnæ (leaflets) radiating in 4 planes (a), (b), (c), and (d) from its main axis (f), *i.e.*, in 2 planes from either side.

Near the base of the main axis of the leaf the pinnæ are poorly developed, hard, and form thorns (e).

(*See page* **7**.)

ILLUSTRATION No. 9.

Base of leaf showing edges of the main axis extended into a thin wall of tissue (*a*) which in the bud, forms a cylinder completely encircling all the younger leaves.

(*See page* 7.)

covering of old leaf bases adds to the strength of the trunk, and is a protection of the tissues within it from the excessive heat to which the plant must be exposed in order to enable it to ripen its fruits properly.

4. The stem is surmounted by a large terminal bud, from which fresh young leaves are continually being
Leaves. developed to replace the older leaves that are withering up. Full-grown leaves are usually 9 to 17 feet long. They may be described as feather-shaped ; each leaf having a long tough main axis and a large number of narrow leaflets, arranged along either side of it like the pinnæ of a feather. Collectively these pinnæ give far less resistance to winds than a single large undivided leaf blade would have done, and there is, therefore, less risk of the tree being overthrown, or its stem broken during a wind storm. Instead of the pinnæ being arranged in one plane on either side of the main axis as in the case of the pinnæ of a feather, they are usually arranged in two, and sometimes three or more, more or less distinct planes on either side of it (see illustration No. 8, page 6c). This arrangement also facilitates the passage of the wind between the leaflets. The edges of the base of the main axis of the leaf for about ¾ feet up its length are extended into a thin wall of soft tissue which in the bud forms a cylinder completely encircling all the younger leaves (see illustration No. 9, page 6d). The wall of this cylinder or leaf-sheath is composed of a close network of long interwoven tough sclerenchymatous fibres and sap-conducting tissues lying in a matrix of soft walled cells. As each leaf-base is provided with this sort of sheath and the apical bud of the palm is composed of a series of leaves, the sheaths of which each envelope the younger ones, the undeveloped leaves are protected in their youngest and most tender stage in a series of cylinders fitted over each other like the sections of a nearly closed telescope.

With the development of the younger leaves in the bud, the sheaths at the bases of the older leaf-stalks become stretched wider and wider to accommodate them, eventually being split open ; also the matrix of soft tissue in the sheath wall soon decays, and only the network of tough fibres is left. With the further growth of the plant the sheath is still further stretched so that even when the stem has attained its maximum thickness the fibres pass a considerable distance round it.

The cylindrical young leaf-sheaths bind the very young leaves firmly in a perpendicular position on the tree-top, but as their age increases the stretching and splitting of the sheaths allow the leaves to assume positions more and more near the horizontal till withering up they become reflexed downwards on the stem, or are pruned off (*see* illustration No. 29, page 86*a*). Thus the youngest and most tender of the leaves are most crowded together and protected by older ones, while the older they become the wider apart they spread, the less they overshadow each other, and the more they can make use of the energy of the sunlight for their work of elaboration of food for the plant. When the leaves have withered, the sheath fibres belonging to them are still strong and are used by the people for various purposes (*see* page 119, para. 89).

The central or main axis of the leaf, besides having an internal structure of the same general principle as that of the stem, has a shape admirably fitted to make the best use of its strength in the directions most required.

On the main axis below the level of the leaflets are a number of long, sharp thorns (*see* illustration No. 8, page 6*c*) which would assist in protecting the tender young terminal bud from damage by the larger animals. In the wild state of the palm the flowers and developing fruits would also be protected by these thorns from some animals.

The blades of the leaflets are rather thick, and sections of one of them under a microscope show a large number of tough sclerenchymatous bands of tissue running lengthwise in them which make it impossible for winds to break these leaflets across (*see* illustration No. 10, opposite). The margins of each leaflet are specially strengthened with tough bands of tissue of this sort,

ILLUSTRATION No. 10.

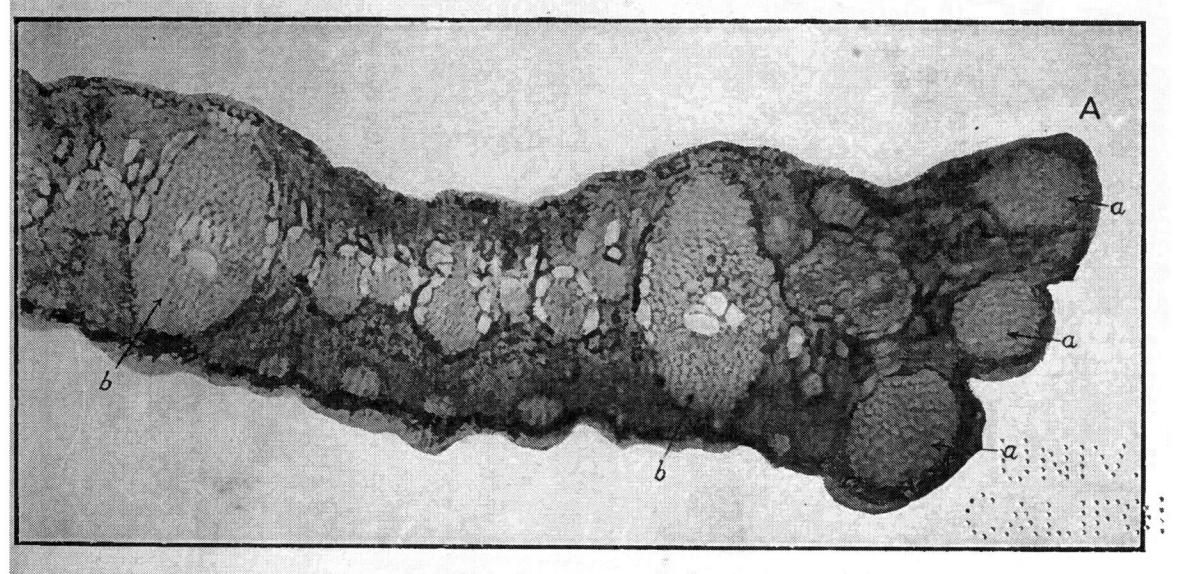

Transverse section of a small part of the blade of a leaflet of the date palm (*Phœnix dactylifera*) × 116 diameters.
A is the outer margin of the blade. The more or less round or oval patches of lighter coloured tissue are the sclerenchymatous bands referred to in para. 4, page 8. Three strong bands of sclerenchyma(a) are seen on the outer margin of the blade. At regular intervals throughout the breadth of the leaflet there are very strong bands, oval in transverse section (two marked *b* are seen in the photo) and between these much thinner bands.
It is from the tough sclerenchymatous bands that ropes, etc., are made.

(See para. 4, page 8, and para. 89, page 119.)

ILLUSTRATION No. 11.

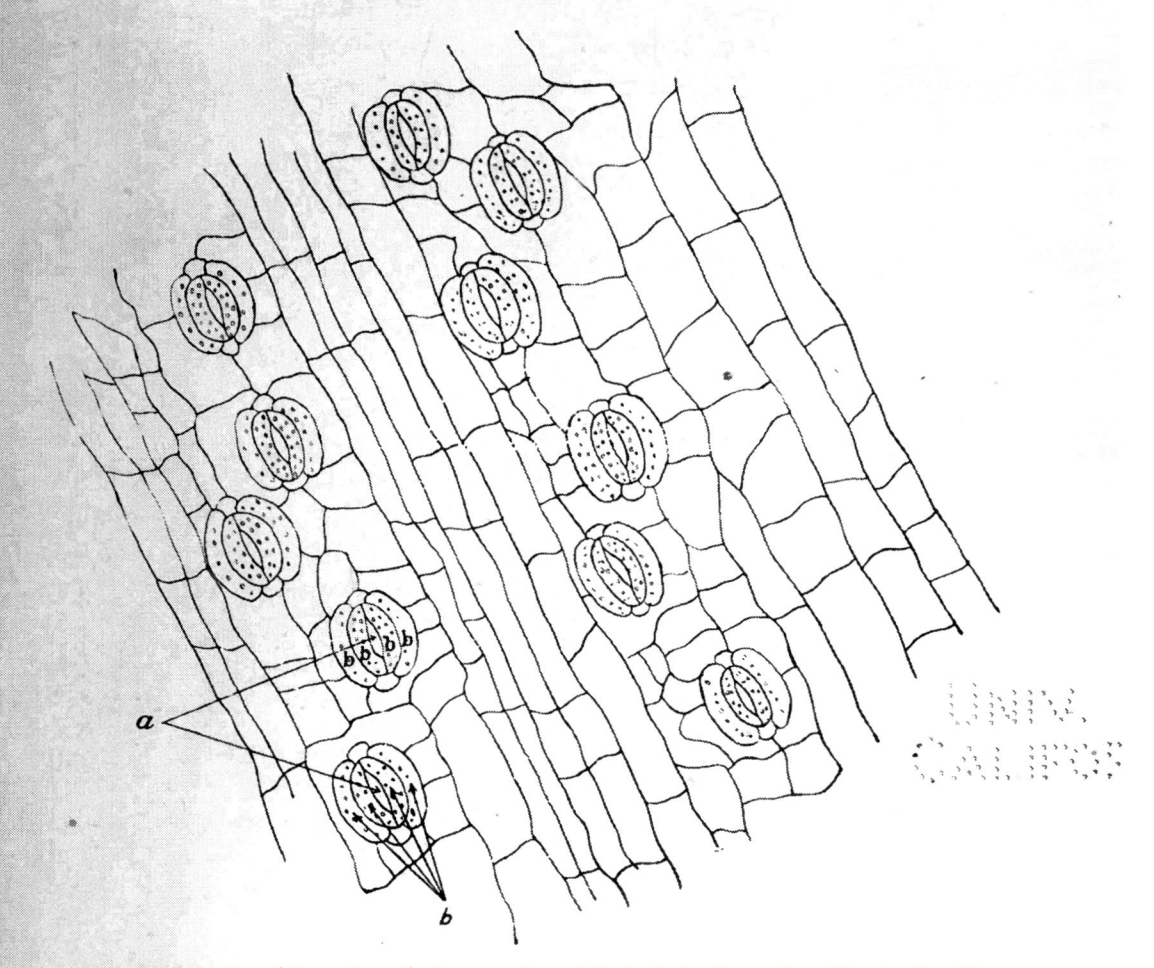

A small portion of tissue from the lower surface of the leaf of a date palm (*Phœnix dactylifera*) magnified 600 diameters.

(*a*) Stomata (mouths) through which the plant takes in from the atmosphere various gases necessary for the elaboration or digestion of its foods, and passes out its gaseous waste products and excess of water in the form of vapour.

(*b*) Guard cells—cells which control the opening and closing of the stomata.

(*See para. 4, page* 9.)

which eventually meet together and form a sharp, almost thorny tip to the leaflet, thus making it also difficult for the wind to start tearing the blade lengthwise (*see* illustration No. 12, page 10*a*). As in the case of other trees there is a cuticle (skin) on both the upper and lower surfaces of the leaflet, but in the case of the date palm the cuticle is specially thick. The cuticle is the outer layer of the outer wall of the external row of cells. It is thickly impregnated with a substance known as " cutin " which makes it tough and impervious to air and water. This cuticle protects the more delicate cells lying under it to a greater or less extent from abrasion from such bodies as wind-blown sand grains, etc., and prevents these cells from being dried up by dry air outside.

In the cuticle, there are rows of very tiny openings or mouths known as " stomata " through which the plant transpires its excess of water in the form of vapour into the atmosphere and also passes various gases necessary for its existence (*see* illustration No. 11, page 8*b*). These stomata are so tiny that a magnification of nearly 300 diameters is required to examine their structure—a pin-prick is large in comparison. Like the stomata in other plants, these open when their guard cells become turgid with sap and close when they become flaccid. In this case, however, they are sunken below the general level of the surface of the leaf blade in small pits as is common only in xerophytic (drought-resisting) plants. In plants the leaves of which lie roughly horizontal, and therefore expose only their upper surfaces to the sun's incident rays, the stomata are usually mostly confined to the back (lower surface) of the leaf while the internal structure shows the part near the face (upper surface) to be specially constructed to allow the chlorophyll granules (green colouring matter) to collect the maximum energy from the sun's rays for the work of food elaboration, tissue building, etc.

In the date palm the stomata are about as numerous on the face as on the back of the leaflet ; also there is no marked difference in the internal structure of the leaflet towards one surface or the other. The last two characters are common in many other plants, the leaves of which stand more or less vertical and which present about as many of the backs as the faces of the leaves towards the sun.

The leaflets of the date palm are folded once lengthwise, the two edges being turned upwards (*see* illustration No. 12, figure II, (*a*), opposite). At the base of the leaflet where it joins the main axis the fold is fixed, and is nearly complete, *i.e.*, the two edges of the leaflet almost meet each other. When the palm has a plentiful water-supply and other conditions are favourable, each leaflet beyond its basal part is unfolded to expose as large a surface area as possible to the sun, thus allowing the chlorophyll to do its maximum work and to give the stomata on both the face and back of the leaflet the freest action (*see* illustration No. 12, figure II, opposite), but when there is a scarcity of water the leaflet folds itself more or less tightly along its whole length, and the two halves of the face of the leaflet come together, thus protecting that surface of the leaflet from the dry winds and reducing the amount of moisture transpired from the plant (*see* illustration No. 12, figure I, opposite). At the same time the leaflets tend to swing round and crowd more together, thus sheltering each other from the dry winds. These closing movements are caused by the contraction of a small pad of a yellowish tissue called a " pulvinus " situated at the base of each leaflet.

With a fair water-supply and other normal conditions there seems to be no marked diurnal change in the degree of folding of the leaflets.

5.   The stem is surmounted by a terminal bud which continues to produce fresh young leaves throughout the life of the palm. If these young leaves are taken carefully apart from the stem, a very poorly developed bud, which usually looks like a mere pustule, is generally to be found in the axil of each leaf, *i.e.*, directly at the base of the main axis of the leaf, in the upper angle formed by that axis and the stem. By far the most of these tiny axillary buds never develop

Buds.

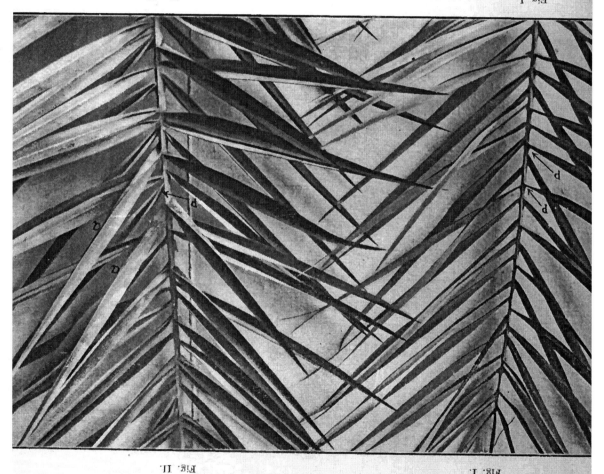

ILLUSTRATION No. 12.

Fig. I.

Fig. II.

Fig. II.

Leaf just cut from the same date tree.
Note that both upper and lower surfaces of t[he]
leaflets are freely exposed to the air.

P.—Pulvinus.

(See para. 4, page 1..)

Fig. I.

...ut from date tree and exposed to a hot sun for two hours approximately.
...that the leaflets have closed along their longitudinal fold, owing to
...ss of water. The stomata on the normal upper surface of the leaflet
...ing now enclosed in the fold and sheltered from the dry air, trans-
ration is reduced.

...lvinus.

ILLUSTRATION No. 13.

Date tree at Multan showing suckers (*a*) growing out of the stems at various heights
from the ground.

(*See para. 5, page* 10.)

ILLUSTRATION No. 14.

Date tree growing on the border of the Taleri Bagh, Muzaffargarh, which has 5 heads.
Continued wet weather in some year has apparently kept the *kabal* (fibre) and
debris near the apex of the stem damp for a sufficiently long time to stimulate the
parent buds into active growth.

Major Buck, Deputy Commissioner, Muzaffargarh District, has a photograph of a date tree
growing in the Karnal District which has 8 similar heads.

(*See para.* 5, *page* 10.)

further, and when the large terminal bud of the palm is destroyed the tree usually dies. Those that do develop give rise to "suckers" (off-shoots). They seem to require lengthened contact with some moist surface to stimulate them to do so. "Suckers" are, therefore, usually produced at the base of the stem where the soil keeps the axillary buds moist. On rare occasions, however, suckers are to be seen developing high above the level of the soil surface (*see* illustrations Nos. 13 and 14, pages 10*b* & 10*c*). The axillary buds, protected as they are by the old leaf bases, often lie dormant for many years before developing into suckers, but those that are to develop have generally begun to do so within 20 years (*see* page 89, para. 56).

6. The sexes of the date palm are usually on separate trees. Perhaps for our purpose this statement is sufficiently explained by saying that one tree bears only flowers which cannot develop into fruits but which produce a yellowish powder-like substance called "pollen" (*see* para. 7, page 12), while another tree produces only flowers which produce no pollen and must be fertilised (*see* para. 8, page 12) by pollen from flowers of the former class, before they can develop fruits. The trees which produce the pollen-bearing flowers are known as males, while those that produce the fruit-bearing flowers are known as females.

The inflorescence or flower-cluster.

In spring a number of structures, at first greenish, and later brown, more or less lens-shaped in transverse section, and measuring 3 to 5 inches across and a foot or more in length, make their appearance between the bases of the leaves which crown the palm. These structures are called "spathes," and each spathe encloses a cluster of flowers. When the spathe has become brown in colour and has attained something like the size mentioned above, it splits open and exposes the cluster of flowers which it contains (*see* illustrations Nos. 15 and 16, pages 12*a* & 12*b*). Each flower-cluster consists of a central stem with usually some 50 to 150, or more, lateral branches radiating from near its end, and each of these small branches carries on it a large number of tiny flowers (*see* illustrations Nos. 15, 16, 17 and 18, pages 12*a*, 12*b*, 12*c* & 12*d*). The spathe has tough leathery walls, and, completely enclosing the whole inflorescence, it protects the comparatively delicate flowers from being shrivelled up with the intense heat until they are quite ready to perform their functions.

7. When the spathe just described bursts, the male flower-cluster is disclosed. Its small lateral branches
The male flower-cluster. are about 6 inches long, and if the cluster is shaken, about the time that the spathe splits open, a dense cloud of yellowish pollen dust will fall from it. On examination it will be seen that in every little flower there are 6 stamens standing up like little pillars, each composed of 2 little yellowish pollen sacs and around the 6 little pillar-like stamens are 6 little waxy-looking scale-like structures which represent the sepals and petals in familiar flowers. These scales close over and help to protect the stamens until the pollen sacs have matured their pollen grains and are ready to burst and set the pollen free (*see* illustrations Nos. 15 and 17, pages 12*a* & 12*c*). Very soon after the large brown spathe splits open, the scales (sepals and petals), which covered and protected the stamens, open out and the pollen sacs burst. The opening of the scales and the bursting of the pollen sacs are due to the cells of their outer or epidermal tissues drying and contracting under the heat of the sun. The pollen sacs usually open within an hour or two of the bursting of the spathe.

8. The spathe which encloses the female flower-cluster is
Female flower-cluster. very similar to that which encloses the male cluster, and it bursts in the same way when the female cluster is ready for fertilisation. The small branches of the female cluster are, however, less confined to the end of its main axis and are very much longer than the small branches in the male flower-cluster (*see* illustrations Nos. 15 and 16, pages 12*a* & 12*b*). The female flower also differs very much from the male flower (*see* illustrations Nos. 17 and 18, pages 12*c* & 12*d*). It is an oval looking body, and might at first be mistaken for a

ILLUSTRATION No. 15.

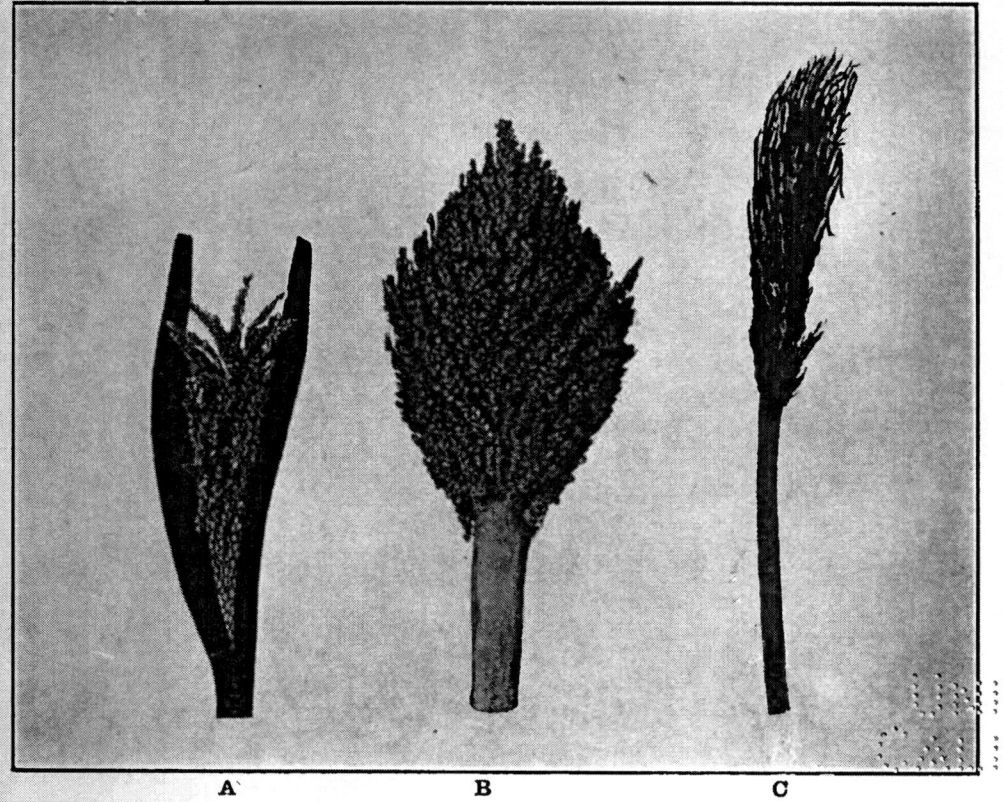

(A) Inflorescence showing the dark brown spathe just splitting open and showing the male flowers which it contains.

(B) Male inflorescence free from the brown spathe.

(C) A past year's male inflorescence showing the comparatively short lateral branches crowded near the top of the main axis.

(See paras. 6 & 7, pages 11 & 12.)

ILLUSTRATION No. 16.

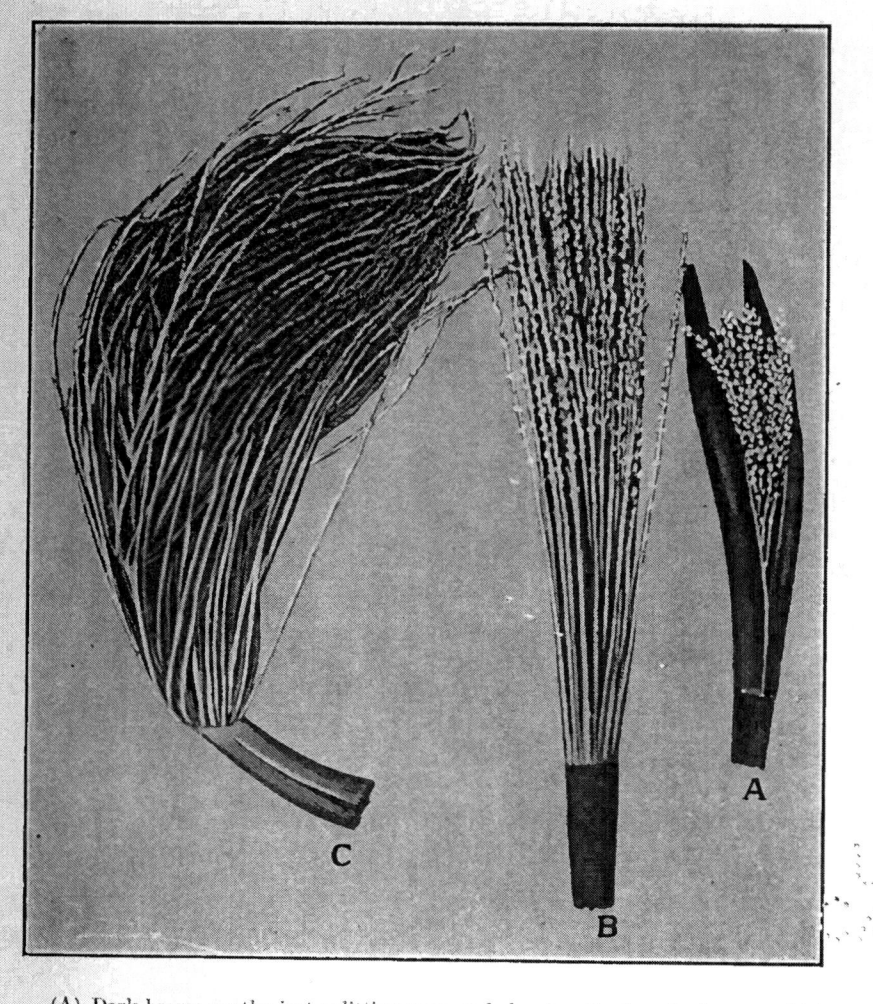

(A) Dark brown spathe just splitting open and showing the female flowers which it contains.

(B) Female inflorescence free from the spathe.

(C) A past year's female inflorescence showing the comparatively long lateral branches less crowded on the top of the main axis than in the case of the male inflorescence.

(*See paras.* 6 & 8, *pages* 11 & 12.)

СУГЬОІ
ПИЛ

ILLUSTRATION No. 17.

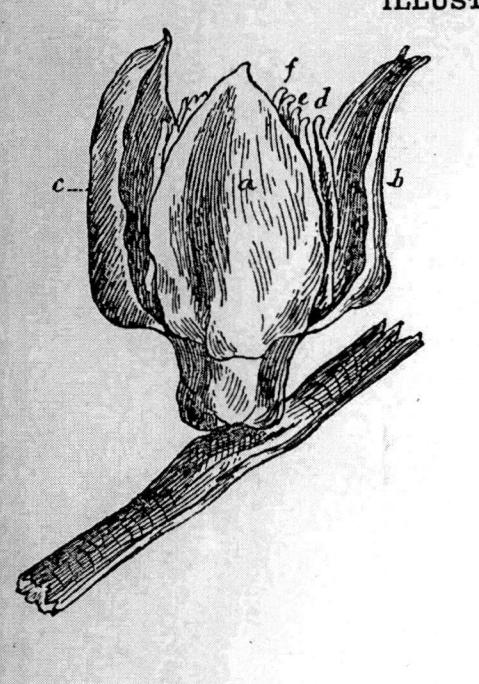

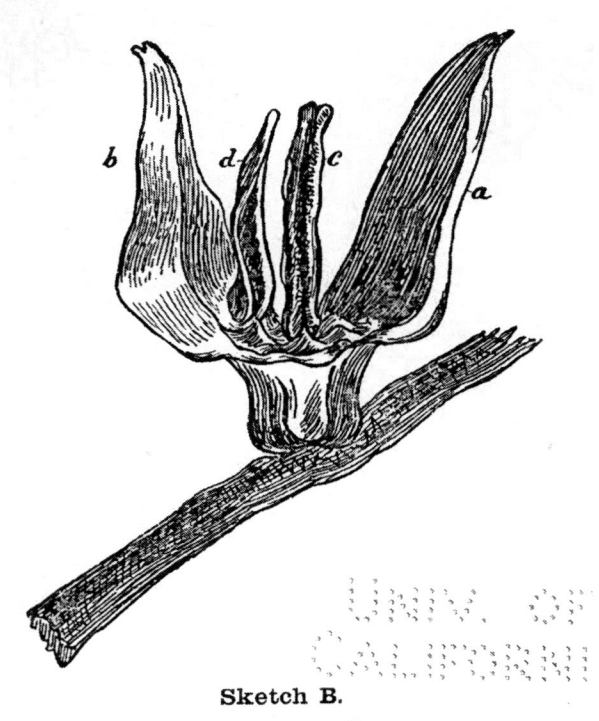

Sketch A.

Male Flower (×6½ diameters)
Scales (Sepals & Petals)....a. b. & c.
Stamens..................d. e. f. etc.

Sketch B.

Part of Male Flower (×7½ diameters)
Scales.....a. & b.
Stamens....c. & d.

(See paras. 6, 7 & 9, pages 11 to 13.)

ILLUSTRATION No. 18.

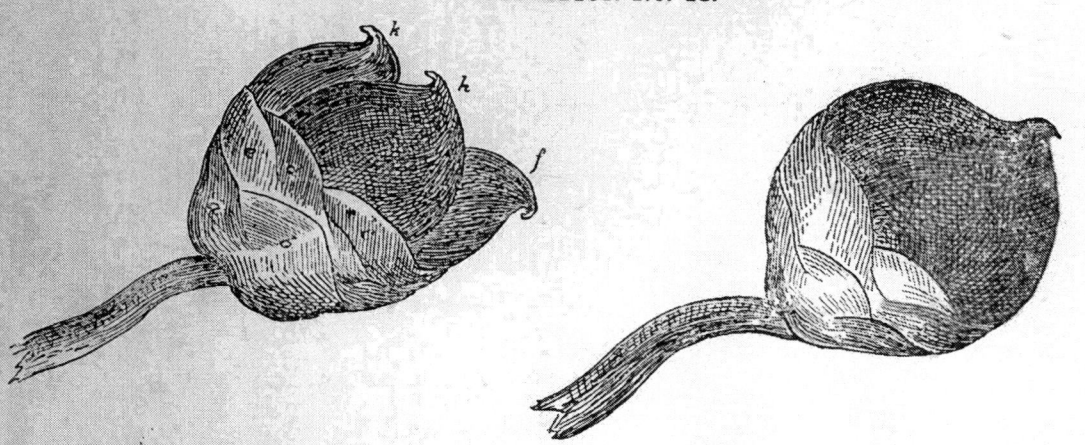

Sketch C.

Female Flower (×8 diameters)
Scales (Sepals & Petals)....a. b. c. d. e.
Carpels.................f. h. k.
The sharp hooked portion at the tip of
the carpel is the stigma.

Sketch D.

*Female Flower after two of the three carpels
have been shed* (× 5½ *diameters). The
single remaining carpel will form the date
fruit.*

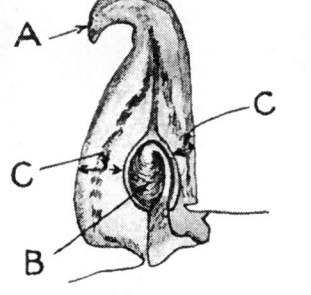

Sketch E.

Vertical Section of a Carpel (× 8 diameters).

(A) Stigma.   The part which receives the pollen grain.
(B) Ovule.   After fertilisation it becomes the seed.
(C) Carpel wall.   After the ovule is fertilised it becomes the edible part of the fruit.

(*See paras.* 6, 8, 9 & 69, *pages* 11 *to* 13, & *page* 98.)

male flower in which the white scales (petals and sepals) had not opened out. On dissecting it, however, it will be found that the central and main part of the flower is formed of three solid bodies closely applied to each other on their adjacent faces and forming what appeared like one oval body. Each of these three solid bodies is called a " carpel," and contains a structure called an " ovule " which when fertilised by the pollen gives rise to a seed, the carpel giving rise to the edible part of the fruit at the same time. At the bases of the three carpels are six scale-like structures similar to the protecting scaly sepals and petals found in the male flower, but very much smaller and clinging very closely to the carpels. A mass of female flowers therefore never has the very waxy white appearance which a mass of open male flowers has.

9. At a distance the flower-clusters may be distinguished by the fact that the small branches in the male cluster are about 6 inches long and densely crowded at the end of the axis, while those of the female are usually twice or more times that length and less densely crowded at the end of the axis (see illustrations Nos. 15 and 16, pages 12a & 12b). When the flowers newly open they may also be distinguished at a distance by the waxy white colour of the male flowers and the more yellowish hue and less crowded appearance of the female flowers. If taken in the hand at this stage a dense cloud of pollen dust will be produced from the male cluster by a slight shake, while none will come from the female cluster. Also six stamens with six comparatively large waxy-looking scales will constitute each male flower, while the female flower will be composed of three carpels closely applied to each other forming what looks like a single solid oval body and having six very tiny scales closely applied to its base (see illustrations Nos. 17 and 18, pages 12c & 12d). The flower-clusters can also be distinguished at that stage by their smell.

Brief comparison of male and female flower-clusters and flowers.

10. The above is the usual condition of affairs, but in my tours in Multan, Muzaffargarh, and Dera Ghazi Khan in the date flowering seasons, I have

Hermaphrodite flowers and polygamous trees.

found a considerable number of trees in which both male flowers and female flowers were met with on the same branch of an inflorescence. In the same inflorescence I have usually found hermaphrodite flowers, *i.e.*, containing both carpels and stamens. Such flowers each contained three, more or less functional carpels and two to six more or less functional stamens (*see* illustration No. 19, opposite). In cases where the number of functional stamens was near the maximum, the number of functional carpels was usually nearly *nil* and *vice versâ*. Trees which contain both unisexual and hermaphrodite flowers are described as " polygamous."

In polygamous trees the lengths of the small branches of the flower-clusters are usually between the lengths of the small branches of the ordinary male flower-cluster and those of corresponding branches of the ordinary female flower-cluster. Other characters which can be detected at a distance are also rather mixed. These trees are very interesting, and I should be glad if people seeing them would mark them and inform us of them. If they are marked with white paint at a height of six or seven feet from the ground so as to be out of reach of farm animals and not accessible without effort to small boys, the marks usually persist for several years.

Differences between male and female suckers.

11. In purchasing suckers (off-shoots) one may be supplied with—

(*i*) male off-shoots ;

(*ii*) female off-shoots from inferior varieties of trees ; and

(*iii*) seedling plants ;

in place of good female suckers.

Male trees have usually more thorny and stiffer leaflets than females. Every variety of female date plant, however, differs to a greater or less extent in these respects from every other variety. Differences of this sort between varieties of females are fairly constant—the plants where varieties are bred being propagated by off-shoots—but they are often very slight. Male trees are usually propagated by seeds, therefore these

ILLUSTRATION No. 19.

Branches from an inflorescence of a polygamous tree.
(a) Purely female flowers.
(b) Flowers showing pronounced male characteristics.
(*Natural size approx.*)
(*See page 13*)

characters differ considerably in males (*see* paras. 27 & 29, pages 66 & 67). To distinguish date suckers by their leaves and spines is consequently often a very difficult task. Only people who are very intimately acquainted with the vegetative characters of the date palms of a locality can hope to identify the cultivated varieties by these means, and even they may fail to do so. It can be done, however, as I have been connected with cases in which hundreds of suckers, including a number of varieties, have been accidentally mixed, and then separated out with wonderful accuracy as was shown when they bore fruits.

The lower end of an off-shoot has a mark showing where it has been severed from its parent, while the lower end of a seedling has no such mark normally. Fraudulent people, however, sometimes cut a piece off the lower end of a seedling to make it appear like an off-shoot, but a seedling plant usually has a straight stem, while that of an off-shoot usually has a slight bend at its base where it curved inwards to join the parent stem (*see* illustration No. 26, page 80*a*). The direction of the cut with regard to the main axis of the young plant and the angle at which it cuts the sap-conducting vessels of the wood also usually differ in the two cases. In the case of the off-shoot the cut is made approximately in the plane of the main axis of the parent plant and owing to the base of the off-shoot stem bending towards its mother in order to join with her tissues, the cut across the off-shoot at that point will be more or less at right-angles to the direction of its sap-conducting vessels there. In the seedling if the cut is made at right-angles to the direction of the vessels, it will be at right-angles to the main axis of the young plant, there being no bend at the base of its stem ; and if it is cut in a plane anywhere approaching that of the main axis of the young plant, it will not be in the proper direction with regard to the vessels, and the cut end will probably show a more or less distinctive outline. Male off-shoots, female off-shoots from inferior trees, and seedling plants, if skilfully cut, are all extremely difficult to distinguish, however, even by the most experienced people, and as the trees will only be distinguished with certainty when they begin to bear flowers and fruits five to ten years afterwards, I strongly advise that where possible the parent trees should be marked when in fruit (*see* para. 31, page 68), and that the suckers should be detached from their parents at the planting season under personal or reliable supervision.

12. Adult male trees in addition to having more spiny leaves and stiffer leaflets are said to have thicker stems and more leaves on their tops as a rule. As thickness of stem depends on the number and degree of development of the functional leaves which a tree bears, the stem, when grown on poor soil with scanty water-supply or under other unfavourable conditions, may not reach the same thickness as it does when conditions are more favourable. A group of trees growing from the same thadda (stool) and which had apparently originated as off-shoots from the taller central one gave the following measurements :—

Differences between adult male and female trees not in flower.

Stem (*a*) 2 feet and 5 inches in circumference.
  ,,   (*b*) 4 feet and 10 inches in circumference.
  ,,   (*c*) 3 feet and 6 inches in circumference.

The plantation was a rather dense one near that point.

The thickness of an individual stem may even differ considerably at different heights if the conditions of growth at different periods in the life of the tree have been markedly unequal. The circumference of such a tree was less than 2 feet at one height while it was 3 feet at another. (*See* also illustrations Nos. 20 and 21, pages 16*a* & 16*b*.) Minor differences in thickness of a stem at different heights can frequently be seen in trees growing where conditions of growth are not very constant. In fair circumstances, however, the stem of a date tree is approximately equal in thickness along its whole length, and different varieties of dates have a tendency to produce a stem of a certain thickness but the tendency to form thick stems is not confined to males. Numbers of male trees have been seen with quite thin stems ; others with very thick stems ; while both thick stemmed and

ILLUSTRATION No. 20.

Female tree at Muzaffargarh showing unequal thickness of stem.

(*See page* 16.)

ILLUSTRATION No. 21.

Vertical sections through centres of two date trees.

The stem of (a) is normal and rather thick.

The stem of (b) is thin and very unequal in thickness.

(*See page* 16.)

thin stemmed female trees have also been seen. The Alipore Chhohāra, for example, which is the finest local date, has usually a very thick stem—quite as thick as any male tree that I have ever seen, and a great deal thicker than in the case of some males. The following are a few measurements of the circumferences of stems and the numbers of functional leaves borne by the tree :—

Statement showing circumferences of the stems and numbers of leaves on a few trees, growing in Muzaffargarh District.

Sex of tree.	Circumference near top of stem.		Number of properly opened functional leaves on the tree.	REMARKS.
	Ft.	in.		
Female	5	0	52	
Female	4	6	52	
Male	4	4	48	
Female	4	2	46	4 leaves were drying up.
Female	3	10	43	5 leaves were drying up.
Female	3	9	42	
Male	3	3½	32	
Female	2	8	24	

Statement showing circumferences of the stems and numbers of leaves on a few trees in the Pucca Mari Railway garden, Lyallpur.

Sex of tree.	Circumference of tree.		Number of functional leaves on the tree.	REMARKS.
	Ft.	in.		
Female ..	3	3	34	Very much overshadowed by other trees, and leaves long but central axis of leaf markedly narrow near base.
Male ..	4	1	39	Very broad bases of leaves. Midribs also thick ; not shaded.
Female ..	4	8	65	Midribs and bases of leaves narrow ; rather overshadowed by other trees.
Female ..	5	1½	73	Not much overshadowed ; leaf bases normal. Tips of some of the leaves withering.

NOTE.—*In measuring the circumferences of date stems for comparisons of the above nature, care has to be taken that nearly the same amount of leaf bases, fibre, etc., is left on each tree at the places where the circumference measurements are taken. These measurements must necessarily be taken near the base of the lowest functional leaves. Care should be taken to count leaves in each case up to the same degree of senility.*

Differences in the thicknesses of the stems and in the number of functional leaves borne by the plants can, therefore, only be of use as identifying factors where the varieties of date trees to be compared are known ; where their stems normally differ materially in thickness, and where they are growing under similar conditions. Very frequently parts of old flower-clusters remain attached to the tree after the flowering and fruiting seasons are over, and in such cases the sex of the tree can usually be identified with certainty. (For structure of the inflorescences and flowers *see* pages 11—13, paras. 6—10, and for date that the trees come into flower (*see* page 92, para. 59).

CHAPTER II.

SOIL AND CLIMATE.

13. The date-palm appears to grow and produce fruit
Soils.   almost equally well on sandy, loamy, or clayey
              soils.   The soils of the Punjab plains are alluvial
varying from light sands to stiff clays, and often contain a large
percentage of lime. The soils of the famous date-growing oases
in the Libyan desert are alluvial, contain much lime, being derived
from the limestone cliffs around them, and vary in physical
character from free sands to stiff clays. Most date-growing
soils are of this general nature.

The physical character of the soil appears to have little
influence on the plant, except that the flowers and fruit may be
a little earlier on sandy lands. The soils of the Saharan oases
are mostly of a sandy nature ; those of the Mesopotamian tract
and in Egypt are mostly of very dense clays, while some of the
date groves on the coast of Egypt are growing on almost pure
sand. On the whole, sandy loams are best suited for date cultivation. A plantation of young off-shoots is much more easily
started on a sandy loam than on other soils (*see* page 81, para 43).
Practically any soil on which ordinary farm crops can be grown
is suitable for the date-palm.

14. After investigations by the Department of Agriculture,
              United States of America, on the soils of the
Resistance to   Algerian date-palm tracts, W. T. Swingle states
   alkali.
              that " although this plant can grow in soils
containing 3 to 4 per cent. of their weights of alkali, it does not
produce fruits unless its roots reach a stratum of soil where the
alkali content is below 1 per cent., and does not yield regular and
abundant crops unless there are layers in the soil with less than
0·6 per cent. of alkali." The alkali referred to is white alkali

consisting chiefly of sulphates of sodium and magnesium and a little of the chlorides of these metals. These soils also contain a great deal of sulphate of lime, which is believed to counteract the poisonous effects of the magnesium salts, and to prevent the formation of the very injurious black alkali. Swingle states : " If a soil at all depths contains over 0·6 per cent. of alkali, the growth is slower and the yield is less than on better lands, and where the alkali content is everywhere over 1 per cent., date-palms do not bear fruits regularly, and their growth is very slow." These figures exclude salts accumulated on the immediate surface of the soil. Unlike many other plants, the adult date-palm can withstand very large accumulations of alkali on the surface of the ground. In laying out a young date plantation, however, the risks of the plants dying before becoming established will be greater if there is a surface accumulation of these salts. It may not be convenient to have all soils analysed before starting a plantation, but as wheat, corn, and lucerne, crops, peach, orange, prune trees, etc., are all believed to be unable to flourish in 0·6 per cent. of alkali, young date trees may be planted where one or other of the above can grow well. Barley, sorghum, sugar-beets, grape-vines and possibly pomegranates are believed to stand from 0·6 to 1 per cent. of alkali, but unlike well-established date-palms these plants are easily killed by an accumulation of the alkali on the soil surface.

I recently took 9 samples of soil from the Arabian date plantation in the garden of the Victoria Memorial Hall, Muzaffargarh, where crops of barley have regularly been a failure. The Agricultural Chemist, Punjab, kindly analysed the samples for me and the chemical results which he gave have been incorporated by me in the table on next page.

TABLE I.

Analysis of Samples of Soil taken from the Arabian Date Plantation, Victoria Memorial Hall, Muzaffargarh, on 22nd February 1916.

Note.—Percentages are calculated on the weight of undried soil.

Sections of soil showing the depths at which the samples were taken.

Soil surface

Section B. Section A.

Note.—Scale ⅛th.
Note.—Scale 6 inches = 1 ft.

	Percentage of matter soluble in water.	Percentage of moisture in soil dried off at 100°C.	Nature of the salts present.	Further Remarks.
Sample No. 1	1·34	13·14	The salts found in the soil extracts are the chlorides, sulphates and carbonates of sodium and calcium. But in samples Nos. 5, 6, 8, and 9, chlorides are only in traces; and in samples Nos. 2, 5, 6, and 8, sulphates are in traces.	The soil was a light water loam. The water table at the time of taking samples was at a depth of 7½ ft.
Sample No. 2	0·24	17·41		
Sample No. 3	0·12	19·01		
Sample No. 4	0·104	18·94		
Sample No. 5	0·116	21·58		
Sample No. 6	0·094	23·45		
Sample No. 7	0·12	22·17		
Sample No. 8	0·046	23·92		
Sample No. 9	0·102	23·00		

(Sample depths: 6 inches, 1 inch, 2 ft. depth, 3 ft. depth, 4 ft. depth, 5 ft. depth, 6 ft. depth.)

The samples were all taken from one pit : the first three samples from one side of it and the remaining six samples from the other. The depths at which they were taken are shown in the above diagrams of the two soil sections. The ground was white with salt when the samples were taken. Twenty-one date off-shoots were planted in this land in 1910 and 230 in 1912, making 251 in all. There are now only 60 plants alive, *i.e.*, the death-rate was approximately 76 per cent. instead of the 20—30 per cent. or less usually got with fair treatment on ordinary lands. On our periodic inspections the plants in the Memorial Hall garden always appeared to be well-watered, and as far as could be seen the heavy mortality among these trees was due to the salts in the soil. The plants which are still alive in this plantation are now growing vigorously. Some of them bore fruits last season (1915) and several more are in flower this year.

In arid districts, when dates are planted on lands containing much alkali and the trees obtain their water from a high subsoil water table and no irrigations are given to land between the trees, either to crops or for other reasons, a white crust of salt very soon forms on the surface of the soil. This is due to the fact that water is constantly depositing its load of salt as it is being evaporated from the surface of the land, and as the evaporating current in such a case is always upwards, the salt deposit at the soil surface continues to be added to. In this way a very large crust of salt may accumulate on the surface of the soil of a date plantation, even when the soil below the surface contains very little salt. Where ordinary crops can be grown between the trees and these are irrigated occasionally, the surface deposit of salt is dissolved by the water, carried down into the subsoil and redistributed to some extent at each irrigation. A thick surface crust of salt, therefore, does not form in such cases unless the land contains a large amount of alkali. A surface deposit of salt similar to that described above collects on the bare land between the date-palms in arid undrained places where the land is not flooded, but the trees are planted in small channels or small circular basins and receive their water directly from these. In

ILLUSTRATION No. 22.

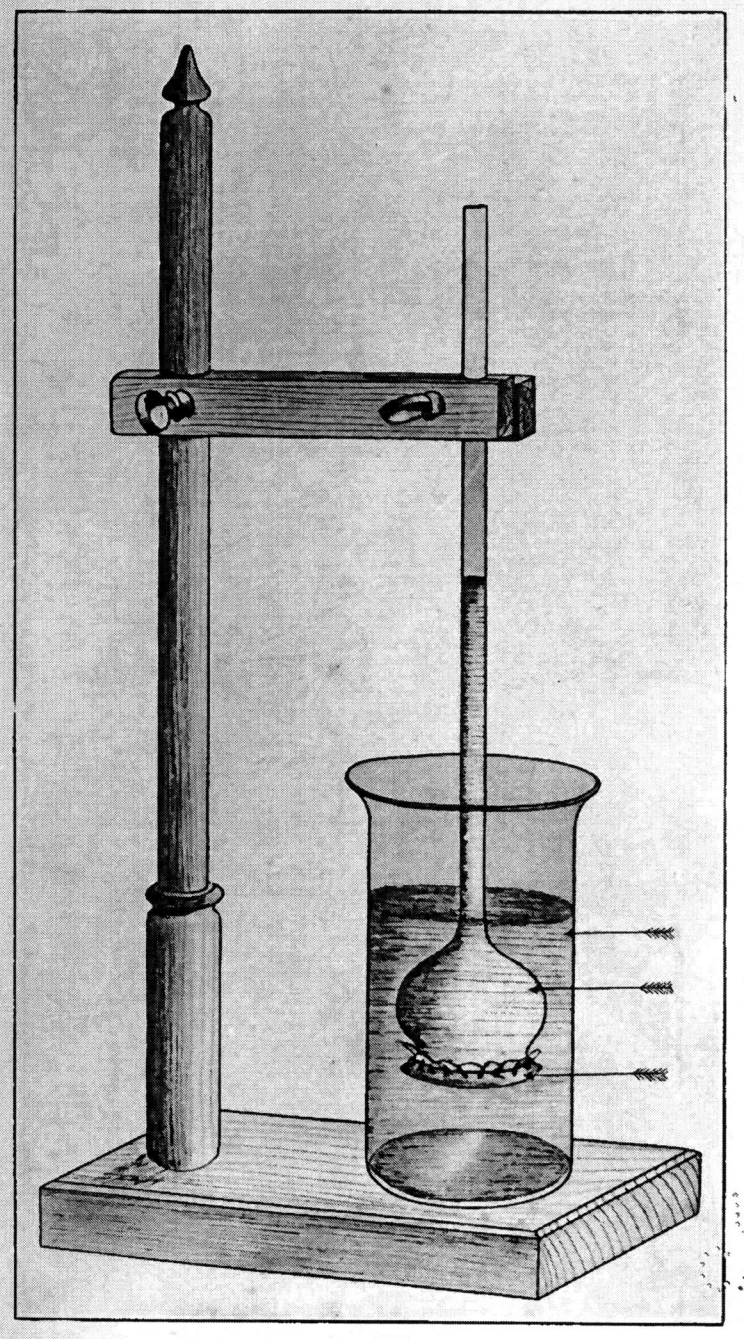

Glass containing water only.

Thistle Funnel containing salt and water.

Permeable membrane.

Apparatus showing Osmotic action.

(See para. 14, page 23.)

this case the water soaks into the earth in the channels or basins only, but in soaking into the earth is distributed more or less evenly throughout the subsoil of the plantation, and all that escapes being taken up by the roots of plants rises again and evaporates over the whole surface of the plantation, depositing any salts that it may then contain on the surface of the soil as in the previous case. In such conditions we often find date trees growing lustily in a soil the surface of which is covered with a thick deposit of salt. This has given the idea to some people that excess of salt does not harm date trees of any age. The roots of the trees may, however, be feeding in a stratum from which practically all the salt has been removed and deposited on the surface of the soil where it does not affect the plants. Very great damage may be done to such a plantation by heavy rains or by flooding the land artificially. The reason of this is that the salt deposit on the soil surface is dissolved and a very strong solution of salt is carried down to the roots of the palms. This solution may quite easily be strong enough to be fatal even to vigorous well-grown trees.

It is believed that the harmful action of the salt on the palm is chiefly one of "plasmolysis." What takes place in such a case, may be roughly illustrated as follows :—

Tie a piece of permeable vegetable or animal membrane—a piece of animal bladder will do—over the top of a glass thistle funnel ; invert it ; fill some solution of salt and water into it, and place the funnel, broad end down, in a vessel of pure water, immersing the funnel till the level of the liquid inside it and that in the outer vessel are the same. Shortly afterwards it will be found that the liquid in the outer vessel tastes saltish and that the level of the liquid in the funnel has become higher than that of the outer vessel ; in fact that there has been an interchange of liquids going on, and that more liquid has flowed from the outer vessel into the funnel than in the reverse way (see illustration No. 22, page 22a). The rates of flow of solutions through such membranes have been measured by scientists and found to be $\sqrt{\frac{1}{\text{density}}}$. There are no visible holes in the membrane separating the two liquids and the mode of interchange of the liquids is known as "osmosis."

Plants require a constant supply of water and salts for the elaboration of their food and to enable them to carry on their vital functions. The supplies of water and salts are obtained in solution from the soil through the cell walls of the roots by osmosis; these cell-walls acting as the permeable membranes.

As soon, therefore, as a solution of salt in the soil becomes more dense than that of the cell sap in the plant, the flow of water and salts into the plant becomes inhibited or reversed, and if the solution is strong enough, and its action continues sufficiently long, the state of plasmolysis is produced and the plant dies.

Great damage has frequently been done to date plantations in the Sahara by heavy rains and floods where the surface soil has been covered with a thick layer of salt. When such a layer accumulates, one way of getting rid of it is to scrape it off and cart it away. If only the layer of salt on the surface of the soil is taken away, this costs little and may be done repeatedly if necessary. In the attempt to get rid of these salts, people sometimes cart away the surface soil to a depth of 6 inches or more, but as will be seen from Table I page 21 it will be as effective and much less expensive to merely scrape the surface whenever a crust of salt forms. If, before a crust of salt has formed on the land, ordinary farm crops can be grown between the trees, and the land is irrigated for these in the usual manner, or if the land is simply flooded occasionally, the upward current of water due to evaporation from the surface of the land is reversed, the salts are carried down and to some extent redistributed in the soil and a large accumulation of salts at the surface of the soil is retarded or prevented.

Possibly one variety of date-palm may resist more alkali than others, just as one variety ripens later than another, and it may be possible, therefore, to obtain a variety specially suited for growing on salty lands.

15. It is recorded that in some oases in northern latitudes

Effect of winds.
the date trees fail to produce a crop if hot winds do not blow frequently. Certainly the body of the plant does not appear to be harmed by winds, even if they are of considerable violence. The roots have great tensile strength (*see* page 1, para. 2). The tree has a very large number of them. Most descend at sharp angles, but a suitable proportion of them spread out all round the stem at small angles to the horizon, finally descending well into the soil; the stem, when healthy, is exceptionally difficult to break across (*see* page 6, para. 3), and the leaves are so built that it is hardly possible for the wind to break or tear them, or for the wind-driven sand to abrade them (*see* page 7, para. 4). Indeed, although I have seen sand-storms in date-growing oases against which one could hardly stand upright or see a yard in front of one, and during which the wind-driven sand has stripped cereal crops into fragments leaving nothing but their stumps in the ground, I have rarely seen a healthy date tree overturned or broken by wind, or the leaves of one abraded by the sand. Sometimes, however, the stems of old trees get broken by high winds when heavily laden with fruits.

Sandstorms may cause damage when they come at the time that the fruit on the tree is in its final ripening stage and the dust sticks to the fruits. Those fruits which are most sticky at that period suffer most. The dust cannot be removed easily from the fruits and may spoil a crop for first class market purposes. In the Persian Gulf and other large date-growing localities, damage of this sort is occasionally met with. Some damage is occasionally done to date fruits in the Punjab in the same way.

16. Well-established palms do not appear to suffer from

General remarks on temperature.
excessive heat or excessive dryness of the air if the roots have a sufficient supply of water. Date trees have been reported to stand as low a temperature as 20°F. in winter without harm, and to be able to live even where it occasionally gets as low as 12°F., but when

the temperature is low in the fruiting season the fruits will not ripen properly.

The development of the fruits appears to suffer no check from cool nights, however, unless the temperature falls below a point somewhere about 64·4°F. (De Candolle, *vide* Swingle, page 63). Certain varieties of dates ripen at lower temperatures than others, and those varieties that ripen only in the hotter climates generally appear to be superior in quality to those that ripen in cooler climates. In most parts of the world, the fruits begin to form about the end of April. If the climate is hot and the variety of date is one that requires comparatively little heat to ripen it, the fruits may be ripe as early as June, while if the climate is cooler, or the variety one that requires more heat to ripen it, the fruits may ripen as late as October or even November. In some oases where harvesting labour is scarce, and the season dry, or where there is some other reason for not collecting the fruit as soon as ripe, it may be left on the trees for several weeks after that. The world's date fruiting season is generally reckoned as between 1st May and 31st October.

Tables II, III, and IV on pages 27, 28, and 29 give as nearly as the data to my hand will allow the monthly normal maximum and minimum temperatures of date-growing localities in Tunis, Egypt, Mesopotamia, and Persia. Table V, pages 30 and 31, gives similar data for ten stations in the Punjab for comparison.

TABLE II.

Normal monthly maximum and minimum temperatures in degrees Fahr. at five Date-growing Centres in Tunis.

Stations	Altitude in feet.	North Latitude.	JAN. Mean maximum.	JAN. Mean minimum.	FEB. Mean maximum.	FEB. Mean minimum.	MAR. Mean maximum.	MAR. Mean minimum.	APRIL. Mean maximum.	APRIL. Mean minimum.	MAY. Mean maximum.	MAY. Mean minimum.	JUNE. Mean maximum.	JUNE. Mean minimum.	JULY. Mean maximum.	JULY. Mean minimum.	AUG. Mean maximum.	AUG. Mean minimum.	SEPT. Mean maximum.	SEPT. Mean minimum.	OCT. Mean maximum.	OCT. Mean minimum.	NOV. Mean maximum.	NOV. Mean minimum.	DEC. Mean maximum.	DEC. Mean minimum.	REMARKS.
Tozer	158	33° 56'	59·4	42·8	65·5	46·5	72·5	52·3	81·3	58·8	89·7	65·3	99·7	74·1	107·1	77·8	104·6	79·5	93·7	72·5	83·2	63·1	70·5	53·2	60·3	44·7	Observations from 9 to 13 years.
Nefta	160	33° 54'	63·7	31·7	70·0	37·6	76·1	47·3	84·1	54·1	89·0	60·2	99·2	69·2	104·9	73·2	103·8	74·4	98·3	69·3	86·1	55·1	76·1	60·5	1·0	40·1	Observations from 3 to 6 years.
Kebili (Nefzaoua oasis)	Not to hand	33° 41'	57·9	39·2	65·8	41·9	72·5	48·2	84·4	56·8	88·3	60·3	96·9	63·2	103·8	73·4	101·3	75·2	96·1	69·3	82·0	60·6	70·6	48·2	61·0	42·4	Ditto.
Gabes	Do.	33° 57'	62·7	40·7	67·6	43·6	71·3	48·6	76·0	53·5	78·9	56·3	89·3	67·2	90·8	71·0	91·4	73·3	95·1	71·0	83·6	61·5	73·3	50·5	65·6	48·2	Observations ex-tending over 15 years.
Gafsa	1150	34° 26'	59·5	39·5	65·2	39·3	70·4	44·0	80·7	43·9	85·2	56·3	96·5	63·9	102·8	48·7	101·2	49·1	96·2	66·0	84·0	57·8	75·0	47·2	60·2	37·7	Ditto.

The data for this table were taken from pages 21 and 22 of the Department of Agriculture, United States of America, Bulletin No. 92, Date Varieties and Date Culture in Tunis, by T. H. Kearney.

TABLE

Normal monthly maximum and minimum temperatures in degrees Fahr.

Stations.	Altitude in feet.	North latitude.	JAN.		FEB.		MAR.		APL.		MAY.	
			Mean maximum.	Mean minimum.	Mean maximum.	Mean minimum.	Mean maximum.	Mean minimum.	Mean maximum.	Mean minimum.	Mean maximum.	Mean minimum.
Alexandria ...	104	31° 12′	64·4	50·6	66·8	52·4	69·8	55·9	74·5	58·4	79·0	63·5
Port Said ...	11	31° 16′	66·4	47·8	68·9	49·6	71·8	52·5	76·3	56·3	81·2	62·5
Abbassia ...	98	30° 5′	64·8	44·2	69·2	46·8	74·8	49·8	83·3	55·0	90·3	60·8
Gizah	72	30° 2′	66·6	42·2	70·9	44·2	74·6	47·1	83·8	53·2	90·0	58·3
Helwan ...	379	29° 52′	63·8	44·6	67·4	45·0	72·5	49·8	83·0	57·2	89·2	62·4
Assiut ...	182	27° 11′	69·2	40·8	74·8	43·0	82·0	48·2	92·0	56·8	98·8	65·0
Dakhla oasis	426	25° 29′	71·2	43·4	74·8	45·3	82·4	49·4	92·3	58·8	99·5	64·4
Aswan ...	326	24° 2′	74·0	48·9	78·4	50·4	88·0	57·6	95·2	65·6	103·8	71·2

The figures for the above table were obtained from data given in the Meteoro-

TABLE

Normal monthly maximum and minimum temperatures in degrees Fahr.
Persian

Stations.	Altitude in feet.	North Latitude.	JAN.		FEB.		MAR.		APL.		MAY.	
			Mean maximum.	Mean minimum.	Mean maximum.	Mean minimum.	Mean maximum.	Mean minimum.	Mean maximum.	Mean minimum.	Mean maximum.	Mean minimum.
Baghdad ...	131	33° 0′	60·1	38·3	64·7	41·8	72·3	48·2	81·6	56·9	91·8	67·9
Basra	25	30° 34′	59·2	43·8	64·8	43·7	73·4	56·1	83·5	65·1	94·1	74·6
Mohammerah ...	20	30° 27′	63·1	46·1	67·1	49·8	74·8	56·5	84·1	65·3	93·6	74·9
Koweit ...	15	29° 21′	59·9	49·3	63·8	50·8	71·3	58·3	83·5	66·6	94·7	75·8
Bahrein ...	18	26° 18′	66·1	56·4	66·7	57·2	72·8	62·9	81·3	70·0	90·2	78·0

The data for the above table were kindly supplied

III.

(over seven years' observations) at eight Date-growing Centres in Egypt.

JUNE.		JULY.		AUG.		SEPT.		OCT.		NOV.		DEC.		REMARKS.
Mean maximum.	Mean minimum.	Mean maximum.	Mean minimum.	Mean maximum.	Mean minimum.	Mean maximum.	Mean minimum.	Mean maximum.	Mean minimum.	Mean maximum.	Mean minimum.	Mean maximum	Mean minimum.	
82·4	68·9	86·7	73·0	86·7	74·1	84·8	72·0	81·5	68·7	74·8	61·9	68·0	54·3	
85·6	67·1	91·0	70·7	91·0	72·3	88·5	70·5	85·6	67·6	77·6	59·9	70·0	51·8	
94·6	65·5	97·0	69·6	94·8	69·4	90·0	66·0	86·0	62·8	75·8	54·5	68·4	47·0	
93·8	63·8	96·2	67·3	96·4	68·0	90·5	64·6	86·7	61·5	77·9	53·8	70·0	46·2	
93·6	67·8	96·2	70·4	94·3	70·2	90·2	67·4	86·6	65·5	76·1	56·8	67·3	48·4	
100·8	70·0	100·2	72·0	99·5	72·5	93·8	69·1	88·9	63·3	81·0	52·0	72·8	44·0	
104·6	71·2	102·9	73·0	103·6	73·2	98·6	69·4	94·8	64·6	84·0	57·6	74·1	45·3	
106·4	74·6	106·9	78·1	104·7	77·0	100·0	73·0	97·5	70·0	85·1	60·4	76·4	51·8	

logical Report for 1907 of the Survey Department, Ministry of Finance, Egypt.

IV.

(averages of ten years) at the undermentioned stations in Mesopotamia and Gulf.

JUNE.		JULY.		AUG.		SEPT.		OCT.		NOV.		DEC.		REMARKS.
Mean maximum.	Mean minimum.	Mean maximum.	Mean minimum.	Mean maximum.	Mean minimum.	Mean maximum.	Mean minimum.	Mean maximum.	Mean minimum.	Mean maximum.	Mean minimum.	Mean maximum.	Mean minimum.	
101·8	75·4	107·3	79·4	108·4	78·8	101·9	71·8	92·8	62·3	74·7	19·5	63·4	42·9	
100·4	81·0	103·6	81·7	104·7	81·0	100·3	75·1	90·0	67·3	75·3	57·2	63·3	48·9	
99·7	79·7	101·0	81·9	102·7	81·9	99·8	76·8	92·8	70·7	79·7	59·0	65·4	49·2	
96·6	81·3	101·1	84·6	102·4	85·4	99·9	80·4	89·8	72·4	76·1	62·2	63·7	51·5	
93·5	83·1	96·9	85·1	97·6	85·6	94·1	82·0	88·5	76·0	79·8	69·0	70·6	60·4	

to me by the Meteorological Department, India.

THE DATE PALM.

Normal monthly maximum and minimum temperatures in degrees Fahr.

Stations.	Altitude in feet.	North Latitude.	JAN.		FEB.		MAR.		APL.		MAY.	
			Mean maximum.	Mean minimum.	Mean maximum.	Mean minimum.	Mean maximum.	Mean minimum.	Mean maximum.	Mean minimum.	Mean maximum.	Mean minimum.
Montgomery ...	558	30° 44′	68·5	42·2	72·8	46·4	85·7	55·9	100·1	68·1	108·3	78·4
Multan ...	420	30° 12′	70·2	43·3	73·7	47·5	86·5	58·4	99·0	68·6	106·6	77·6
Khushab ...	612	32° 18′	67·6	41·3	68·7	46·1	80·6	56·8	95·3	68·0	104·9	77·3
Sirsa ...	662	29° 30′	71·0	43·1	75·2	46·8	88·6	57·2	101·1	68·5	107·2	77·4
*Delhi ...	718	28° 36′	70·7	47·9	74·8	51·8	87·4	62·2	99·7	73·5	104·7	80·2
Lahore ...	702	31° 36′	69·0	40·7	72·7	44·1	85·1	54·2	98·2	64·3	105·7	72·6
Ludhiana ...	812	30° 50′	67·2	44·3	71·2	47·5	84·4	57·5	97·4	67·2	104·4	75·4
Sialkot ...	830	32° 30′	66·2	42·8	69·6	46·1	81·7	55·6	95·2	66·3	103·1	74·8
Amballa ...	892	30° 24′	67·8	43·3	71·5	47·8	83·9	57·1	97·7	66·2	105·2	76·9
Rawalpindi ...	1,674	33° 39′	63·1	37·9	64·8	41·4	76·5	50·7	88·4	59·9	98·1	68·6

* Delhi City is not now in the Punjab, but the temperatures

SOIL AND CLIMATE.

V.

(average of ten years' observations) at ten stations in the Punjab.

| June | | July | | Aug. | | Sept. | | Oct. | | Nov. | | Dec. | | Remarks. |
Mean maximum.	Mean minimum.	Mean maximum.	Mean minimum.	Mean maximum.	Mean minimum.	Mean maximum.	Mean minimum.	Mean maximum.	Mean minimum.	Mean maximum.	Mean minimum.	Mean maximum.	Mean minimum.	
110.0	84.1	101.7	83.9	102.0	81.6	101.7	76.1	96.6	62.2	84.2	50.9	72.9	43.0	
107.8	83.7	103.8	83.7	100.7	82.1	100.3	77.6	95.5	64.4	81.4	52.4	73.9	44.4	
107.1	82.4	102.6	82.1	100.2	80.8	99.6	75.8	93.8	61.9	82.8	49.7	71.7	41.9	
106.7	83.1	100.6	81.8	98.2	80.2	98.9	75.7	96.1	62.6	84.9	49.5	74.9	42.7	
103.2	83.3	94.0	80.7	91.8	79.3	93.0	77.0	92.1	67.2	82.9	66.2	73.1	48.9	
107.4	79.3	100.6	79.4	98.2	77.8	98.9	72.6	95.1	59.1	83.6	46.8	73.2	40.3	
104.8	80.7	97.0	80.3	95.0	79.0	94.9	74.8	91.9	63.0	80.6	50.9	71.0	44.0	
102.5	80.5	97.6	79.6	94.1	77.7	95.7	73.8	92.3	61.9	80.9	49.9	70.1	42.6	
101.4	80.2	93.3	78.8	92.8	78.1	93.7	73.9	92.2	60.8	82.3	50.9	72.1	43.5	
102.8	75.3	97.6	76.7	93.9	75.2	93.6	68.9	88.2	55.8	77.2	43.3	67.6	37.1	

are representative of those of the Punjab lands near it.

Regarding the places mentioned in Tables II, III, and IV, the following points may be noted :—

    (*i*) The very finest dates known in the world can be grown at Tozer and Nefta in the Jerid oases, Tunis ; in Dakhla oasis, Egypt ; and in Baghdad, Mesopotamia. Nefta has the lowest temperatures of any of those places, and until we have further information we may take its temperatures as the lowest under which the finest dates may be grown, provided that humidity, rainfall, and all other factors in date growing are entirely satisfactory.

    (*ii*) The fruits produced at Alexandria would have to be relegated to the lowest class as regards quality. There is some reason to believe that certain varieties of dates can be ripened under even lower temperatures than those of Alexandria, but detailed tables of these temperatures are not to hand, therefore the Alexandria temperatures may be taken here as the criterion for low grade fruits. Where other conditions do not interfere, the places above referred to which have temperatures between those of Nefta and Alexandria produce, as a rule, an intermediate grade of fruits.

17. The chief point to note about winter temperatures is that they are not so low that the trees may be killed or harmed by the cold. Where harm is done, it is the younger leaves, especially those just issuing from the terminal buds that are affected ; therefore most harm is done if heavy frosts occur after fresh tender young leaves have begun to appear in spring. Small date plants are more susceptible to harm than tall ones, as the terminal buds of the former are nearer the ground than those of the latter, and cold frosty air being heavier than warm air tends to lie lower down.

Winter temperatures.

The temperatures at all the ten Punjab stations in winter seem very comparable to those of date-growing regions and are apparently suitable for date culture. The minimum temperatures at none of our stations get down to 20°F. (*see* also page 25, para. 16); the lowest yet recorded are 23·9°F. at Rawalpindi and 24°F. at Ludhiana.

18. Regarding summer temperatures it may be noted that the hottest month of the season in the Punjab is June; in Tunis and Lower Egypt it is July; and in Upper Egypt and Baghdad it is August. Also that May—approximately the beginning of the date fruiting season here as elsewhere—is hotter in the Punjab than at any of the date-growing centres quoted. The Indian Meteorological Department have kindly given me the following explanation of this :—

Summer temperatures.

"Northern Africa and Mesopotamia possess normal continental or marine climates, and the hottest part of the year is accordingly the end of July or the beginning of August."
.... " In that month (May) the solar heat is expended in heating up the dry land surface of the Punjab and as the air above is prevented largely from moving away, by the bordering mountains, it reaches very high temperatures. On the other hand, strong and relatively cool northerly and north-westerly winds prevail at that time over the north of Africa and tend to keep down the temperature. There is a change of wind in the autumn, the prevailing direction being then south-west, and therefore a land wind with the result that the months of September and October are as warm in Northern Africa as those of June and May."

The rains and cloudy weather in the Punjab in July and August reduce the daily maximum temperatures here in these months, and also prevent the daily minimum temperatures from falling as low as they otherwise would in that part of the season.

The following table is of interest in this connection.

TABLE VI

Showing the diurnal ranges of temperature in degrees Fahr. in May, August, and October in the Punjab.

				May.	August.	October.
Montgomery	..	..	..	29·9	20·4	34·4
Multan	..	..	..	29·0	18·6	31·1
Khushab	..	..	..	27·6	19·4	31·9
Sirsa	..	..	..	29·8	18·2	33·5
Delhi	..	..	..	24·5	12·5	24·2
Lahore	..	..	..	33·1	20·4	36·0
Ludhiana	..	..	..	29·0	16·0	28·9
Sialkot	..	..	..	28·3	17·0	30·4
Amballa	..	..	..	28·3	14·7	32·4
Rawalpindi	..	..	..	29·5	18·7	22·4

August is our dampest month (*see* Table XVII, pages 50 and 51), and in it the diurnal range of temperature is least. Our climate is drier towards both May and October; therefore the diurnal range is greater towards these months. Alexandria (*see* Table XV, pages 48 and 49), is very humid and gets gradually more so from May to October. There, as we expect, the diurnal range is small, being only 15·5°F. in May and gradually falls to 12·5 in October while Nefta, with its comparatively dry atmosphere all summer, has a diurnal range of about 30·7°F. throughout the fruiting season. A great diurnal range is apparently not necessary to the production of good fruits, however, as Bahrein, which produces very good fruits, has only a diurnal range of 9·5°F, in February to 12·5°F. in October. Most of the date varieties at present growing in the Punjab mature between 20th July and the end of August, therefore although intending growers should take notice of the temperatures in the broader date-fruiting period—May to October inclusive—in case varieties are introduced which will ripen later than those now growing, it should be noted that May to August, inclusive, is at present the important date-fruiting season in this province. Whether we limit the Punjab fruiting season to August or October, however, we find that the minimum temperatures at all the Punjab stations quoted are more than satisfactory. Even those at Rawalpindi—the coldest of these stations— are higher than the minimum temperatures at Nefta, except in September when they are about equal, and in October when they are only 2·3°F. lower; are rather higher—except in October— than those of Dakhla oasis; and little short of those for Baghdad. To further compare the temperatures in the date-fruiting season at the ten Punjab stations with those of the same period at the other centres already referred to, we will consider the monthly mean temperatures and the mean temperatures of the whole fruiting period at all these stations (see Tables VII, VIII, IX and X, pages 36, 37, 38 and 39). This comparison gives a better idea of the amount of heat to which the palm is exposed than a consideration of the maximum temperatures alone, but as equal mean temperatures for any particular month at two separate stations could obviously be made up of very different maxima and minima, a comparison of mean temperatures is of use only where, as in the cases quoted above, the minimum temperatures are satisfactory. They are naturally of most use when the maximum and minimum temperatures are also before us so that any marked difference in the heights of these or in the diurnal range of temperature may be noted.

TABLE VII.

Normal monthly mean temperatures in degrees Fahr. at Date-growing Centres in Tunis and Algeria.

Stations.	Altitude in feet.	North Latitude.	January.	February.	March.	April.	May.	June.	July.	August.	September.	October.	November.	December.	Mean temperature between 1st May and 31st October.
Tunis.															
Tozer	133	33° 56′	51·3	55·9	62·1	68·7	76·1	86·2	92·0	92·0	83·1	73·0	61·7	52·3	83·7
Nefta	150	33° 54′	50·5	56·3	61·1	69·2	74·5	84·3	89·1	88·8	83·8	72·9	61·4	53·0	82·2
Kebili	Unknown	33° 41′	49·6	56·5	61·7	71·9	74·8	84·1	89·4	87·0	82·5	72·5	59·8	52·0	81·7
Gabes	Do.	33° 57′	51·8	55·6	59·7	64·2	69·2	76·3	81·3	81·0	80·0	72·8	62·9	54·3	76·7
Gafsa	1150	34° 26′	49·2	53·7	58·1	64·2	71·4	80·4	85·6	85·4	81·7	71·3	59·8	48·6	79·2
Algeria.															
Biskra	449	34° 50′	50·5	53·2	58·3	63·1	71·8	80·6	87·1	85·8	78·6	67·6	57·2	51·3	78·6
Tougourt	..	33° 10′	47·3	49·8	54·9	64·0	74·8	86·0	92·1	85·1	83·7	68·4	58·5	48·9	81·7
Ouargla	..	31° 56′	46·8	51·8	59·9	66·4	73·6	82·4	90·7	86·0	78·1	63·5	52·9	45·0	79·0
Orleansville	422	36° 10′	49·8	61·6	55·4	60·6	69·2	77·3	86·0	84·6	76·6	66·9	56·5	49·6	76·7
Algeria	72	36° 47′	53·9	55·0	56·1	61·1	63·8	70·7	76·6	78·0	73·4	67·6	59·6	54·7	71·8

NOTE.—*The figures for the above Table were got from the same source as those of Table II., excepting those for Orleansville and Algeria, which were taken from "The Climate of the Continent of Africa" by Alex. Knox, Pub. Univ. Press, Cambridge.*

TABLE VIII.

Normal monthly mean temperatures in degrees Fahr., at eight Date-growing Centres in Egypt.

Stations.	Altitude in feet.	North Latitude.	January.	February.	March.	April.	May.	June.	July.	August.	September.	October.	November.	December.	Mean temperature between 1st May and 31st October.
Alexandria ..	104	31° 12'	57·4	58·4	61·0	65·1	69·8	74·5	78·1	78·8	77·2	74·0	67·4	61·2	75·4
Port Said ..	11	31° 16'	56·5	58·3	61·0	65·3	70·5	75·8	79·5	80·4	78·4	75·4	67·6	60·2	76·6
Abbassia ..	98	30° 5'	53·6	56·6	61·9	69·4	76·4	81·5	83·3	82·4	77·9	73·0	63·0	57·6	79·1
Gizah ..	72	30° 2'	51·2	54·3	58·4	66·8	72·8	77·6	79·9	79·5	75·9	71·6	63·0	54·8	76·2
Helvan ..	379	29° 52'	52·4	55·4	59·4	68·2	74·3	79·5	81·7	80·6	77·2	74·1	64·8	56·0	77·9
Asuit ..	182	27° 11'	51·1	54·8	61·2	70·9	78·8	83·6	84·6	83·8	78·8	74·1	63·5	56·3	78·9
Dakhla oasis ..	426	25° 29'	56·8	59·0	66·2	76·6	83·5	88·2	89·2	87·2	83·0	78·4	69·4	59·6	84·9
Aswan ..	326	24° 2'	60·8	63·3	72·7	81·5	90·7	93·8	95·4	93·4	89·0	84·8	73·6	65·0	91·2

NOTE.—The figures for the above Table were got from the same source as those of Table III.

TABLE IX.

Normal monthly mean temperatures in degrees Fahr. at Date-growing Centres in Mesopotamia and Persian Gulf.

Stations.	Altitude in feet.	North Latitude.	January.	February.	March.	April.	May.	June.	July.	August.	September.	October.	November.	December.	Mean temperature between 1st May and 31st October.
Baghdad	131	33° 25'	49·2	53·3	60·3	69·3	79·9	88·6	93·3	93·6	86·9	77·5	62·1	53·1	86·6
Basrah	25	30° 34'	51·5	56·7	64·7	74·3	84·3	90·7	92·7	92·9	87·7	78·7	66·3	56·1	87·8
Mohammerah ..	20	30° 27'	54·6	58·5	65·7	74·7	84·3	89·7	91·5	92·3	88·3	81·7	69·3	57·3	87·9
Koweit	15	29° 21'	54·6	57·3	64·8	75·1	85·3	88·9	92·9	93·9	90·1	81·1	66·3	57·6	88·7
Bahrein	18	26° 18'	61·3	61·9	67·9	75·7	84·1	88·3	91·0	91·6	88·1	82·3	74·4	65·5	87·5

NOTE.—*The figures for the above Table were got from the same source as those for Table IV.*

TABLE X.

Normal monthly mean temperatures in degrees Fahr. (average of ten years' observations) at ten stations in the Punjab.

Stations.	Altitude in feet.	North Latitude.	January.	February.	March.	April.	May.	June.	July.	August.	September.	October.	November.	December.	Mean temperature between 1st May and 31st October.
Montgomery	558	30° 44′	55·4	59·6	70·8	84·1	93·4	97·1	94·3	91·8	88·9	79·4	67·6	58·0	90·8
Multan	420	30° 12′	56·8	60·6	72·5	83·8	92·1	95·8	93·8	91·4	89·0	80·0	68·4	59·2	90·3
Khushab	612	32° 18′	54·5	57·4	68·7	81·7	91·1	94·8	92·4	90·5	87·7	77·9	66·3	56·8	89·06
Sirsa	662	29° 30′	57·1	61·0	72·9	84·8	92·3	94·9	91·2	89·3	87·3	79·4	67·2	58·8	89·06
*Delhi	718	28° 36′	59·3	63·3	74·8	86·6	92·5	93·3	87·4	85·8	85·0	80·0	69·6	61·3	87·29
Lahore	702	31° 36′	54·9	58·4	69·7	81·3	89·2	93·4	90·0	88·0	85·8	77·1	65·2	56·8	87·25
Ludhiana	812	30° 50′	55·8	59·4	71·0	82·3	89·9	92·8	88·7	87·0	84·9	77·5	65·8	57·5	86·8
Sialkote	830	32° 30′	54·5	57·9	68·7	80·8	89·0	93·0	88·6	86·2	84·8	77·1	65·4	56·3	86·45
Amballa	892	30° 24′	55·6	59·7	70·5	82·0	91·1	90·8	86·1	85·5	83·8	77·0	66·6	57·8	85·7
Rawalpindi	1,674	33° 39′	50·5	53·1	63·6	74·2	83·4	89·1	87·0	84·6	81·3	72·0	60·3	52·4	82·9

NOTE.—*Data from Meteorological Department, India.*
**Delhi is not now in the Punjab, but the temperatures are representative of those of the Punjab lands near it.*

From a comparison of the above tables, it appears that the mean temperatures for the whole of the world's date-fruiting season (1st May to 31st October) at all the Punjab stations are higher than that at Nefta ; that the monthly mean temperatures in the same season are higher at Montgomery, Multan, Khushab, and Sirsa than those at Nefta ; that those at Lahore and Ludhiana are all higher than at Nefta, except in August when they are only 0·8°F. and 1·8°F. lower, respectively ; that those at Delhi, Sialkote, and Amballa are higher, except in July and August, when they are lower by less than 3·5°F. ; that at Rawalpindi they are only short of those at Nefta by 2·1°F. in July, 4·2°F. in August, 2·5°F. in September, 0·9°F. in October, and are far better than those at Cairo where many date trees are successfully farmed.

So far as mean temperatures in the date-fruiting season are concerned, therefore, it seems that the very best dates known could be grown at Montgomery, Multan, Khushab, and Sirsa ; probably also at Lahore and Ludhiana, while Delhi, Sialkote, and Amballa fall little short of the standard required for first class dates ; and even at Rawalpindi the temperatures are quite suitable for date farming.

19. It has been stated that, with certain reservations, certain amounts of heat are required to produce

Comparison of Heat-Units at Punjab stations with those at stations in Algeria, Tunis, Egypt, and Mesopotamia.

flowers and to mature the fruits of particular crops. People holding this view have made comparison of the sums of daily temperatures with a view to throwing light on whether a plant would mature in a certain district, and if so, on what date it would be likely to mature. The daily mean temperatures are usually added for this purpose. The value of comparisons of this sort has been severely criticised. It has been contended that these comparisons can only be made between regions of somewhat similar climates, and some people deny the value of that, pointing out that the amount and nature of the plant's food supply, the supply of water, the amount of light, etc., are equally vital factors in the development of the plant. Where the sunshine is little interrupted by cloud, etc., and the plants are in moderately rich soil, well supplied by irrigation water or water rising from below as is often the case where date palms are grown, a comparison of the heat factors is considered of importance. This factor has therefore been considered. It should be noted, however, that a weak point in comparisons made on those lines is that no indication is given of the height of the temperature at different stages of the plant's life cycle. In date culture, for example, high temperatures are much more essential at the fruit ripening period than early in the fruiting season, and where such comparisons are being made it should also be seen that there is no considerable discrepancy in this respect.

The amount of heat necessary to ripen the fruits of the date palm has generally been calculated by adding together the daily mean temperatures during the months when the dates are developing, the developing period being considered as extending from 1st May to 31st October. Following W. T. Swingle of the United States of America, Department of Agriculture, I have, for convenience, added only the degrees of temperature above $64\cdot4°F$. The Deglet Noor date referred to below is supposed to be the finest date known, and the most difficult date to ripen.

TABLE XI.

Stations.	Sum of daily mean temperatures above 64·4°F. between 1st May and 31st October in Degrees F.	REMARKS.
	Algeria.	
1. Algiers	1,373*	No dates ripen here.
2. Orleansville	2,276*	Very early sorts mature.
3. Biskra	3,165*	Average of ten years' observations; many dates ripen regularly, Deglet Noor dates ripen but are not of best quality. Date culture, the leading industry.
4. Ayata (1889)	3,764	Deglet Noor dates ripen well.
5. Ayata (1890)	3,269	Deglet Noor dates ripened very imperfectly.
6. Ayata (1891)	3,431	Deglet Noor dates ripened very slowly and imperfectly. At Ayata a speciality is made of the culture of choice Deglet Noor dates for the export trade.

*Data from Swingle, United States of America, Department of Agriculture, Bulletin No. 53, except those marked * which are from " Climate of the Continent of Africa," by A. Knox.*

TABLE XI—*contd.*

Stations.	Sum of daily mean temperatures above 64·4°F. between 1st May and 31st October in Degrees F.	REMARKS.
Tunis.		
7. Tozer ⎱ Jerid oasis	3,555	Observations nine to thirteen years : all varieties of dates including Deglet Noor ripen perfectly.
8. Nefta ⎰	3,277	Observations three to six years ; date fruits as at Tozar.
9. Kebili. (Nefzaoua oasis)	3,183	Observations four to five years ; several first class varieties ripen perfectly. Deglet Noor not yet grown.
10. Gabes oases	2,272	Observations fifteen years. Finest varieties do not ripen well, even second and third class dates do not always ripen perfectly.
11. Gafsa oasis	2,738	Observations fifteen years. 50,000 to 65,000 date trees in the oasis. Fruits mediocre quality, elevation 1,150 feet. Not suited for choice varieties because of its high elevation.

Data from Kearney, United States of America, Department of Agriculture, Bulletin No. 92.

Egypt (observations over seven years).

Stations.		REMARKS.
12. Alexandria	2,035 ⎫	
13. Port Said	2,266 ⎪	Dates ripen regularly, but are not as good as the dates grown higher up in Egypt.
14. Abbassia	2,702 ⎬	
15. Gizah	2,168 ⎪	
16. Helwan	2,480 ⎭	
17. Assuit	2,982	Good dates ripen regularly.
18. Dakhla oasis	3,772	First class dates ripen regularly.
19. Asswan	4,851	First class dates ripen regularly.

Meteorological data from Report 1907, Survey Department, Egypt,

Mesopotamia and Persian Gulf.

Stations.		REMARKS.
20. Baghdad	4,088	Observations ten years ; first class dates ripen regularly.
21. Basrah	4,309	Observations fifteen years ; first class dates ripen.
22. Mohammerah	4,386	Observations five years ; first class dates ripen.
23. Koweit	4,447	Observations seven years ; first class dates ripen.
24. Bahrein Island	4,261	Observations thirteen years ; first class dates ripen.

Meteorological data from Meteorological Department, India.

The above data are interesting. From Kearney we understand that the fruits of the Deglet Noor ripen perfectly where the heat units above 64°F. between 1st May and 31st October amount to 3,277°F. (*vide* Nefta), while Swingle states " From three years' observations, it is considered that about 2,000°C. (3,600°F.) are required to ripen the Deglet Noor satisfactorily."

Assuming that the data from both investigators are correct, it seems that the explanation of the case would most likely be found from a comparison either of the heights of the temperatures at the different stages of the fruiting season, or of the amounts of rainfall at the ripening time. Unfortunately Swingle does not give the monthly rainfalls and maximum and minimum temperatures at Ayata for the particular years which he refers to, and I have not yet got these to hand, so I am not able to say whether they throw any light on the point.

He notes, however, that in 1889 when the dates are said to have ripened well at Ayata, the rainfall for the whole year was only 2·52 inches; in 1890, when they ripened very imperfectly, it was 9·32 inches, and that again in 1891, when they ripened imperfectly, it was 4·16 inches. It appears to me possible, therefore, that in 1890 and 1891 enough rain may have fallen, when the fruits were ripening, to have spoiled them somewhat. This suspicion is strengthened by the fact that the finest dates can be grown at Nefta, where there is practically no rain under 3,277°F. units, and that several first class varieties are grown at Kebili which is practically rainless until October or November, under 3,183°F. units. Our data indicate that 2,738°F. units is too little heat to ripen first class dates properly, as at Gafsa, which is practically rainless, the finest dates do not appear to do so. From the Alexandria figures, it appears that lower qualities of dates can be ripened where there are about 2,000 units of heat properly distributed between 1st May and 31st October.* No dates appear to ripen under 1,373 units distributed throughout the season as at Algiers (For monthly mean temperatures at Nefta, Kebili, Gafsa, Biskra, Orleansville, Algiers, etc., see page 31, Table VII, and for a comparison of the data to hand concerning humidity and rainfall, see Tables XIII, XIV, XV, XVI and XVII, pages 46, 47, 48, 49, 50 and 51). The relative qualities of date fruits grown at the places where the sums of the heat units lie between those of Alexandria and Nefta appear to correspond roughly with these sums.

---

* Some dates in Alexandria ripen in early September.

We have seen (*see* para. 18, page 33), that the minimum and mean temperatures in the fruiting season at all the Punjab stations mentioned above are quite satisfactory, and if other factors are equal and if first class dates ripen under 3,277 units of heat, then the finest dates should ripen in the Punjab, at the places and by the dates given in the following table :—

TABLE XII.

Stations.	Sum of daily mean temperatures above 64° F. from 1st May to 31st October in degrees F.	Date on which the Deglet Noor dates might be expected to ripen if 3,277 heat units are necessary.
Montgomery...	4,856	18th August.
Multan	4,770	21st August.
Khushab	4,534	26th August.
Sirsa	4,534	27th August.
Delhi	4,216	8th September.*
Lahore	4,199	6th September.
Ludhiana	4,117	9th September.
Sialkote	4,052	12th September.
Amballa	3,919	18th September.
Rawalpindi	3,399	17th October.

* *Lahore is hotter than Delhi before 6th September, see Table X, page 39.*

So far as temperature is concerned, then, the finest dates ought to ripen at all the ten stations mentioned.

The amount of heat required to ripen date fruits has been calculated by various other methods, but we need not deal at greater length with the subject here. No amount of heat has yet been found too much for date trees when properly established.

20. In order that the date palm may produce abundant fruits of the best quality, it is essential that the air be very dry from the time the flowers open to the time the fruits ripen. Rains or a damp atmosphere at other times of the year may be beneficial. The presence of water vapour in the air has been considered to cause harm to the date palm in the fruiting season by absorbing heat from the sun's rays and thereby preventing the temperature from rising to the great height necessary to develop and ripen the fruits properly. It would appear from the Tables V, X and XII, however, that we need not fear insufficient heat in most parts of

Rainfall and humidity.

the Punjab. The dry atmosphere, which allows an excessive heating during the day, allows an equally great fall of temperature at night by radiation of heat into a cloudless sky; therefore the diurnal range of temperature in dry parts of the season is much greater than it is in damp weather (*see* page 33, para. 18). Damp or rainy weather is directly injurious to date palms in preventing the fertilisation of the flowers in spring and in causing decay or dropping of the fruit when it is developing and ripening in summer. Tables XIII, XIV, XV, XVI and XVII, on pages 46—51 show the mean relative humidities and normal rainfalls at stations in Tunis, Algeria, Egypt, Mesopotamia, Persian Gulf, and the Punjab.

21. The date flowering season in the Tunis oases appears to be from about the middle of March to the middle of April (*see* Kearney, page 53, Bulletin No. 92, United States of America, Department of Agriculture); that for the Algerian oases appears to begin in April and extend to the end of May (*see* Swingle, page 27, Bulletin No. 53, United States of America, Department of Agriculture); April-May cover the chief flowering seasons in Lower Egypt, and March-April that of Upper Egypt, Dakhla oasis, Baghdad, and the Punjab. For our purpose, we may take the spring months, March, April, and May, as the world's flowering season.

The world's date flowering season.

22. From the figures to hand an average humidity of 63 in the spring months apparently does not interfere with date culture, as Tozer, where large quantities of some of the finest dates known are cultivated, has that degree of humidity. A normal mean humidity of 73-74, even at that season, does not appear to be a serious objection, as at Port Said under that humidity, hand pollination is successfully carried on. The point for intending date growers to note when comparing climates as regards humidity and rainfall in the flowering season is whether hand pollination ensures fertilisation in a sufficiently high percentage of cases. Contrasted with the places just referred to, the mean relative humidities at all the Punjab stations in that season seem satisfactory.

Humidities in the flowering season.

TABLE XIII.

Monthly mean rainfall in inches and mean relative humidities at Date-growing Centres in Tunis.

RAINFALL.

Stations.	Altitude in feet.	North Latitude.	January.	February.	March.	April.	May.	June.	July.	August.	September.	October.	November.	December.	Total for the year.	Observations extending over—
Tozer or Nefta..	153	33° 56′	·62	·35	·70	1·02	·23	·15	··	··	·15	·27	·31	·47	4·33	Several years.
Kebili	Not to hand	33° 43′	1·77	1·49	1·33	·78	·86	·23	·03	·03	·66	1·53	2·87	1·57	13·15	14 years.
Gabes	Ditto	33° 57′	·90	·94	·98	·70	·19	·07	·03	·03	·55	1·02	·90	·82	7·20	Several years.
Gafsa	1,150	34° 26′	·47	·74	·66	·74	·35	·31	·11	·07	·74	·47	·59	·39	5·64	14 years.

NOTE.—*Data for rainfalls from the Meteorological Department, India.*
Data for Humidities from Kearney, Agricultural Department, United States of America, Bulletin No. 92.

HUMIDITIES.

Stations.	Spring.	Summer.	Autumn.	Winter.
Tozer or Nefta	63·0	52·0	59·6	70·6
Gabes	65·0	64·1	67·6	70·1
Gafsa	57·6	47·0	59·6	64·0

NOTE.—*Spring includes the months of March, April, and May.*
Summer includes the months of June, July, and August.
Autumn includes the months of September, October, and November.
Winter includes the months of December, January, and February.

TABLE XIV.

Monthly mean rainfalls in inches and mean relative Humidities at stations in Algeria.

RAINFALLS.

Stations.	Altitude in feet.	North Latitude.	January.	February.	March.	April.	May.	June.	July.	August.	September.	October.	November.	December.	Total for the year.	REMARKS.
Algeria ..	Not to hand	36° 47'	3·82	3·31	3·11	2·01	1·30	0·59	0·08	0·28	1·02	2·87	3·90	4·61	26·90	Average of fifty-four years' observations.
Orleansville ..	422	36° 10'	1·34	2·91	2·32	2·72	1·54	0·59	0·08	0·08	0·79	1·89	2·40	2·40	19·06	Average of fifteen years' observations.
Ayata (Oued Rirh region).	Not to hand	33°	0·87	0·55	1·06	0·32	0·28	0·04	..	..	0·10	0·32	0·12	1·14	4·86	Average of five years' observations (1888–1892).
Biskra ..	446	34° 5'	0·43	0·95	1·02	1·18	1·22	0·24	0·04	0·12	0·83	0·75	0·39	0·67	7·91	Average of nineteen years' observations. Greatest rainfall 16·30 inches in 1884. Least rainfall 2·44 inches in 1878.

NOTE.—Data for rainfalls from the Climate of the Continent of Africa by Alexander Knox. Humidities from Kearney, Department of Agriculture, United States of America, Bulletin No. 92.

HUMIDITIES.

Station.	Spring.	Summer.	Autumn.	Winter.
Biskra	47·7	34·9	51·3	59·8

NOTE.—Spring includes March, April, May.
Summer includes June, July, August.
Autumn includes September, October, November.
Winter includes December, January, February.

THE DATE PALM.

Monthly mean rainfalls in inches and mean relative

Stations.	Altitude in feet.	North Latitude.	JAN.		FEB.		MAR.		APL.		MAY.	
			Humidity.	Rainfall.	Humidity.	Rainfall.	Humidity.	Rainfall.	Humidity.	Rainfall.	Humidity.	Rainfall.
Alexandria ..	104	31° 1′	69	2·3	68	1·2	68	0·68	69	0·12	72	0·04
Port Said ...	11	31° 16′	76	0·88	75	0·36	74	0·4	73	0·2	73	0·04
Abbassia ...	98	30° 5′	68	0·36	64	0·2	58	0·16	50	0·08	46	0·04
Gizah ...	72	30° 2′	82	0·36	73	0·16	70	0·12	60	0·16	57	0·04
Helwan ...	379	29° 52′	63	0·56	54	0·08	53	0·16	44	0·04	43	0·08
Assuit ...	182	27° 11′	72	...	66	..	57	...	43	..	35	...
Dakhla oasis	426	25° 29′	42	..	39	...	35	. .	28	...	27	...
Asswan ...	326	24° 2′	52	...	44	...	37	...	32	...	34	...

Data from Meteorological Report

Monthly mean rainfalls in inches and mean relative Humidities

Stations.	Altitude in feet.	North Latitude.	JAN.		FEB.		MAR.		APL.		MAY.	
			Humidity.	Rainfall.	Humidity.	Rainfall.	Humidity.	Rainfall.	Humidity.	Rainfall.	Humidity.	Rainfall.
Baghdad ...	131	33°	80	1·04	70	1·37	70	1·41	62	0·81	56	0·23
Basrah ...	25	30° 34′	80	1·22	77	0·97	71	1·59	65	0·44	59	0·33
Bahrein ...	18	26° 18′	80	0·41	80	0·68	77	0·52	72	0·23	65	0·07
Koweit * ...	15	29° 21′	...	1·05	...	0·63	...	0·98	...	0·16	...	0·10
Mohamerah *	20	30° 27′	...	1·19	...	1·06	...	1·48	...	0·35	...	0·14

Data from Meteorologica
* Humidity figure

XV.

Humidities at Date-growing Centres in Egypt.

JUNE.		JULY.		AUG.		SEPT.		OCT.		NOV.		DEC.		Mean relative humidities between 1st April and 30th November.	Total rainfall in inches from 1st April to 31st October.
Humidity.	Rainfall.	Humidity.	Rainfall.	Humidity.	Rainfall.	Humidity.	Rainfall.	Humidity.	Rainfall.	Humidity.	Rainfall.	Humidity.	Rainfall.		
74	..	76	...	75	...	71	0·08	71	0·32	69	1·52	70	2·48	72	1·56
74	..	76	...	75	...	74	...	74	0·08	73	0·48	76	0·84	74	0·32
46	..	50	...	55	...	61	...	65	0·04	68	0·16	70	0·24	55	0·16
58	...	62	..	67	...	71	...	75	0·04	78	0·04	81	0·12	66	0·24
44	...	48	..	54	...	58	..	58	0·04	62	0·04	64	0·01	51	0·16
35	...	40	...	45	...	57	..	62	...	68	...	67	...	48	...
26	...	28	...	30	...	35	...	34	...	39	...	43	...	31	...
31	...	29	...	30	...	35	...	39	...	48	...	52		35	...

for 1907, Survey Department, Egypt.

XVI.

at Date-growing Centres in Mesopotamia and Persian Gulf.

JUNE.		JULY.		AUG.		SEPT.		OCT.		NOV.		DEC.		Mean relative humidities between 1st April to 30th November.	Total rainfall in inches between 1st April and 31st October.
Humidity.	Rainfall.	Humidity.	Rainfall.	Humidity.	Rainfall.	Humidity.	Rainfall.	Humidity.	Rainfall.	Humidity.	Rainfall.	Humidity.	Rainfall.		
40	...	42	...	45	0·05	48	...	55	0·08	64	0·79	78	1·17	50	1·12
56	...	54	...	53	...	58	0·12	63	0·07	69	0·96	79	1·18	60	0·96
63	...	65	...	71	...	73	...	76	0·01	78	0·24	81	0·82	70	0·31
...	.	...	...	...	...	...	...	...	0·20	...	0·46	..	1·23	...	0·46
...	...	...	..	...	...	...	...	...	0·14	...	1·17	...	2·59	...	0·63

Department, India.
not to hand.

M, DP

THE DATE PALM.

Monthly mean rainfalls and mean

Stations.	JAN.		FEB.		MAR.		APRIL.		MAY.	
	Humidity.	Rainfall.	Humidity.	Rainfall.	Humidity.	Rainfall.	Humidity.	Rainfall.	Humidity.	Rainfall.
Delhi	68	1·23	65	0·71	49	0·50	36	0·20	38	0·72
Sirsa	76	0·84	73	0·33	57	0·32	39	0·26	37	0·71
Amballa	87	1·62	84	2·41	63	0·37	53	0·31	49	0·73
Ludhiana	82	1·84	78	1·80	63	0·79	45	0·71	40	0·61
Lahore	82	1·12	78	1·10	65	0·65	47	0·42	41	0·82
Sialkote	82	2·51	79	1·80	67	1·14	48	0·80	41	1·03
Rawalpindi	84	2·74	82	2·24	72	1·89	56	1·70	44	1·47
Khushab	70	0·82	70	0·69	58	1·13	42	0·62	32	0·78
Montgomery	75	0·84	69	0·67	52	0·35	38	0·13	36	0·27
Multan	71	0·45	68	0·43	59	0·39	48	0·10	44	0·30

NOTE.—*Data from the*

XVII.

relative Humidities in the Punjab.

JUNE.		JULY.		AUG.		SEPT.		OCT.		NOV.		DEC.		Mean relative humidity from 1st March to 31st August.	Total rainfall from 1st March to 31st August.
Humidity.	Rainfall.	Humidity.	Rainfall.	Humidity.	Rainfall.	Humidity.	Rainfall.	Humidity.	Rainfall.	Humidity.	Rainfall.	Humidity.	Rainfall.		
56	3·41	75	8·48	78	8·52	69	3·61	50	0·06	52	0·11	61	0·53	55·3	21·84
51	1·79	67	4·14	71	3·87	64	1·74	50	0·11	59	0·01	69	0·31	53·6	11·09
67	6·29	86	7·65	88	8·03	82	4·24	70	0·03	75	0·46	82	0·82	67·6	23·38
56	3·02	76	9·29	79	6·35	75	3·61	61	0·33	64	0·06	76	0·78	59·8	20·75
52	2·09	71	5·96	75	5·30	67	1·99	57	0·20	67	0·07	78	0·38	58·3	15·24
52	3·08	74	8·01	79	9·69	70	2·83	59	0·25	65	0·09	74	0·52	60·1	23·75
50	2·01	72	8·53	80	8·70	72	3·23	62	0·44	65	0·29	74	0·74	62·3	24·30
43	1·72	65	4·52	69	2·73	60	0·55	45	0·01	48	0·02	60	0·54	51·5	11·50
43	1·14	60	2·48	63	2·99	59	0·87	46	0·03	58	0·06	65	0·42	48·6	7·36
48	0·62	62	2·41	68	2·02	65	0·32	56	...	62	0·07	70	0·19	54·8	5·84

Meteorological Department, India.

23. Actual rainfall is much more to be feared than high
humidity short of precipitation in the flowering
season, as it may wash the pollen from the
flowers and may do damage in other ways;
therefore the less rain in that season, the better for date farmers.

The total normal rainfall at the date-growing centres quoted
in the above tables in the spring months (March, April, and May)
is highest at Biskra. There it is 3·42 inches. This rain evidently
does not preclude date culture, for date culture is the leading
industry there (*see* Table No. XI, page 41). Kebili comes
second with 2·97 inches; Baghdad comes next with 2·45 inches,
while rainfalls at the other stations are lower. In the Punjab
the totals for the same three months are less than 0·8 inches at
Montgomery and Multan; less than 1·5 inches at Lahore and
Ludhiana; 2·5 to 3 inches at Khushab and Sialkote, and over
5 inches at Rawalpindi. So far, then, as can be seen from the
above data, the climate in the flowering season in most parts
of the Punjab seems suitable for date culture. Where date
trees are already growing that are either pollinated by hand or
are in suitable positions with regard to male trees, or where other
conditions are suitable, people can set the point at rest for themselves by noting whether a fair number of fruits on such trees
develop seeds annually (*see* also page 98, para. 70). The test
is most severe where female trees are grown with few or no males
near them, and the plants are hand pollinated (*see* page 96,
para. 64), because if rain washes the pollen off the female flower
after hand pollination, more pollen is not brought by the wind
to replace it as may be the case where the trees are habitually
wind pollinated. In the young Arabian date plantations at
Multan, and Lyallpur however, where trees have been hand
pollinated for the last three years and where very few male trees
are growing near, hand pollination has been quite successful.

24. Although the temperatures may be entirely satisfactory, excess of atmospheric moisture, including
actual rainfall in the fruit developing and
ripening season, may damage the crop by causing

the fruits to decay and drop from the trees before they are ready
for harvesting ; also possibly in other ways.   As already stated,
the world's fruit developing and ripening season may be taken
as extending between 1st May and 31st October, and the most
critical stage is the ripening period.   Excluding special cases the
ripening periods may be taken roughly as September-October in
Mesopotamia, Algeria, Tunis, and Egypt ; and July-August in
the Punjab. The greater heat in early summer probably hastens
the ripening season here. From figures for Tozer and Basra
we may conclude that a humidity of 60 approximately in the fruit
ripening season will not hinder the culture of the finest dates,
while most excellent dates are ripened in the Island of Bahrein,
where the humidity is recorded as 73 in September and 76 in
October. The poorer quality of fruits got at some of the date-
growing places mentioned in the above tables, for example at
Gafsa, Port Said, and Alexandria, seems therefore to be due to
the lower temperatures at these places. I believe also that if
readings were taken in many plantations in Egypt in which trees,
which annually yield good crops of fruits, stand in a sea of water
while the Nile is in full flood in September-October, the humidity
figures would be much higher than those recorded above for the
stations there.

The   same is probably true of Basra in the   Persian
Gulf, which grows large quantities of excellent dates. Even
the very high figures given above for Bahrein apparently understate the case. Major Keys, Political Agent there, in reply
to a letter of mine enquiring regarding date culture in the island,
informs me that he believes the humidity in the date groves to
be considerably in excess of that reported from the observatory,
as the observatory is at Manama which is at a much higher
level than the date plantations. He also writes :—" The people
begin to eat the dates when ' ratab ' (literally moist) but ' ratab '
dates are also gathered and allowed to ripen on the ground,
which they do in a few days. Those intended for export or for
keeping are not gathered till they are ripe. In very damp years
when there is a danger of mildew, they are gathered when half

' ratab ', half ' tamar '* ". This stage of ripeness appears to be approximately that at which date fruits are habitually harvested in the Punjab.

The case of Bahrein is very interesting, as there is an excessively high humidity in the date-ripening season there with practically no rainfall to complicate our interpretations. In the light of the fact that excellent qualities of date fruits are grown at Bahrein, the mean relative humidities at most of our Punjab stations do not appear to be above the limits for successful date cultivation.

In the fruiting season actual rainfall in excess, coupled with a normally damp air which does not allow the rain to dry up rapidly, is what is to be most feared. The ripening period, from the time the dates begin to soften till they are harvested, is the part of the fruiting season in which these conditions do most damage. Of the places referred to in Tables Nos. XIII to XVII, those that produce the best dates, i.e., Tozer, Nefta, Dakhla oasis, Baghdad, and Persian Gulf stations, have practically no rainfall in the ripening season. Kebili has the highest normal rainfall in autumn (September, October, and November). There it is 5·06 inches. Gabes comes next with 2·47 inches : Biskra has 1·97 inches, Gafsa 1·8 inches, and Ayata 0·6 inches.

25. A glance at Table No. XVII shows that rainfall is the

The limiting factor of date farming in the Punjab.

limiting factor for date farming in the Punjab. None of the Punjab stations are rainless in our date ripening season (July and August). Multan and Montgomery have the lightest rainfall in these months, but even these are higher than those of the date ripening seasons at the date-growing centres outside India quoted above. We know, however, that at Multan, Muzaffargarh, Dera Ghazi Khan and elsewhere, trees fertilised by wind and left very much to care for themselves do produce crops of dates annually. The explanation of this is that date fruits are much more susceptible to damage by wet weather in the final ripening

---

* Tamar = ripe.

stage which begins after the fruits begin to soften, than before it ; and that in the Punjab they are plucked from the trees as soon as this stage commences, the final ripening and curing being done by spreading the fruits on mats in the sun. The people thus avoid the risk of the heavy damage that may be done in wet weather to fruits which are left on the trees till they are fully ripened. This custom has been in vogue as long back as we can get authentic information for, and probably arose as early as the introduction of dates into the province. That a marketable quality of fruits can be got when dates are plucked at this stage of ripeness is shown in paras. 85 and 86, pages 113 and 115, and also can be seen by reference to literature dealing with the curing and marketing of date fruits plucked at the same stage of maturity in other parts of the world. The questions before us then are—"What is the extent, if any, of the damage done to the crop by rains in years of normal and excessive rainfall in the western side of the Punjab ; and what are the extreme conditions of rainfall under which dates can be cultivated when the fruits are harvested and cured in the above way ?"

A consideration of the case shows that a record of the monthly amounts of rainfall may be misleading in this connection, as a heavy rainfall continuing for a very short time will do much less damage than a lighter rainfall extending over a longer period ; the effects will also be less if the rain falls before the fruits begin to soften, etc. In the following records of rainfall at Multan, Muzaffargarh, Dera Ghazi Khan, and Lahore, the dates on which rain fell, as well as the amounts, have therefore been given.

TABLE

Rainfalls during the date-harvesting months

Date.	1902.		1903.		1904.		1905		1906.		1907.		1908	
	JULY.	AUG.	JULY.	AUG.	JULY.	AUG.	JULY.	AUG.	JULY.	AUG.	JULY.	AUG.	JULY.	AUG.
	Rainfall in inches.	Rainfall in inches.	Rainfall in inches.	Rainfall in inches.	Rainfall in inches.	Rainfall in inches.	Rainfall in inches.	Rainfall in inches.	Rainfall in inches.	Rainfall in inches.	Rainfall in inches.	Rainfall in inches.	Rainfall in inches.	Rainfall in inches.
1	...	...			...	...	...			...		...	...	...
2	...	...	0·47		...	...	...	...		...		...	...	...
3	...	...		0·03	...	...	...	...	0·07	...		...	...	...
4	0·96	.	...	0·10	...	...	...	...	...	...	...	...	...	0·14
5	0·50	...		...	...	...	...	...	...	...	...	...	...	0·75
6	...	...	0·02	0·04	...	...	...	...	...	...	...	...	...	...
7	...	...	...	...	...	...	...	...	...	...	...	...	0·15	...
8	..	...	...	...	...	...	...	...	...	...	...	0·02	...	...
9	...	...	...	...	...	...	...	...	...	...	...	...	1·93	...
10	...	...	...	...	...	...	...	...	...	...	..	1·80	...	...
11	...	...	...	...	...	...	...	...	...	...	...	...	...	...
12	...	...	...	...	...	...	1·24	...	...	...	...	...	...	1·43
13	...	...	...	...	...	...	0·04	...	...	...	...	...	...	...
14	...	0·09	...	...	...	0·32	...	...	...	...	..	...	...	...
15	...	..	...	...	...	...	...	...	...	...	...	1·37	0·18	...
16	...	..	0·02	...	...	...	...	...	...	...	...	...	...	...
17	...	...	0·08	1·16	...	...	...	...	...	...	...	...	...	...
18	...	...	0·10	...	...	...	...	...	...	...	...	...	..	...
19	...	...	...	...	...	...	...	...	...	...	...	...	...	...
20	...	...	0·50	...	...	...	...	...	...	...	...	...	...	...
21	...	...	1·98	...	...	...	...	...	...	...	...	...	...	0·16
22	...	...	...	...	...	...	...	...	...	...	...	...	...	...
23	...	...	...	...	...	...	...	...	...	...	...	0·08	...	...
24	...	...	...	...	...	...	...	...	...	...	...	...	...	...
25	...	...	...	...	...	...	0·01	...	...	0·52	...	...	...	...
26	...	...	..	0·41	...	...	...	...	...	0·02	0·04	...	...	...
27	...	...	...	...	...	...	...	...	...	...	...	...	0·03	0·03
28	...	...	...	...	...	...	...	...	...	...	...	...	...	...
29	...	...	0·21	...	..	...	...	...	...	...	...	...	...	...
30	...	...	...	...	...	...	..	...	...	..	...	...	...	...
31	...	...	...	...	...	...	..	...	..		...	...	...	...
Total	1·46	0·09	3·38	1·74	...	0·32	1·29	...	0·07	0·54	0·04	3·27	2·29	2·51

Data from Director of

XVIII.

for the past 14 years in Multan.

1909.		1910.		1911.		1912.		1913.		1914.		1915.	
JULY.	AUG.	JULY.	AUG.	JULY.	AUG.	JULY.	AUG.	JULY.	AUG.	JULY.	AUG.	JULY.	AUG.
Rainfall in inches.	Rainfall in inches.	Rainfall in inches.	Rainfall in inches.	Rainfall in inches.	Rainfall in inches.	Rainfall in inches.	Rainfall in inches.	Rainfall in inches.	Rainfall in inches.	Rainfall in inches.	Rainfall in inches.	Rainfall in inches.	Rainfall in inches.
…	…	…	…	…	…	…	…	0·83	…	0·09	1·42	…	…
…	0·10	…	…	…	…	…	…	…	…	0·02	…	…	0·11
…	…	…	…	…	…	…	…	0·28	…	1·71	…	…	…
…	…	…	…	…	…	…	0·89	0·30	…	0·09	…	…	…
0·63	…	0·17	…	…	…	…	…	0·04	…	…	…	…	…
3·19	…	…	…	…	…	…	0·77	…	1·70	…	…	…	…
…	…	0·07	…	…	…	…	…	…	…	…	…	…	…
…	…	…	…	…	…	0·11	…	…	…	0·48	1·03	…	…
0·02	…	…	…	…	…	…	…	0·16	…	…	…	…	…
0·06	…	…	…	…	…	…	…	…	…	…	…	…	…
…	…	…	…	…	…	1·14	…	1·45	…	…	…	…	…
…	…	…	…	…	…	…	…	…	…	0·03	…	…	…
0·02	…	…	0·11	…	…	…	…	…	…	0·39	…	…	…
…	…	…	0·16	…	…	…	…	…	2·18	1·09	…	…	…
…	…	…	0·09	…	…	…	…	…	0·12	1·95	…	…	…
…	…	…	…	…	…	…	…	…	0·24	0·13	…	…	…
…	…	…	…	…	0·23	…	…	…	0·01	…	…	…	…
3·92	**0·10**	**0·24**	**0·36**	**…**	**0·23**	**1·25**	**1·66**	**3·06**	**4·25**	**5·98**	**2·45**	**…**	**0·11**

Land Records, Punjab.

Rainfalls during the date-harvesting months

Date.	1902.		1903.		1904.		1905.		1906.		1907.		1908.	
	JULY.	AUG.	JULY.	AUG.	JULY.	AUG.	JULY.	AUG.	JULY.	AUG.	JULY.	AUG.	JULY	AUG.
	Rainfall in inches.	Rainfall in inches.	Rainfall in inches.	Rainfall in inches.	Rainfall in inches.	Rainfall in inches.	Rainfall in inches.	Rainfall in inches.	Rainfall in inches.	Rainfall in inches.	Rainfall in inches.	Rainfall in inches.	Rainfall in inches.	Rainfall in inches.
1	...	...	...	...	...	...	...	...	...	...	...	...	...	...
2	...	...	9·05	...	...	...	...	...	...	...	...	...	...	...
3	...	...	...	...	...	...	...	...	...	...	...	...	...	...
4	0·12	...	0·22	0·20	...	...	...	...	...	...	...	...	...	...
5	...	...	...	...	...	...	...	...	...	...	...	...	...	0·15
6	0·68	...	...	...	...	...	...	...	...	...	...	...	...	0·11
7	...	...	...	...	...	...	...	...	...	...	...	...	...	...
8	...	...	...	...	...	...	...	...	...	...	...	...	0·05	...
9	...	...	...	...	...	...	...	...	...	...	...	...	...	...
10	...	...	...	...	...	...	...	...	...	...	...	1·45	...	...
11	...	...	...	...	...	...	...	...	...	...	...	...	...	1·08
12	...	...	...	...	...	...	...	...	...	...	...	...	...	...
13	...	...	...	...	...	...	0·27	...	...	...	...	...	0·09	...
14	...	0·30	...	...	...	...	...	...	...	...	...	...	0·06	...
15	...	...	...	...	...	...	0·20	...	...	...	...	...	...	...
16	...	...	...	...	...	...	...	...	...	...	...	...	...	...
17	...	...	1·05	0·33	...	...	...	...	...	...	...	...	...	...
18	...	...	0·15	...	...	...	...	...	...	...	...	...	...	...
19	...	...	...	...	...	...	...	...	...	...	...	...	0·62	...
20	...	...	1·56	...	...	...	...	...	...	...	...	...	...	...
21	...	...	3·29	...	...	...	...	...	...	...	...	...	...	...
22	...	...	...	...	...	...	...	...	...	...	...	...	...	...
23	...	...	...	...	...	...	...	...	...	...	...	0·93	...	...
24	...	...	...	...	...	...	...	...	...	...	...	...	...	...
25	...	...	...	...	...	...	...	...	...	1·29	...	...	...	...
26	...	...	...	1·09	...	...	...	...	...	...	...	0·33	...	...
27	...	...	...	...	...	...	...	...	...	...	...	...	...	0·43
28	...	...	...	...	...	...	...	...	...	...	...	...	0·48	...
29	...	...	...	...	...	...	...	...	...	...	...	...	...	...
30	...	...	...	...	...	...	...	...	...	0·14	0·18	...	...	0·90
31	...	...	...	...	...	...	...	...	...	...	...	...	...	...
Total	0·80	0·30	6·23	1·62	...	...	0·47	...	...	1·43	0·51	2·38	1·50	2·27

Data from Director of

XIX.

for the past 14 years in Muzaffargarh.

1909		1910.		1911.		1912.		1913.		1914.		1915.	
JULY.	AUG.	JULY.	AUG.	JULY.	AUG.	JULY.	AUG.	JULY.	AUG.	JULY.	AUG.	JULY.	AUG.
Rainfall in inches.	Rainfall in inches.	Rainfall in inches.	Rainfall in inches.	Rainfall in inches.	Rainfall in inches.	Rainfall in inches.	Rainfall in inches.	Rainfall in inches.	Rainfall in inches.	Rainfall in inches.	Rainfall in inches.	Rainfall in inches.	Rainfall in inches.
...	...	...	...	...	...	...	...	0·51	...	...	0·37	...	...
...	...	...	...	...	...	...	...	...	...	0·03	...	...	...
...	...	...	...	...	...	...	...	0·04	...	0·05	0·03	...	...
...	...	...	...	...	...	...	...	0·11	...	2·10	0·86	...	...
...	...	...	...	...	...	...	0·40	...	...	0·06	...	...	...
0·19	...	0·04	...	...	...	...	...	...	0·95	...	...	...	...
0·04	...	...	...	...	...	...	...	...	...	...	...	...	...
...	...	...	...	...	...	...	0·09	...	...	...	...	...	...
...	...	...	...	...	...	1·05	...	...	...	0·11	...	...	...
...	...	...	...	...	...	0·04	...	...	...	...	...	...	...
0·15	...	...	...	...	...	...	...	0·53	...	...	...	...	...
3·53	...	...	...	...	...	...	...	0·20	...	...	...	...	...
...	...	...	...	...	...	...	...	...	...	...	0·10	...	...
...	...	...	...	...	...	...	...	0·46	...	...	...	...	...
...	...	...	...	...	...	...	...	...	...	0·07	...	0·65	...
...	...	...	...	...	...	...	...	...	...	0·22	...	...	...
...	...	...	...	...	...	...	...	...	...	0·60	...	...	...
0·38	...	...	0·07	...	...	...	...	...	...	0·23	...	...	...
0·38	...	...	0·06	...	...	...	...	...	2·92	0·21	...	...	...
...	...	...	...	...	...	...	...	...	0·04	...	...	...	...
...	...	...	...	...	...	...	0·31	...	0·19	...	...	...	...
...	...	...	...	...	0·29	...	...	...	0·36	...	...	...	...
4·29	...	0·04	0·13	...	0·29	1·09	0·80	1·85	4·46	3·68	1·36	0·65	...

Land Records, Punjab.

THE DATE PALM.

Rainfalls during the date-harvesting months

Date.	1902. July	1902. Aug.	1903. July	1903. Aug.	1904. July	1904. Aug.	1905. July	1905. Aug.	1906. July	1906. Aug.	1907. July	1907. Aug.	1908. July	1908. Aug.
	Rainfall in inches.	Rainfall in inches.	Rainfall in inches.	Rainfall in inches.	Rainfall in inches.	Rainfall in inches.	Rainfall in inches.	Rainfall in inches.	Rainfall in inches.	Rainfall in inches.	Rainfall in inches.	Rainfall in inches.	Rainfall in inches.	Rainfall in inches.
1														
2														
3														
4						0·21								
5														
6	0·11													
7														
8													0·25	
9											0·55			
10												0·56		
11														1·88
12							0·03							
13							0·10					0·12		
14		0·34					0·14							
15							0·02					0·02	0·28	
16														
17														
18														0·18
19														
20			0·30											
21														
22														
23												1·16		
24														
25										0·71				
26		1·94		0·41										
27														
28														2·10
29														
30										0·35				
31														
Total	0·11	2·28	0·50	0·41	...	0·21	0·29	...	...	1·06	0·55	1·86	0·53	4·16

Data from Director of

XX.

for the past 14 years in Dera Ghazi Khan.

	1909.		1910.		1911.		1912.		1913.		1914.		1915.
	JULY.	AUG.	JULY.	AUG.	JULY.	AUG.	JULY.	AUG.	JULY.	AUG.	JULY.	AUG.	JULY.	AUG.
	Rainfall in inches.	Rainfall in inches.	Rainfall in inches.	Rainfall in inches.	Rainfall in inches.	Rainfall in inches.	Rainfall in inches.	Rainfall in inches.	Rainfall in inches.	Rainfall in inches.	Rainfall in inches.	Rainfall in inches.	Rainfall in inches.	Rainfall in inches.
	...	...	...	...	...	...	...	...	0·63	...	...	...	...	...
	...	...	...	...	0·03	...	...	...	...	...	0·03	0·85	...	...
	0·03	...	...	...	...	...	...	...	...	...	0·42	0·55	...	...
	...	...	...	...	...	...	...	...	...	...	0·56	...	...	...
	...	...	...	...	...	...	...	...	0·33	...	...	...	...	...
	...	...	0·51	0·01	...	...	...	...	...	0·01	...	...	...	...
	...	...	0·01	...	...	...	...	...	...	0·25	...	...	...	...
	...	...	...	...	...	...	...	...	...	0·12	...	...	...	...
	...	...	...	...	...	...	...	...	0·14	...	...	0·52	...	...
	0·02	...	...	...	...	...	...	...	...	...	...	...	...	...
	...	...	...	...	...	...	...	...	...	...	...	...	...	...
	0·05	...	...	...	...	...	...	...	...	...	...	...	...	...
	...	...	...	...	...	...	...	...	0·02	...	...	...	...	...
	...	...	...	...	...	...	...	...	0·32	...	...	...	...	...
	...	...	...	...	...	...	...	...	2·50	...	...	...	...	...
	...	...	...	...	...	...	...	...	0·03	...	0·55	...	...	...
	...	...	...	...	...	...	...	...	...	...	0·85	...	...	...
	...	...	...	1·00	...	...	...	...	...	...	2·67	...	...	...
	0·20	...	...	...	...	...	...	...	...	...	0·30	...	...	...
	0·13	...	...	...	...	...	...	...	...	1·40	0·33	...	...	0·21
	...	...	...	...	...	...	...	...	...	0·95	0·02	...	...	...
	...	...	...	...	...	...	...	...	...	0·41	...	...	...	...
	...	...	...	...	...	...	...	...	...	...	...	...	...	...
	...	...	...	...	...	...	...	...	...	...	...	...	...	...
	0·43	...	0·52	1·01	0·03	...	...	...	3·97	3·14	5·73	1·92	...	0·21

Land Records, Punjab,

Rainfalls during the date-harvesting months

Date.	1902. JULY.	1902. AUG.	1903. JULY.	1903. AUG.	1904. JULY.	1904. AUG.	1905. JULY.	1905. AUG.	1906. JULY.	1906. AUG.	1907. JULY.	1907. AUG.	1908. JULY.	1908. AUG.
	Rainfall in inches.	Rainfall in inches.	Rainfall in inches.	Rainfall in inches.	Rainfall in inches.	Rainfall in inches.	Rainfall in inches.	Rainfall in inches.	Rainfall in inches.	Rainfall in inches.	Rainfall in inches.	Rainfall in inches.	Rainfall in inches.	Rainfall in inches.
1	...	0·02	...	...	...	...	...	...	...	0·16	...	...	0·90	...
2	...	...	...	...	...	...	...	...	...	...	...	...	...	0·31
3	...	0·71	0·08	...	...	...	...	...	0·14	...	...	0·26	...	4·21
4	...	...	...	0·42	...	...	...	...	...	...	...	0·79	...	2·49
5	...	...	...	0·31	...	...	...	...	...	...	...	0·29	...	0·69
6	0·06	...	...	...	...	...	...	...	...	...	...	...	...	0·09
7	...	...	...	...	...	...	...	...	0·04	...	...	...	0·58	...
8	...	...	...	...	...	...	...	...	0·01	...	...	...	0 04	2·24
9	...	...	...	0·26	...	0·71	...	...	0·30	...	...	0·75	1·62	...
10	0·08	...	...	0·08	...	...	...	...	...	...	0·03	...	...	...
11	...	...	...	...	...	...	0·54	...	0·23	0·46	...	1·32	...	0·06
12	...	0·22	...	...	...	...	2·43	...	...	R*	0·04	...	...	0·07
13	...	...	...	...	0·18	...	0·04	...	...	R*	...	0·06	...	...
14	...	...	...	...	...	0·36	0·05	...	...	...	...	0·03	0·01	...
15	...	...	0·44	...	...	...	...	...	...	...	...	R*	0·69	...
16	...	...	0·84	...	...	...	...	...	...	...	...	0·48	...	...
17	...	...	0·39	...	...	...	...	...	...	...	...	...	...	0·02
18	...	...	...	...	...	...	...	...	...	...	...	0·34	...	1·27
19	...	...	...	...	0·57	...	...	...	0·51	...	...	...	0·04	0·14
20	...	...	0·08	...	...	...	...	...	0·12	...	...	...	0·04	...
21	...	...	...	...	...	0·08	...	...	...	...	...	...	...	...
22	0·27	0·46	...	...	...	...	...	...	...	...	0·69	...	...	...
23	...	...	0·91	...	...	...	...	...	...	...	...	0·10	0·02	...
24	...	...	1·48	...	...	...	0·37	...	...	1·59	...	...	1 12	...
25	...	2·21	...	0·25	...	...	...	...	...	...	...	0·36	0·41	3·04
26	...	...	...	0·55	...	...	...	...	0·31	...	...	...	...	0·05
27	0·65	...	...	0·21	...	...	...	...	...	1·73	...	...	0·28	...
28	0·90	...	...	...	...	...	...	...	0·02	...	...	...	...	...
29	...	...	...	...	...	...	...	...	...	0·25	...	...	...	1·54
30	...	...	...	...	...	...	...	...	...	0·71	...	...	0 95	...
31	...	...	1·09	...	...	...	...	...	...	...	...	...	...	1·25
Total	1·96	3·62	5·31	2·08	0·75	1·15	3·46	...	1·68	4·90	0·76	4·78	6·70	17·47

Data from Director of
* NOTE.—R denotes a few

XXI.

for the past 14 years in Lahore.

1909.		1910.		1911.		1912.		1913.		1914.		1915.	
JULY.	AUG.	JULY.	AUG.	JULY.	AUG.	JULY.	AUG.	JULY.	AUG.	JULY.	AUG.	JULY.	AUG.
Rainfall in inches.	Rainfall in inches.	Rainfall in inches.	Rainfall in inches.	Rainfall in inches.	Rainfall in inches.	Rainfall in inches.	Rainfall in inches.	Rainfall in inches.	Rainfall in inches.	Rainfall in inches.	Rainfall in inches.	Rainfall in inches.	Rainfall in inches.
...	...	0·11	...	...	...	...	3·50	...	...	...	...	...	...
0·35	...	...	...	...	...	...	3·24	0·80	...	...	...	...	...
...	...	...	...	...	...	...	0·10	...	...	...	...	...	...
...	0·35	...	...	...	...	...	...	...	...	0·18	0·06	0·38	...
...	...	...	...	...	...	...	...	0·63	...	...	...	0·06	...
...	0·85	...	0·68	...	...	0·02	...	0·49	0·31	...	...	...	...
...	...	...	...	...	...	...	...	...	2·02	0·26	...	...	...
...	...	...	0·94	...	...	...	...	...	3·36	...	...	...	...
...	...	...	0·02	...	...	...	...	...	...	...	...	...	...
...	...	...	...	...	...	0·18	0·35	...	...	0·22	2·05	...	...
...	...	0·91	...	...	...	...	...	...	...	...	0·09	...	...
...	...	0·15	0·02	...	...	...	...	0·35	...	0·20	...	...	...
...	...	0·50	0·07	0·48	...	...	...	1·06	...	...	...	...	...
...	...	2·27	...	0·08	...	...	...	2·50	...	...	...	...	...
...	...	...	0·28	0·02	...	0·45	...	...	...	...	...	...	...
...	...	...	...	...	...	0·07	...	...	...	0·16	...	...	...
0·13	...	...	...	...	...	0·22	...	...	...	...	...	...	...
0·20	0·01	...	...	...	...	...	0·36	...	...	...	...	0·30	...
...	...	...	...	...	...	0·07	...	...	...	0·60	...	...	0·70
1·63	0·07	...	...	...	...	...	0·40	1·80	...	...	...	...	0·17
3·48	...	...	...	...	...	...	...	0·16	...	2·34	...	...	...
...	...	...	...	...	...	...	...	0·85	...	2·38	...	...	...
...	0·04	...	...	...	0·01	...	...	...	...	2·67	...	...	...
0·40	...	...	...	...	...	0·56	...	...	...	0·32	...	...	...
0·02	...	0·20	1·01	...	0·37	...	...	...	...	0·02	...	...	...
0·12	...	...	1·11	...	...	...	...	0·98	0·13	0·31	...	...	...
2·29	...	...	0·08	...	...	...	...	0·37	2·52	0·48	...	...	...
...	0·14	...	...	...	0·01	...	...	...	0·10	0·10	...	...	...
...	...	...	0·90	...	...	...	...	...	...	...	...	...	...
...	0·21	...	...	...	0·21	...	...	...	...	0·82	...	...	...
0·13	1·32	...	...	...	2·65	...	0·01	...	0·57	...	...	...	...
8·75	2·99	4·14	5·11	0·58	3·25	1·57	7·96	9·99	9·01	11·06	2·20	0·74	0·87

Land Records, Punjab.
drops of rainfall.

To enable us to interpret these figures properly, we require very accurate and detailed information regarding any damage done to the fruits by rains in these years. Authentic information of this sort, or indeed concerning the crop in any way, is very difficult to collect from the smaller owners of date groves, as they are apt to suspect that the Government revenue on the trees may be raised if they show that they are obtaining large crops, while larger owners having let their gardens to tenants do not know exactly what amount of crops the tenants get. It is usually just as difficult to get information from the tenant, as he is afraid that the owner will raise his rent for the garden if he shows that he is getting large crops. We must therefore look to the model plantations which we planted in 1910 and later (*see* page 111, para. 83) to give us the exact information required, or get it from a qualified assistant who will actually stay in local plantations throughout the fruit-developing and harvesting season. So far we have not been able to spare a man to do this. Meantime, I may say that date growers in Multan, Muzaffargarh, and Dera Ghazi Khan are unanimous in stating that in average years little or no harm is done to the fruits there by rains. They also inform me that more harm was done to the date crop in those districts by rains in 1914 than in any year for a long time past. We would expect the greatest damage to be done by rains falling between the 20th July and 20th August, that being the chief harvesting period (*see* para. 74, page 100), and referring to the above rainfall records we find that in 1914 in Multan and Muzaffargarh there were apparently five consecutive rainy days at the beginning of this period, and in Dera Ghazi Khan rain fell every day, except one, for a week then, while in no other of the past 14 years were there as many consecutive rainy days within the main harvesting period. At Lahore the conditions for date culture are evidently very much worse than in the previously mentioned districts. There also 1914 was apparently a very bad year, rain having fallen almost every day from the 21st July to the end of the month, but 1908, which had few consecutive dry days throughout the whole harvesting time, was probably worse. The rainfalls in several others of the years referred to in this table are also most interesting, but we must have more information regarding the damage done to the crop before we can say much more on the subject. Date-growers in Lahore, however, maintain that they got a considerable proportion of their crop even in 1914, and that they do not remember a year in which their crop was totally destroyed by rains.

In reply to enquiries made through the Deputy Commissioner, Lahore, the Extra Assistant Settlement Officer, Lahore, in December 1915, writes :—" The trees at Lahore fruit regularly ; the crop of one year is heavier than that of the second, but the difference is not very marked. The fruit does not fall off in the rains, but a year of excessive rainfall is a bad year for fruiting generally."

We may therefore expect to improve date culture in Multan, Muzaffargarh, and Dera Ghazi Khan districts at least, and there are other districts which are promising. All data to hand indicate that date trees will grow lustily over a large portion of the Punjab, but that the successful cultivation of the crop may be limited to a comparatively small area owing only to the fruits being damaged by rain in the ripening season. It may, however, be possible to extend the area of successful date cultivation somewhat by selecting and propagating off-shoots from those varieties which ripen before the rainy season commences, or even which ripen after the rains are over.

26. There are already date trees to be seen growing in many parts of the province, and observations on these would give very valuable evidence as to whether date cultivation could be profitably taken up in those districts. Information regarding such cases would be of great value to the Agricultural Department.

Useful informa- tion that might be collected.

CHAPTER III.

*Propagation of date-plants from seeds and suckers (off-shoots);
care of young plantations ; manuring, interculture, pruning
and water requirements of established plantations.*

27. If 100 seeds are sown, 50 or more of the seedling
Propagation by
seeds. plants will probably be male trees and will of
course bear no fruits. If 50 females are got,
perhaps ten trees or fewer will yield passable fruits, five or six
of these will probably yield fruits of a quality equal to that
of the mother tree, and one or more, usually not even one,
may yield fruits superior to her. The characters of the male
and female palms used to produce the seeds will of course
materially affect the number of useful seedlings got. (*See*
page 95, para. 62.) The sexes cannot be known with certainty
till the trees bear flowers (*see* also page 14, para. 11), and as
this will occur five to ten years after the seeds are sown, land,
labour, and water will have to be provided for 100 trees for
from five to ten years before the 90 more or less useless trees
can be weeded out and the ten or fewer passable ones can be
selected.

The reason that so few good female trees are got from
ordinary seeds is that the female trees are generally pollinated
by male trees of inferior quality, and they of course influence
the offspring. As the female date trees are almost always propagated by off-shoots in date-growing countries and the edible
part of the fruit formed as the immediate result of pollination
is not affected by the character of the male used (*see* page 95,
para. 62), date-growers have ordinarily no incentive to breed
good male trees. If good males were bred, much better results
from female seedlings would be got.

28. The land on which the seedlings are to be reared should not contain alkali to an extent that **Rearing of date seedlings.** will harm ordinary farm crops. The seed bed should be prepared in March or April as for an ordinary crop. The seeds should be planted in it to a depth of 1 to 2 inches and 3 to 4 feet apart, in rows 3 to 4 feet between the rows, and then irrigated. The bed should be watered once per week till the seedlings show above ground and should then be watered as frequently as to keep the ground moist enough to grow any ordinary garden crop. The seedlings are extremely hardy and I have seen them germinate and come to a foot or more in height in deserts where nothing else was growing. If they are well treated, they will grow faster and come into flower sooner. They repay good treatment well, as only when they come into flower and fruit can the fruitless males and worthless females be weeded out. The weeding out should be done with all possible speed to prevent the worthless trees choking the others up and so retarding their growth. Transplanting may be done as in the case of off-shoots (*see* pages 10, 68 and 73, paras. 5, 31, 38 *et seq.*).

29. The rearing of date trees from seeds is not advisable for ordinary date cultivators when good off-**Advantages of planting by off-shoots.** shoots can be obtained. No useless trees have to be cultivated if the off-shoot method is adopted, as all off-shoots from female trees will become female trees and will yield fruits of the same quality as the mother tree would in the same conditions. Consequently by planting off-shoots of the same variety, it is possible to obtain a plantation of trees, all yielding fruits of the same sort. Where the date trees are reared from seeds, no individual tree bears fruits, the inherent qualities of which are like those borne by any other tree, and therefore the cultivator cannot supply a large quantity of fruits of the same grade to buyers. This is a very important disadvantage for trading purposes. Although new and improved varieties of dates may be produced by careful breeding and propagation from seeds, it will usually take many years to evolve an improved variety, and many more years to

multiply it to a number of trees fit to produce a considerable consignment of fruits for the market, as that variety will then have to be propagated from suckers got from the original improved seedling tree.

30. Off-shoots should be selected when fruits are ripe and hanging on the mother trees, as at that time there can be no doubt about the quality of the fruits that the off-shoot will bear. The trees from which off-shoots are required, should then be marked with paint or in any other convenient way, and their positions recorded in a note-book, a rough plan of the positions being made if necessary. To help identification the approximate height of the parent tree, the number of off-shoots at its base, the approximate size of the off-shoots, their age, etc., should all be noted.

Time of year to select off-shoots.

31. It is essential that a sucker before being removed from a tree, should have its leaves trimmed back as in illustration No. 26, page 80a. Practically nothing but the tender young unopened leaves in the central bud and parts of the bare stalks of the old leaves necessary to protect the bud should be kept on the plant. Water is transpired from plants through the medium of the leaves (*see* page 7, para. 4), and the object in this severe pruning is to prevent as far as possible the drying up of the off-shoots through loss of water between the time when it is severed from the parent plant and that when, after being replanted, it has developed a root system of its own able to supply sufficient water to replace the amount transpired by a more full leaf system.

Trimming of suckers and detaching them from parent trees.

If a large number of leaves are left on the off-shoot after it has been severed from the parent plant, drying up before replanting will obviously be accelerated. Even after replanting the off-shoot, a large leaf system on it is fatal, as such off-shoots usually have few or no roots ; it takes the plant some time to develop a vigorous root system, and if the amount of water given off by the leaves is greater than that taken up from the soil, the plant *must* dry up and die.

The pruning of the off-shoot before detaching it from the parent tree both facilitates the detaching operations and decreases the weight of the off-shoot for transport. Off-shoots are usually severed from the tree by means of an ordinary axe or large chisel, the cutting being done in a plane parallel to the stem of the parent tree. The cut should be made as near to the parent tree as is possible without unduly harming it. The detaching implement should be sharp and the blows light. Every care should be taken not to shatter the off-shoot in removing it from the mother. The wound on the mother should be earthed up at once, and it is strongly advisable to first coat the wound with coal tar or other material generally used to cover plant wounds (*see* para. 93, page 126).

32. After the adult leaves have been trimmed back, the off-shoot should not weigh less than six

Size of suckers to be planted.

pounds. Off-shoots less than this usually die when transplanted, because if by any chance the amount of moisture in the soil around the off-shoots becomes less than what is required, the plant has not a sufficient store of food and vitality in it to replace those rootlets that may have been dried up. From the weighment of a large number of plants I find that the average weight of an off-shoot when trimmed and ready for planting is 12 to 15 lbs. Off-shoots may be fit for transplanting when they are 3 to 4 years old, but the larger the shoot is the better, as there will be less danger in shattering it when removing it from the parent tree, more strength in its substance, and more chance of it doing well when transplanted.

33. Six months to a year before the off-shoots are removed,

To induce off-shoots to form roots.

earth is sometimes piled up round the bases of the mother trees and kept moist. This induces the off-shoots to send out rootlets and increases their chances of taking root when planted out (*see* also page 10, para. 5).

34. When suckers are transported long distances and a considerable time elapses before they can be planted, it is imperative that their leaf systems should be severely cut back. It is also advisable to coat the bases of the plants with mud and cover them with palm fibre, grass and straw, or matting, leaving the crown of the off-shoot exposed. The palm fibre, etc., should be kept damp by occasional sprinkling with water. The water must be applied lightly, otherwise the mud tends to be washed off the palms. The mud used should have rather more sand than clay in it, and should be about as thick as cream when applied. The coating is done in a box or in a hole in the ground which should be at least 6 inches wider than the diameter of the largest sucker and 6 inches deeper than the largest base to be coated. The box or hole is filled with mud and a sucker is placed into it and withdrawn. It is then immediately bound in wet fibre, straw, etc. If many trees are to be treated a larger hole is much better, as it has to be re-filled with mud less frequently. Care is taken not to admit the mud into the crown of the plant. This process is called " puddling " by gardeners. Suckers have been known to keep healthy for about three months when treated in this manner. (Gaskin.) The bases of the off-shoots may be simply bound up with a covering of palm fibre to protect them during transport to where they are to be transplanted. More frequently no packing of any sort is done. Whether the plants are to be specially packed or not, it is very important that their lower ends not higher than the base of the central bud should be placed in water on the same day as they are removed from the parent tree. They should be left there until the moment for packing or transport has arrived. Also as soon as they arrive at their destination they should again be similarly placed in water. If the off-shoots are strong and they are kept in water in this way, or are kept damp, little harm seems to happen to them if they are not planted for a month. We have repeatedly had off-shoots sent here from Basra which on being cut from their parents were stood in water till ready for transport; were sent without any packing—the journey occupying about 10 days;

Care of off-shoots after removal from parent tree until planted.

were placed in water at once on arrival, and were planted in good condition 4 to 6 weeks after they were cut from the trees. During transport the plants should not be placed on the deck of a ship without shade, and so be exposed to the withering effect of the hot sun, nor be stored in a space so badly ventilated that fermentation will set in.

Swingle (*see* page 47 of United States of America Bulletin No. 53, The Date Palm) states that 75 per cent. of 384 off-shoots lived which were obtained in Algeria, packed simply in boxes in charcoal or straw with damp moss about their bases, no more moisture being added, and planted 2 months' later in Arizona, United States of America.

It is well, however, to plant date off-shoots as soon after detaching them from the parent tree as possible.

35. Many Egyptian people believe that the best results are got by planting date off-shoots in March. Our late Arab date overseer (Hassan-el-Atman) informed me that the best results are got in Arabia if the off-sets are planted when the wheat is beginning to ripen, *i.e.*, in the end of March. In Baluchistan the time of planting is recorded as between the end of February and beginning of April. Of 24 off-shoots from foreign trees which arrived at the end of January in 1913, 12 were planted at Lyallpur and 12 at Muzaffargarh. All died. About 50 off-shoots were planted in the end of March one year at Muzaffargarh and a similar lot were planted at the same time in Multan. Both lots failed. These were got from local trees and planted immediately after removal from their parents. Where fair attention has been given to the plants, very good results have been got by planting Basra off-shoots in the first week of September in Lyallpur, Muzaffargarh, and elsewhere, and I should advise planting being done in Multan, Muzaffargarh, and neighbouring districts in the first week of September until we have reason to do otherwise.

Time of year to plant off-shoots.

The heat of summer is very trying to the plants before they have established themselves, and the excessive heat in May and June in the Punjab (*see* para. 18, page 33) may make early September a better planting season than March here.

36. In Basra in 1910 the cost per 100 date suckers fit for
Cost of off-shoots in Arabia.
transplanting ranged from Rs.* 50 to Rs. 75. In September 1910, 1,000 off-shoots of assorted varieties were obtained from Basra and cost at Multan, after all expenses were paid, Rs. 1,020, or practically Re. 1 per tree. The consignments got from Basra in 1911 and 1912 cost approximately the same. Prices like Rs. 5 per tree have been charged by people in the Punjab for off-shoots from trees on their land. These local off-shoots are from trees bearing fruits of lower quality than those that can be had at Rs. 50 per 100 in Basra and elsewhere. For varieties of date palms being imported (*see* para. 83, page 111).

37. If date trees are grown on the edges of water-courses
The advantages and disadvantages of having dates in plantations as compared with having the trees around the borders of fields.
or fields where the permanent water-level is well within 20 feet of the soil surface, a large number of palms may be grown without diminishing the area of land under other crops. Once established they can also be grown with little special water-supply. When palm trees are grown in a plantation, a large number of plants can be more easily watered and attended to when young than if scattered around the edges of fields, and when the trees are bearing fruits they can be more easily guarded from birds and other enemies. The death-rate among young date-suckers in the first two years after being planted out is so alarming where water has not been regularly given in suitable quantities and where the trees have not been properly attended to that, in cases in which these attentions cannot be insured, it would probably be better to plant the trees in a nursery and grow them there till they have developed a good root system and then transplant them into their permanent places with a ball of the nursery earth undetached from their bases. A year's growth or more may be lost in this way owing to the planting

---

* Re. 1 (one rupee) = 16 pence.

ILLUSTRATION No. 23.

The two date trees in the foreground have had their bases continuously covered with water for the past 6 years. The photograph was taken in the fruit-bearing season and shows that they are bearing practically no fruits. The leaf systems also look miserable and their roots were found to be considerably decayed.

(See page 73).

of the trees a second time, and they will have to be well attended to till they establish themselves in their new positions, but the death-rate among the plants will be very much decreased. Much less water will be required for a number of trees in a nursery than if they are widely scattered over a large area. Even where old trees have to be replaced in a date plantation, it may be advisable to grow the suckers in a nursery for a time before planting them in their permanent positions, as these young plants require much more water and attention than the older trees, and they are very apt to be neglected if scattered about in odd places. In suitable localities dates are probably a more paying crop than most others, and if vegetables, lucerne, and other crops are grown between the trees, a piece of land laid out in a first class quality of date trees ought to be a very paying investment (*see* para. 88, page 117). Where the difficulty of the enemies can be got over easily, however, and where the subsoil water conditions are suitable, I think it would be well to have a considerable number of trees planted round the edges of the fields and along water channels as well as in plantations. As the many factors involved differ not only in the different districts, but with each individual cultivator, each intending date-grower will have to decide what is best to be done in his own case.

38. In choosing the site for a plantation the question of the water-supply must be carefully considered.

Choosing the site and preparations for laying down a plant-ation.

Although date palms love an abundant supply of water and can stand water-logging to a far greater extent than many other plants (*see* para. 2, page 1), they yield their best crops only when a plentiful supply of water is accompanied by proper æration of the soil. Adult trees which stand in a water-logged soil, or in a sea of stagnant water all the year round, may not die but they do not bear as good crops of fruits as those growing in better selected soils.

In the foreground of illustration No. 23, page 72*a*, are two date trees photographed in the fruit-bearing season and which have been standing in a pond of water for several years, their roots being nearly always submerged and the water standing to a depth of several feet up their stems in summer. They bear most miserable crops of fruits, while the date trees seen in the background of the photo., growing on land, the level of which is about 5 feet higher, bear passable crops. Adult palms appear to stand the bases of their stems being flooded for considerable periods however without much apparent harm. In parts of Egypt, for example, water often to a depth of several feet stands round the trees during September and October every year. Colonel Scott-Moncrieff, R.E., Under-Secretary of State, Public Works Department, Egypt, in a *resumé* of notes on Date Culture in Egypt, writes: "Water may remain over the roots for 70 days, a longer period will damage the produce" (*vide* letter dated 4th July 1887, from Dr. Bonavia to the Secretary to Government, North-West Provinces and Oudh).

We usually find the roots of date trees descending into ordinary loamy soils to a depth of 7 to 10 feet (*see* page 1, para. 2), and if the land is not well drained naturally to about that depth, this should be done artificially if practicable by means of open ditches or by other means. Adult trees may be seen growing luxuriantly without any irrigation where the subsoil water-level is about 14 feet from the soil surface. Where the water-level is at 20 feet depth and no artificial waterings are given, the trees generally look more or less stunted and, although they may exist, they do not bear their maximum crops of fruits. Where, however, irrigations are given to trees in such situations, or where the water-level is rather higher, there is the advantage that if the irrigations are unavoidably or carelessly delayed, the trees will suffer less than they would if the subsoil water was beyond the reach of the roots altogether.

Water in soaking into a soil which is not water-logged fills up the interspaces between the earth's particles, displacing the air from these, and as the liquid descends leaving these interspaces again, fresh air from the atmosphere is drawn into them. Fresh water also contains a certain amount of oxygen dissolved in it. Water is therefore a powerful ærating agent, and judicious applications of it may be beneficial even where the roots can reach a good underground supply. On lands where the subsoil water is far below the reach of the palm roots, excellent crops of date fruits can be got if a regular and plentiful supply of irrigation water is given. The disadvantages of the situation are the expenses incurred before the water can be applied, and the very serious damage that may be done if regular irrigations are not given. In parts of the Persian Gulf the lands are both ærated and irrigated by the rise and fall of the tide in the river, but unfortunately we have no such efficient, cheap, automatic method in the Punjab. When a young plantation is to be laid down, even where the subsoil water is at such a height as to be well within reach of the roots of adult palms, it is absolutely vital to its success that an abundant and regular supply of irrigation water should be provided for the young plants throughout the year during the first 2 to 3 years after they are planted out (see pages 84 and 85, paras. 49, 50, and 51). Should this not be done the death-rate will be appalling. If the plants have been properly treated, they should be growing vigorously by the end of that time and more hardy. They should still receive artificial waterings in accordance with their requirements however. A plentiful water-supply will be well repaid by the trees coming several years earlier into bearing than they otherwise would. By the time well-kept trees have been planted out 5 to 6 years, they ought to have developed a strong root system penetrating into the soil to a depth of 7 to 9 feet (see para. 2, page 1; and illustration No. 1, page XIX), and if there is a good supply of subsoil water well within reach of these, the plants may yield good crops without further artificial waterings. If the natural water-supply is below the reach of the roots of adult trees, permanent arrangements for the necessary waterings (see page 84, para. 49) must be made.

Perhaps the best sites as far as water-supply is concerned, are where the permanent water-level is at a depth somewhere between 9 and 16 feet. Even with a water table at these depths irrigations might improve the crop. With a water table at greater depths it is essential that the requisite amount of irrigation water should be available. According to the data yet at hand a rise of water-level above 9 feet, or even flooding of adult trees for a short time in the fruiting season, does no great harm. Proper æration of the roots and a plentiful supply of fresh water in the fruit developing season are the ideal conditions. Floods will, of course, kill newly planted off-shoots by destroying their terminal buds if the water covers these for any length of time.

As regards texture of the soil, a sandy loam is perhaps best (*see* page 19, para. 13). Such a soil is open enough to allow good drainage and close enough not to allow manurial ingredients to wash out unduly rapidly.

If the land is virgin and is suspected of containing excess of alkali, it should be tested for this. The land may be divided by small banks into suitable sized beds, and the whole surface well flooded. The water will soak into the subsoil, dissolve the salts and that quantity of it which returns to, and is evaporated from, the soil surface will leave its deposit of salts there. If there are water channels across the soil at suitable distances apart ; if these are then filled with water, and the water is simply allowed to soak from these into the subsoil, it will diffuse laterally as it descends, and that part of it which rises to the surface between the channels will evaporate and add its load of salts to those of the first irrigation. Repeated soakage of the land by way of these channels only will soon show an accumulation of salt at the soil surface if excess exists in the land and no rain occurs to wash it in again. Even where a chemical analysis of a virgin soil is to be made for alkali in a rainless tract, more representative samples will be got after a few irrigations, as the irrigations will disseminate any pockets or layers of salts. In many cases the simplest way of testing the soil for excess of alkali, however, is to grow some of the crops mentioned on page 83, para. 46, on it.

The irrigations given to the crop disseminate pockets or layers of salts, and the condition of the crop is an excellent indication of whether there are sufficient salts present to interfere with date culture.

It may be mentioned here that in my experience on the Egyptian oases where salty lands were being reclaimed, rice was the only common crop that would grow on these in the first year ; next year barley and often leguminous crops could be grown. In bad cases rice had to be grown several years in succession before other crops would grow.

The efficacy of this treatment seems to depend on the large quantities of water supplied to the rice crop preventing a concentrated solution coming in contact with the rice plants ; in the water dissolving and disseminating the salts from the pockets and layers in which they were usually deposited ; and in carrying a considerable part of the salt out of reach of the crop by natural drainage. When date suckers are planted in salty lands, a high death-rate must be allowed for (*see* page 19, para. 14).

Before a new plantation is laid down pits should be dug in the soil to see that no hard pans (hard strata more or less impenetrable to roots) are present to a depth of 9 or 10 feet. If the land is not level it should be levelled or contoured. The positions of the trees should then be carefully marked, holes about 2½ feet in diameter and a convenient depth (*see* page 80, para. 41) should be dug, small water channels should be made connecting the holes in each row, and main channels should be made where necessary.

39. Considerable differences of opinion exist as to the most economic distance to plant the trees apart from each other in plantations. All distances between 12 feet and 30 feet have been advised.

Distance between the trees in a plantation, and relative positions of the trees.

F. E. Crow, British Consul at Basra, in an article on the date palm in Mesopotamia dated March 1908 (*see* Kew Bulletin No. 7, 1908) says that the trees are planted 10 to 15 feet apart there. In date-growing countries I have seen many plantations the trees in which had about that interval, but in the best plantations that I have seen, the trees have been 17 to 20 feet apart.

Paul B. Popenoe in his book " Date Growing in the Old and New Worlds " gives opposite page 297 a photograph of a plantation of " Fardh Palms in the Samail Valley, Arabia " under which he writes : " The natives of this region are the most skilful Arab cultivators of the Date " and " the trees are planted 20 feet apart and a subsidiary crop is grown."

The observations referred to on page 1, para. 2 of this note, show that a very large proportion of the roots of the date palm descend at a sharp angle and never spread beyond a radius of a few feet from the tree trunk. As far as the root system is concerned, therefore, the data from these observations would explain why considerable crops of fruits are got even when the trees are planted very close together. They show, however, that there would be a good deal of overlapping of the roots when the plants are planted 10 to 15 feet apart and indicate that the trees would probably bear more heavily if planted at distances apart up to about 20 feet. When the trees are growing 19 or 20 feet apart, the relative positions of the trees are as advised below, and the leaves are fairly developed, there is also neither overcrowding, nor much vacant space left between the tree tops (*see* para. 4, page 7).

If each tree is allowed a circular space having a diameter of about 19 feet, good results should therefore be got. To get most trees into a given area of ground the trees should be set out in lines, and the trees in adjacent lines should not be opposite, but should alternate with each other as in illustration No. 24 opposite. Also the proportional distances apart of the rows and the trees in the rows should be

$$(\tfrac{1}{2}a)^2 + b^2 = a^2$$

When a = the distance apart of the trees in the rows, and b = the distance between the rows.—

With a = 19 feet, b will be about 16·4 feet, and 139 trees approximately will be planted per acre.

ILLUSTRATION No. 24.

DIAGRAM

OF

DATE PLANTATION

SHOWING POSITION OF PLANTS PLANTED, DATE ――――

IN

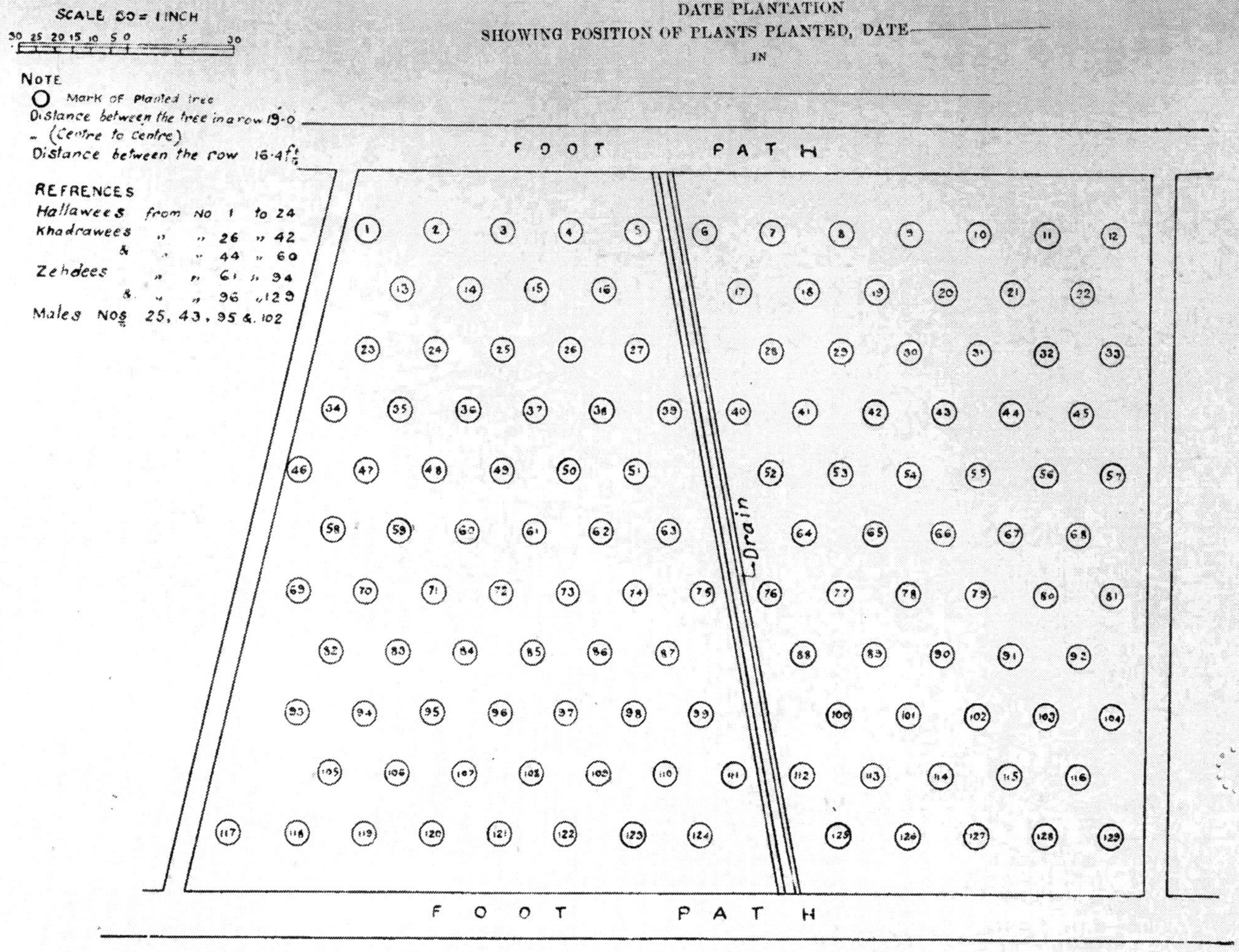

NOTE

O Mark of planted tree

Distance between the tree in a row 19.0

― (centre to centre)

Distance between the row 16.4½

REFRENCES

Hallawees	from	No	1	to	24
Khadrawees	„	„	26	„	42
	„	„	44	„	60
Zahdees	„	„	61	„	94
	„	„	96	„	123
Males Nos	25, 43, 95 & 102				

SCALE 50 = 1 INCH

FOOT PATH

FOOT PATH

FOOT PATH

→Drain

78a

ILLUSTRATION No. 25.

Average sized Arabian date tree in the garden of the Multan Central Jail, growing on a piece of land trenched and highly manured a year or more before the tree was planted as a sucker in September 1910. There is a crop of vegetables 15 inches high growing around this tree.

ILLUSTRATION No. 25A.

Average sized Arabian date tree growing on ordinary untrenched land in the same garden.
The tree was obtained as a sucker from Arabia in the same consignment as that
of Illustration No. 25 on page 78b and was also planted in September 1910.
Both photos were taken on 23rd July 1916.

Where there is a distance of 25 feet or more between the palms in a plantation, other fruit trees are usually grown between them.

40. Many writers advise manure being given to the trees when they are planted, but the Arabs I met in Egypt and our late Arab date-overseer from Basra are all emphatically against manure being used at planting time. When the off-shoot has just been planted, it has lost connection with the roots of the parent tree and has usually no root system of its own by means of which water and dissolved salts from the soil necessary to carry on the vital function of the plant, and to enable it to grow a root system, etc., for itself, can be properly supplied to it. A large quantity of manure closely applied round the off-shoot at planting time would, when wetted, produce a concentrated solution which would retard the passage of water into the plant to an extent depending on the degree of concentration just as strong solutions of the Alkaline salts do (*see* page 19 , para. 14) and so might cause the death of the off-shoot. Apparently this is not a hyper-sensitive point, for in the case of 59 suckers to each of which about 22 lbs. of well-rotted cow-dung were given at planting time well mixed with the earth replaced in the planting pit, the death-rate was no higher than among the plants which got no manure.

The question of applying manure to the plants at planting time.

Until we have further data, however, I should advise planters to be very careful of the use of manure at planting time. In lands of ordinary quality it would be safer to use none then, as anything which will interfere with the passage of water and dissolved salts into the plants at this critical period of their existence is to be avoided. When growth once starts, however, a little well-rotted manure spread round the plant and dug into the soil an inch or two, soon gives a robust appearance to the plants and accelerates their growth greatly. The differences in rates of growth of date plants growing on rich trenched land and on ordinary poor land is shown in illustrations Nos. 25 & 25*a*, pages 78*b* and 78*c*. The trees growing on both plots were got

from Basra in one consignment in 1910 ; were of similar appearance
and size and have received the same water and other treatment
throughout, the only difference being that the land on which
the plant in illustration No. 25 is growing was trenched and
heavily manured about a year or more before the trees in that
plot were planted, while the land on which the plant shown
in illustration No. 25a is growing was not. The trees on the
trenched land have grown much faster and are now practically all in bearing—many having borne two or three crops
of fruits of considerable weight—while many of the trees on the
untrenched lands are just coming into bearing or are not yet
bearing. About $\frac{9}{10}$ths of the crop got so far from the garden
have been got from the trees on the trenched area.

41. Usually the off-shoot is not quite straight, but has a slight
curve on it. Date-growers usually plant the
off-shoots so that their tops lean very slightly
towards the south and the inner side of the curve
on the stem is in that direction. The off-shoot is placed in the
centre of the hole in the position above described, and the earth
is filled in and pressed fairly firmly around it. A basin is usually
made round the plant and a watering is given immediately.
The basin should be about $2\frac{1}{2}$ feet in diameter and the level
of its bottom should be 1 to $1\frac{1}{2}$ inches lower than the bottom
of the irrigation channel which runs into it so as to trap a small
pool of water round the tree and irrigate the soil properly there
(see illustration No. 26 opposite). The water in the pool should
disappear within 6 to 8 hours after the irrigation. In planting,
a very important point to notice is that the crown of the off-shoot
(i.e., the position from which the bud of very young leaves start)
is at least 1 or 2 inches above the level of the irrigation water.
If the crown is below this level the irrigation water will get into
and kill the plant by rotting out the young terminal bud.
Frequently the off-shoots and the soil around it sink considerably
after the first few irrigations owing to the earth settling more
compactly in the hole dug at planting time, and the crown of
the plant may then become covered with water at each irrigation.

Planting the off-shoots.

ILLUSTRATION No. 26.

BASIN SYSTEM.

Fig. I. Vertical Section.

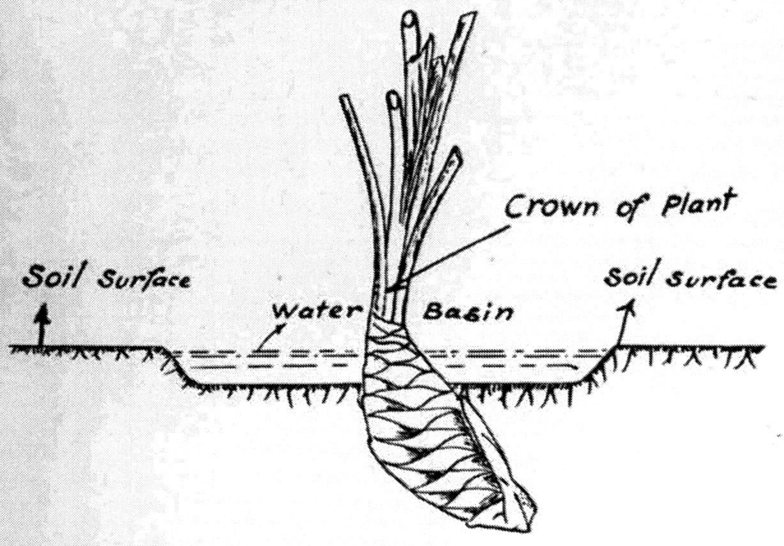

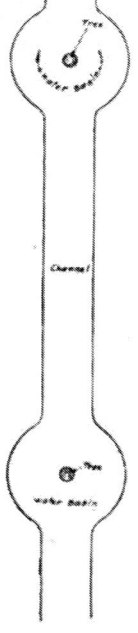

Crown of Plant
Soil Surface
Water
Basin
Soil Surface

Fig. II. Plan.

(On much more reduced scale than Fig. I.)

Channel
Tree
Water Basin
Channel
Tree
Water Basin

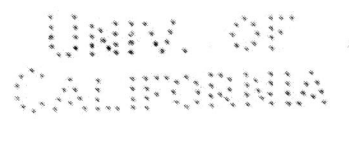

СУГЛОБИ
ПИЛА ОБ

ILLUSTRATION No. 27.
RING SYSTEM.
VERTICAL SECTION.

Fig. I.

Soil surface

Water Ring

Crown of plant

Water Ring

PLAN.
(On much more reduced scale than Fig. I.)

This happens especially where the holes in which the off-shoots were planted have been dug very deep. The hole is perhaps the best depth for planting purposes when on the plant being placed with its lower end resting on the bottom of the hole, the crown of the plant is just at its proper height. As the off-shoots are not all of one size, I find that it is most convenient to have all the holes dug just the correct depth for the smaller plants and then dig out a little more earth where necessary when planting the larger plants. This method of digging holes of course applies only to good loamy well ærated soils. Where there are bands of impervious clays or hard pans, etc., in the soil, the hole should be dug to a depth of 3 feet or more and left for some weeks or months : then some days at least before planting is begun the earth should be replaced and thoroughly packed to the height required in planting the off-shoot, so as to prevent the plant sinking later.

42. If in spite of every thing the plant sinks too low, the irrigating water may be prevented from *To prevent water getting into the crown of the off-shoot when the plant has sunk after planting.* entering the crown of the plant by filling up the basin round the plant with earth and making instead a circular trench round the off-shoot and about 12 inches away from it (*see* illustration No. 27, page 80*b*). The soil around the off-shoot receives water from this trench just as it did from the basin. Care should be taken that earth and dirt does not collect in the crown of the tree, as that is also bad for the plant. Another method of preventing irrigating water entering the crowns of the trees when they have sunk after being planted, is to lower the levels of the water channels and basins around the trees, and then only partly fill the channels with water when irrigating. The previous method is usually the better one, however. Where the crowns have not sunk too low, I prefer the plain basins without the rings (*see* illustration No. 26, page 80*a*).

43. If the soil is of a stiff nature, a mulch of some sort *To prevent cracking of the soil round the plants and excessive evaporation of water.* should be spread on the surface of the soil in the basins around the plants as soon as possible after planting. The mulch may be composed

M, DP

6

of clean river sand that will not run together forming a compact hard cake when it dries, or it may be composed of decaying leaves, refuse litter, straw or any material which will form a loose layer an inch or two in depth on the surface of the soil.

In the Punjab coal ashes perhaps form one of the best materials for spreading round the plant, as they not only form a nice mulch, but retard the attacks of white-ants. The object of a mulch is attained by keeping the upper inch or two of soil loose by very frequent hoeing, etc. The idea is to form a layer of matter which will retain a considerable volume of air in the spaces between its component particles and so retard the swift exchange of dry air of the atmosphere for the more or less moist air that is in contact with the soil surface. If this is done either by frequent hoeing or by an artificial mulch the number of irrigations required to keep the land in a satisfactorily moist state for the plants, will be reduced to an astonishing extent even on medium loams. When the soil is stiff and no mulching is done, the earth around the plants contracts and cracks very readily, and the young tender roots of the off-shoots are apt to be torn during the contraction, or dried up by exposure at the cracks.

44. Immediately the off-shoots are planted each plant should be loosely thatched with sufficient grass to provide a gentle shade for its young terminal bud as the older leaves which naturally formed this shade have been trimmed off (*see* page 68, para. 31).

Newly planted trees must be shaded by thatch.

45. The trees must on no account be shaken or pushed about after being planted, as this breaks the young roots being sent out, or disturbs the proper packing of the soil around the stem so that air spaces are left there into which dry air passes and shrivels up the roots. Ordinary bullock labour, therefore, should not be allowed in the plantation between the time the plants are planted and the time the plants become firmly established.

Trees must not be shaken till firmly established.

ILLUSTRATION No. 28.

Arabian date plantation at Central Jail, Multan, planted in September 1910, photographed about two years later. Onions growing between the lines of dates.

(See para. 46, page 83.)

82a

46. Sometimes in date-growing localities a variety of crops are grown between the trees. While the trees are small only such crops are grown as will not injure the palms by overshading them too much. Common crops grown then are wheat, barley, lucerne, clover, vegetables (*see* illustration No. 28, page 82*a*). Later, such fruits as grapes, pomegranates, figs, peaches, apricots, almonds and similar fruits are often grown under the shade of the palms if there is sufficient space for these. In the Sahara many of these fruits can only be grown successfully under the shade of other trees and do best where grown under the date palm. It is quite common there to see three crops occupying the land at the same time. First the date trees towering above everything, then a mixture of other fruit trees, and under them the more shade loving garden vegetables. Gardens of this sort are of course excellent where the other fruit trees can be grown well, and the fruits from these and the crops of vegetables can be succesfully dealt with. Rice crops should not be grown between newly planted date trees, as until they have become well established the stagnant water of the rice plots harms the young plants.

Auxiliary crops.

47. The great necessity for keeping a minute and accurate record of the trees in a plantation is shown in paragraph 81, page 109. My method of keeping a record is by making a plan of the plantation as in illustration No. 24, page 78*a*, and filing with it all letters and notes of anything of interest connected with the case. Every tree in the plantation is represented on the plan by a small circle with a number inside it and a reference on the margin of the plan shows the name of the variety under that number. The date of planting and a reference are given to the connected correspondence. This plan makes it a simple matter in following years to record when a tree comes in bearing; what its annual yields of fruits are, and any thing of interest about it. The work is greatly facilitated if each tree bears a zinc label with a number on it corresponding with that of the plan.

Method of keeping records of trees in a plantation.

48. A register should also be kept of the number and
Register of waterings. dates of waterings and, if possible, the amount
of water given, as different soils and positions
require different amounts of water. If a record is kept of the
condition of the plantations and compared with different
supplies of water given, the best results can be got eventually
with the most economical water-supply.

49. An irrigation must be given to the date plants as
Water and other requirements of a young plantation on medium soils in Multan. soon as they are planted. A very great stream
of water should not be turned on to the
plantation when irrigations are given, as this
is apt to submerge too much of the plant, carry
dirt into its crown, rot the central bud and kill the plant. The
land must be kept continuously almost wet for the first month
after planting and continuously moist until the plants become
established. Sandy soils will require much more water than
clayey soils will, to keep them in the proper condition, and the
waterings may have to be applied more or less frequently in
different classes of soil, so that the only reliable way to discover
when a young plantation requires watering is to see the dampness
of the soil in the basin round the plants. When plants have been
planted in the first week of September on well drained medium
loams in Multan and neighbouring districts, however, the plants
will stand one watering per day for the first 40 days, one watering
every 2 days for the next 40 days, and one watering every 6 days
till growth starts and the heat commences in spring. After the
frosts in spring are well over and before the weather is very hot
the thatching may be removed from the plants for a week or two
and then fresh thatching put on. Care should be taken, however,
not to shake the plant much while removing the old thatch or
replacing the new. This thatch may finally be removed when
the plants have formed a few strong leaves. From spring the
plants may require a watering every 4 or 5 days till the rains
begin and one watering per week or less after that. One watering
every 6 to 7 days will probably have to be given during the next
hot weather. By the end of that time most of the plants will be

firmly established and will require water less often, the number of waterings depending on the character of soil, the amount of surface hoeing or mulching done, the climate, the height of the permanent water table or the amount of percolation of water if near a river, canal or other body of water (*see* also page 73, para. 38).

50. In Basra the Arabs like to plant date off-shoots in spring when the wheat ripens and they consider the following waterings necessary :—

Water require-ments of young plan-tations in Basra.

(*a*) First 40 days after planting one watering daily.

(*b*) Next 40 days one watering every alternate day.

(*c*) Then one watering every 4 days till end of November.

(*d*) One watering per week in December, January and February.

(*e*) One watering every 4 days during the hot weather.

(*f*) Then once in 10 to 14 days.

(*g*) After two hot seasons and one winter the trees are established and require a watering once in 15 to 30 days.

51. If off-shoots are planted in spring in Multan or neighbouring districts, the above waterings as far as (*e*) would probably be fairly suitable for them also. *f* and *g* would depend on the depth of the subsoil water table (*see* page 73, para. 38). Up to the time the off-shoots have developed the first few well grown leaves they require the most careful and constant attention. If the soil in the basins around the plants has been allowed to dry up once during that time, the death-rate among the plants may be many times multiplied. A remarkably long time elapses before a palm shows very obvious signs of the damage done to it by want of water and it frequently happens that the soil has been kept in excellent condition as regards water for months after the time it was allowed to dry up, before the plant actually withers up completely. The very small proportion of parenchymatous (soft thin walled) tissue in the leaf-blade ; its excessively strong framework of scle-renchyma (hard fibrous tissue) and the thick strong cuticle (skin)

The effects of allowing the soil in a young plantation to dry up.

(*vide* page 7, para. 4) prevent it wilting and drooping at once as a turnip or cabbage leaf does when water is scarce. We have seen cases where the short supply of water took place in July and the plants only began to show very obvious signs of dying off in October and later in the year. If the off-shoots are planted in the first week of September and the plantation receives careful attention, nearly all the weakly plants will have died out and many of the others will have produced several well grown leaves by that time next year. If careful attention is not given some of the plants will not have established themselves till three or four years after planting. Proper attention as regards water, etc., is well repaid by a young date plantation as strong vigorous trees come several years sooner into bearing than weakly ones.

52.   In most parts of the world the death-rate in a young
Death-rate in a   plantation is usually between 20 and 30 per
young plantation.   cent. The results of the past five years' experiments in the Punjab show us that the death-rate could be kept well within these figures by planting fair sized plants on average quality of soil in early September and by giving them the attention prescribed. Forty-three trees out of fifty planted at Lyallpur in September 1910 are now (1916) flourishing vigorously and some have borne three crops of fruits. The Executive Engineer, Lower Sutlej Canals Division, informs me that 42 out of 50 suckers sent to him in 1911 are alive and that some are giving fruits. In other places also where proper attention has been given very low death-rates have been got. In many cases, however, the death-rate has been far higher than it should have been, and in some cases it has practically amounted to total extinction. Shortage of irrigation water, for reasons beyond control, and a want of knowledge of the value of mulching were in some cases the causes of the high death-rate, but failure to realise the absolute necessity of preventing the soil in the plantation from drying up further than prescribed above, even once until the plants become established, was the great stumbling-block. This is not surprising, as most people here have never reared date palms from suckers but have seen from

ILLUSTRATION No. 29.

Date tree growing in Multan. It stands beside a dunghill (*a*) and annually bears several times the amount of fruit borne by date trees of the same age in the same enclosure. It is giving off a sucker (*b*) although its age is about 40 years. The leaves (*c*) are past their useful stage and should be pruned away.

(*See page* 87.)

their birth date trees grow from seeds simply thrown away after the fruits were eaten and receiving no special watering or attention whatsoever. All the above instructions are therefore looked upon as so much empty talk and the carrying out of these instructions but an unnecessary expense. The planter will find, however, that if these are not strictly complied with, he must face a correspondingly high death-rate. On the other hand, all our experience indicates that if vigorous plants are planted in good soil at the proper season, and are given fair attention, there is no reason why the death-rate should not be as low in the Punjab as in any date-growing region in the world. These points cannot be too strongly impressed on intending planters. There is a large number of people, who having seen how very much better the fruits grown in the Punjab on the imported trees are, than those on local trees, are asking us for suckers, but a great number of the plants planted by these people will certainly die off and be a loss to the growers if they are not properly treated when planted.

53. In many cases no manure is given to date palms. In some cases, however, it is given once every 2 to 4 years; in other cases annually, and in a few cases twice a year. Where manure is not given at any other time it is customary to apply it to off-shoots when they have established themselves in the soil after being planted out. Manure seems to very much increase the vigour and rate of growth of young plants and the fruit-bearing capacity of adult trees (*see* illustrations Nos. 25 & 25*a*, pages 78*b* & 78*c* and No. 29, page 86*a*). The tree in illustration No. 29 stands beside a dung heap and the owner informed me that the tree annually yields several maunds of fresh fruits while several other trees of the same age growing a few yards distant only yield 20 seers each.

Manuring and interculture of established date palms.

The manure applied to date trees may be any ordinary farm-yard manure. Cow, horse, donkey, camel, fowl, etc., dungs have been used. It should be well rotted, especially here, where it may attract white-ants if it is not properly decayed. The

amount to be used will vary with the age of the tree, quality of
the soil and the time which will elapse between the applications.
It is better practice to give a small quantity annually than to
give a larger amount only after a lapse of several years.   About 50
lbs. of well-rotted manure per tree annually would be a beneficial
dressing. When applying the manure the earth may be removed
around the tree to a radius of 3 or 4 feet and to a depth of 2 or
3 inches. In this excavation the dung may be spread and covered
up by replacing the soil again. The operation is done before
spring growth commences. The growing and ploughing in of a
crop of green manure between the trees may be resorted to.

San (*Crotolaria juncea*) may be grown for this purpose
when the date plants are big enough not to be too much
overshadowed by it. In Egypt and elsewhere leguminous fodder
crops are grown between the trees. These crops may be fed,
where they grow, to cattle, or may be carried off the land and
fed to cattle elsewhere, but even in the latter case their residue of
roots, etc., left in the land enriches it in nitrogen. In the Punjab,
Lentils (*Ervum lens*) gram (*Cicer arietinum*) peas (*Pisum sativum*)
vetches (*Lathyrus* sp.) senji (*Melilotus parviflora*) etc., may be
grown in winter and moth (*Phaseolus aconitifolius*) mash (*Ph.
radiatus*) mung (*Ph. mungo*) and such crops may be grown in
summer for this purpose. Where vegetables, etc., are grown
between the trees and manure is applied to these crops, the
fertility of the soil is kept up in that way (*see* para. 46, page 83,
for further auxiliary crops, and para. 58, page 91, for cultivation
of the soil where no auxiliary crop is grown).

54. Adult   trees require very little attention and care.

Leaf pruning and
clearing of excess of
off-shoots and rub-
bish from the bases
of the trees.

Where harm from winter frosts is feared, they
should not be severely pruned in autumn, as
a large number of leaves on the top of the plant
protect its inner and more tender young leaves
from the colds in winter. It is especially necessary to remember
this in the case of young plants in such situations, as small plants
are more liable to injury than taller ones (*see* page 32, para. 17).
Special conditions as regards disease, etc., may arise, however,

ILLUSTRATION No. 30.

Date tree growing at Pacca Mari, Lyallpur, 21 years old, and showing a sucker (*a*) at its base ; a large number of leaves on the tree are withered and drooping, and, should be pruned away.

(*See page* 89.)

which would make it advantageous to prune the plants fairly severely and then protect them artificially.

Mr. Gaskin, Assistant for Commerce and Trade, Baghdad, informs me that the Arabs there prune the old leaves from the palms three times a year, *viz.* : (*a*) at the time of pollination, (*b*) when the fruit is well formed but has not turned yellow, and (*c*) when the bunches of fruits are finally cut down. At the time of (*a*) the growers have to climb the trees to " hand-pollinate " the flowers ; at (*b*) they are probably thinning out the fruit bunches and unfertilised fruits ; at (*c*) they are harvesting. Having climbed the trees at these times the people naturally cut away any leaves which have passed their most useful stage of life or are in the way of the worker (*see* illustration No. 29, page 86*a*.)

Usually where the date is cultivated, however, the main pruning is done in spring. When growth commences, the leaves which are withering and hanging limply are cut away and the bases of the trees are cleared of all rubbish and superfluous off-shoots. Four to six off-shoots are usually left on each young tree to provide young plants for planting elsewhere. Young off-shoots while attached to the parent tree obtain water and food materials from the parent, and later when they have developed roots for themselves, these roots take up water and food materials from the soil which would otherwise have been available for the parent tree ; therefore the crop of fruits is diminished if too large a number of off-shoots are allowed to remain attached to a tree.

55. Young date palms grown from seeds which have dropped around the trees, and all other useless plants growing around the bases of the trees should be removed, as they also take up water and food materials from the soil, which would otherwise have been available to the date trees.

Effect of seedling dates and weeds on a plantation.

56. Date trees usually produce off-shoots fit for planting between the ages of 5 and 20 years (*see* illustration No. 38, page 112*b*, and illustration No. 30, page 88*a*). After 20 years of age few or no

Ages between which trees produce off-shoots (suckers) and number of suckers borne.

off-shoots are produced as a rule. Sometimes, however, much older trees give off one or more suckers (*see* illustration No. 29, page 86*a*).

If a tree bears good fruits and off-shoots from it are much wanted, a larger number of off-shoots may be allowed to grow at its base than is quoted in paragraph 54 above. The total number of suckers which a date tree bears during its lifetime varies greatly with the variety of the date, the vigor of the plant, the degree of moisture usual in the surface soil, etc. Imported Arabian trees planted as suckers at Lyallpur 5 years previously are now bearing 1 to 16 suckers each and have an average of about 7 suckers per tree ; trees of the same consignment planted at Muzaffargarh are bearing 1 to 15 suckers each, with an average of about 6 suckers per tree ; and trees of the same lot in the Multan Central Jail Garden now bear 1 to 14 suckers per tree. About 60 per cent. of these suckers are ready for removal from the parent trees.

Twenty is an approximate estimate of the average total number of suckers that a date tree will produce during its normal sucker-producing years, but, as will be seen from the above, the number even on individual five-year old trees varies very widely.

When it is desired to extend the period during which a tree will give off off-shoots, or to increase the number of off-shoots which it is giving off at a younger period, a platform of earth is sometimes raised round its stem and kept moist. Continued contact of the stem with the moisture induces it to give off suckers and roots at that point (*see* page 10, para. 5). In the case of old trees a mass of matting, ropes, etc., is sometimes wound round their stems higher up and kept moist for similar purposes.

Several cases have been met with where old trees have fallen over and suckers have developed from the upper portions of their stems where they remained in contact with damp earth. In the case of one such date tree when found the original base of the tree had disappeared and the lower part of the old stem was quite clear of the ground while much further along it a sucker and a new root system had developed from its side where it lay in contact with the soil.

How far this tendency of the younger parts of date stems to form suckers and roots when in continued damp conditions, after the older more basal parts have ceased to do so, can be made real practical use of to get suckers from old trees, to save trees which have been uprooted by river floods, etc., is being further investigated.

57. As has already been explained in paragraph 38 (page 73) the number of waterings required by adult date trees varies with the height of the permanent water table, the amount of percolation, the character of the soil, climatic conditions, etc., so that no general rule can be given with regard to the amount of water to be applied artificially. It is, however, agreed that the palm requires more water in the fruit-developing period than it does at other times of the year. When the plants are artificially watered here, they should receive liberal supplies between the 1st May and the time when the fruits stop developing in July or August. At the flowering time no water, as a rule, is recommended, as it is believed that an excess of water at that time prevents the proper setting of the fruit. The main aim in watering adult date palms should be to give abundant water in the fruit-developing season and to keep the soil well aerated. Where the plants are not growing in these conditions the crop of fruits will be reduced, the size of the fruits will be smaller and their quality inferior. (*See* also page 111, para. 84, and page 99, para. 72.)

Water requirements of adult trees.

58. If no crops are grown between the trees, it would still be an advantage to irrigate the whole of the land and plough, harrow, or otherwise stir its surface up occasionally. If alkali is present, the occasional irrigations would prevent it collecting in great strength on the surface of the land by washing it down and re-distributing it in the soil, and the ploughings or harrowings would eradicate weeds and retard evaporation. For crops grown between the trees (*see* paragraph 46, page 83, and paragraph 53, page 87). When salts accumulate at the soil surface in a plantation, these should be scraped off and carted away (*see* page 19, para. 14)

Treatment of the soil between the trees where no crops are grown.

CHAPTER IV.

Pollination to Fruit Preservation.

59. In some other parts of the world writers have found that date palms usually come into flower while the mean temperatures are between 68° F. and 77° F. If this were so here, date trees would usually be in flower in Multan from about the beginning to the end of March. What we actually find is that, although a very few date trees may sometimes be seen as early as the first week of January, most date trees come into flower and are pollinated between the 15th March and the end of April in Dera Ghazi Khan, Muzaffargarh and Multan districts, which at present form our principal date-growing area. Date palms in Dera Ghazi Khan generally come into flower a week or so earlier than those in Muzaffargarh, and 10 days approximately earlier than those in Multan. The warmer the winter, the earlier the trees come into flower. The time of flowering of a date tree appears to vary with the variety as well as with the climate, however, and is probably also influenced more or less by its water-supply, etc. One date tree of either sex will produce from 5 to 30 flower-clusters in one season, and a month may elapse between the times that its first and its last flower-cluster are ready for fertilisation.

Date that the trees come into flower in the Punjab and number of flower-clusters produced per annum by a date tree.

60. Pollination is the conveying of pollen grains from the pollen sac of the stamen to the stigma, or receptive point, on the carpel. In the case of the date palm, the receptive part of the carpel is its sharp-hooked tip (*see* illustration No. 18, page 12*d*). In good date-growing countries pollination is facilitated by the cultivator. It is usually done in the following way :—

Artificial pollination.

The male flower-cluster with its enclosing spathe (*see* illustrations Nos. 15 and 17, pages 12*a* and 12*c*), is cut from the tree,

ILLUSTRATION No. 31.

Arabian Date Palm planted at Multan Central Jail, September 1910, being hand-pollinated in March 1912.

(See page 92, para. 60.)

generally immediately before the spathe splits open. The stage at which the spathe is ready to split open may be known by comparing the spathes that are just splitting with those that have not yet reached that stage. It will be seen that when ready to split the spathe will have assumed a brown colour, a soft texture and other characters by which the splitting stage is fairly easily known. By removing the spathe then it will be seen that the waxy scales of the flowers are closed over and protecting the stamens and if these scales are lifted, it will be seen that the pollen sacs have not yet burst. If on removing the spathe the flower-cluster is exposed to the sun, the waxy scales will open out within a few hours and the pollen sacs will burst and shed their pollen. Sometimes the male flower-cluster is cut from the tree just after the spathe opens, but in this case there is a chance that many of the pollen sacs may have opened, and that much of the pollen dust may be shaken out and lost while removing the flower-cluster from the tree and carrying it to the female trees. If the flower-cluster is removed just before the spathe opens, the pollen will not be lost in carrying it about. The spathe must be very near the bursting stage before the male flower-cluster is cut from the tree however, as otherwise the pollen grains will not be mature enough to fertilise the ovules of the female. Having obtained a male flower-cluster in the proper stage of development, a female flower-cluster is next found which is just appearing between the parts of its bursting spathe (*see* illustration No. 16, page 12*b*), and one or two small branches are broken from the male flower-cluster and are inserted among the small branches of the female cluster (*see* illustration No. 31, page 92*a*). In due time the male flowers open, the pollen sacs burst and the pollen is carried by wind or insects to the stigmas of the carpels of the flowers in the female cluster. In most cases the Arabs place one or more branches of the male flower-cluster among the branches of the female cluster and then loosely bind the branches of the female cluster around the inserted male branch ; the binding being done by a strip of palm leaf or string, and in such a way that it will become undone by the time the fruits begin to develop. In Sind two small branches of the male flower-cluster are said to be usually inserted

in the female flower-cluster and no tie is used. It may be noted
here that the placing of the male flower branches in the female
flower-cluster is not strictly speaking pollination, as insects or
winds have still to convey the pollen from these male flowers to
the stigmas of the female flowers. Date cultivators, however,
usually apply the term " pollination " or " hand-pollination "
to this act.

61. Fertilisation may be defined here as the fusion of certain
Fertilisation and its effects. of the contents of the pollen grain of the male
flower with certain of those of the ovule of
the female flower necessary to enable the ovule
to develop into a seed.

So far as I know, this process has not yet been followed in
the case of the date palm, but the generally accepted idea of how
fertilisation is effected in plants of this sort may be roughly
indicated as follows :—

When the tiny pollen grain reaches the stigma (receptive
portion of the carpel, *see* illustration No. 18, page 12*d*), it germi-
nates ; and absorbing food from the carpel, forms a long tube
which makes its way through the carpel tissues into the ovule
which the carpel contains. Two bodies termed gametes,
from the pollen grain, pass down this tube and enter the ovule.
One of these gametes fuses with a certain body (the ovum) in the
ovule, and the fused mass so formed now known as the oospore,
eventually gives rise to the tiny embryo (baby plant). The
other gamete from the pollen grain fuses with another body
(the definite nucleus) in the ovule, and this fused mass gives rise
to the hard tissue (endosperm) which forms the bulk of the seed.

The baby plant while in the seed is a small whitish structure
little bigger than a pin-head. Its position is indicated by a small
circular depression about half way up the seed, on the surface
opposite the large longitudinal groove. Its size, shape, etc., can
be seen if the seed is split along that groove with a chisel or strong
knife (*see* illustration No. 32, opposite). As a result of fertilisation of the ovule, the carpel enclosing it becomes stimulated

ILLUSTRATION No. 32.

COMPLETE SEED

Showing

GROOVED SIDE   PLAIN SIDE

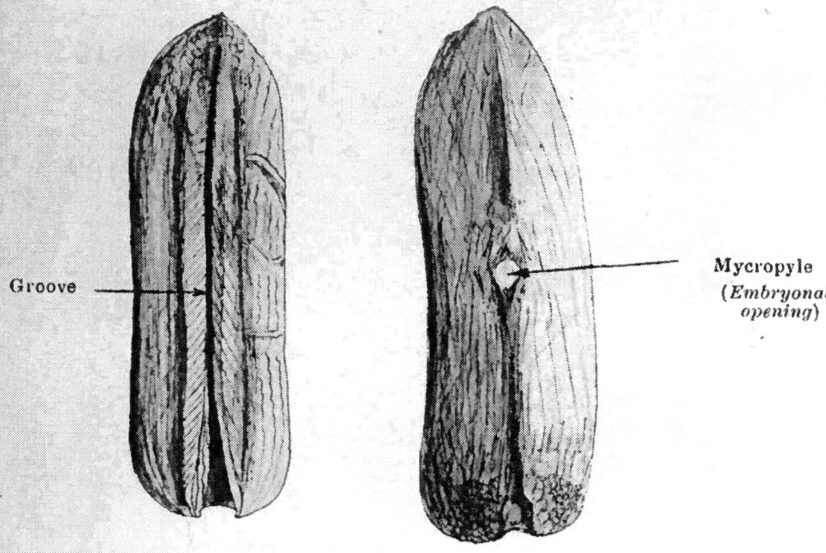

Groove ⟶

Mycropyle
(*Embryonal
opening*)

LONGITUDINAL SECTION OF SEED

PASSING THROUGH EMBRYO

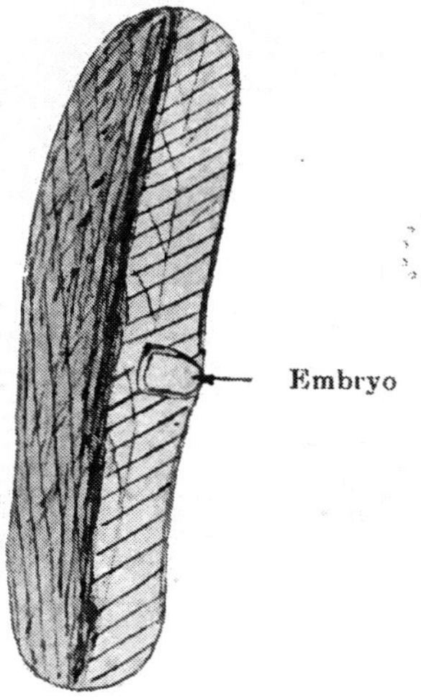

⟶ Embryo

× 3 *Diameters*

(*See page* 94.)

to renewed growth. The carpel increases in size ; its cells become stored with sugar, etc., and it forms the fleshy edible part of the fruit by the time that the hard seed has matured. These sweet walls induce animals to eat the fruits and assist in the dispersal of the seeds, thus helping the palms to multiply in the wild state. When the seeds are sown in suitable conditions, the hard endosperm which forms the bulk of the seed gradually softens and becomes a supply of soluble food which nourishes the baby plant until it can develop a sufficient root and leaf system to collect food materials from the soil and air, and manufacture food for itself.

62. If after pollination the parts of the male plant which

Characters of the male trees are conveyed to the seeds but not to the edible part of the fruits formed as the immediate result of pollination.

pass to the female (*i.e.*, the gametes and accompanying protoplasmic matter) fuse only with bodies which give rise to parts of the seed as they do in other plants, the characters of the male plant used in pollination are not embodied in the edible part of the fruit which encloses the seed ; that part being simply the ripened carpel of the female. I have not yet found any reliable evidence against this view, although it is not uncommon to find date-growers who believe that the characters of the male are conveyed to the edible part of the fruit formed. When seeds of these fruits are sown, the plants produced show characters of the male used, as one would expect.

63. As the number of flower-clusters on both male and

Number of males required per 100 females.

female trees are about equal, and there are one hundred or more branches in a male inflorescence, one male tree will suffice to fertilise 100 female trees approximately where one male branch is used to a female flower-cluster, and will suffice for 50 trees approximately where two male branches are used. It is evident, therefore, that if the male trees produce a fair number of flower-clusters, two male date trees ought to suffice to pollinate 100 female trees. It is safer, however, to have three male trees to every 100 females (*see* also page 97, para. 66).

64. It is essential that pollination is done as soon as possible after the female spathe bursts, as within a few days time the stigmas of the carpels become withered and unreceptive. When the flowers open the stigmas are most fresh and receptive. At that time they are whitish coloured. They become dark as they wither. In very hot dry weather the beginning of the darkening process is apparent after two days ; in cloudy dull weather it may only be apparent after four or five days. For this reason the plantations of good date cultivators are carefully and frequently inspected during the flowering season and every flower-cluster is pollinated as it becomes ready. As hand-pollination is being introduced into the Punjab, I may here emphasise that unless careful and regular attention can be given to the pollination of the female flower-clusters in the flowering season, good results will not be got, where only 3 per cent. of the trees are males, and no wild males are growing near. Pollination is a very simple process, however, consisting merely of thrusting a branch of a male flower-cluster into a female cluster, and two to three visits per week during the flowering season would be sufficient to ensure getting the flowers in the proper stage of development for pollination. With a little practice it is a simple matter to detect spathes which are just about to open, and in order to reduce the number of visits necessary to pollinate all the flower bunches satisfactorily, Arab date-growers cut these open and pollinate them when they are pollinating those which have already opened.

Hand pollination demands regular attention at the flowering season.

65. Pollen may be kept for at least one year with safety if it is stored in a dry place. For storage purposes the flower-cluster is frequently not removed from its spathe, and if it is removed from its spathe, it is usually stored in a paper bag. Where male trees are late in coming into flower and females are early, it is advisable to store a few male flower-clusters, which contain ripe pollen, so that pollen may be at hand when the early females come into flower in the following season.

Preservation of pollen.

66. Some male trees produce more pollen and some come
Selection of male trees. earlier into flower than others. In propagating
male trees, to be used to pollinate female trees
whose fruits are to be sold for consumption, off-shoots should be
taken from trees which produce much pollen, and which come
into flower at or a little before the time that the females are in
flower. It is most convenient if males can be propagated, which
come into flower in succession throughout the female flowering
season. If the trees produce a plentiful supply of pollen in the
proper season, other qualities of the male tree selected are mostly
unimportant if rearing of date trees from seedlings is not
undertaken, as the characters of the male are not transmitted
to the edible part of the fruit formed as the immediate result
of pollination. If new varieties of dates are to be bred, however,
male trees should be used which have been reared from seeds got
from good varieties of trees, and which have had good male and
female ancestors as the seeds of those fruits when sown will give
rise to plants most of which will show some of the characters of
the male used (*see* also pages 94 and 95, paras. 61 and 62).

67. Where pollination is done by natural agencies, *i.e.*,
Percentage of males required for natural pollination. where the pollen is carried from the pollen sacs
of the male tree to the carpels of the female
by wind, insects and other agencies not con-
trolled by the farmer, about 50 per cent. of the date plantation
should be male trees and these should be well mixed with the
female trees to obtain the best results. Cases are on record in
which date pollen is believed to have been carried many miles
by natural agencies and female trees fertilised by it, but where
the distances between the male and female trees are great, good
results could only be expected when the winds are in a direction
which will carry the pollen from the male to the female trees,
the air is not too humid, etc., at flowering time.

68. By what date-growers term " hand pollinating " date
Advantages of " hand pollina- tion." trees, instead of allowing them to be wind-pollinated, the following advantages will be had :—

(1) Fertilisation will be more certain.

(2) 47 per cent. of the trees which in a wind-pollinated plantation would be males and bear no fruit can be replaced by good fruit-bearing females, and therefore practically double the crop of fruits can be got from a given area of land with the same water-supply ; the only difference in annual costs to the growers being those of the labour of hand pollination of the trees and the collection and disposal of the extra fruits.

69. When date-flowers are pollinated, all three carpels in
Falling of two of the three fruits from a female flower.
the female flower are usually fertilised and begin to develop (*see* illustration No. 18, page 12*d*). When the fruits get to about the size of peas, two of the three fruits fall off and one date fruit only is left to develop and ripen in each flower (*see* illustration No. 18D, page 12*d* and illustration No. 33 opposite). This usually happens in April or early May in the western side of the Punjab.

70. If these carpels begin to develop without being
Seedless dates and their relation to pollination.
fertilised, all three dates may remain on the flower, but they will be seedless and generally of poor quality (*see* illustration No. 33 opposite). When a large number of seedless dates are found, it may usually be concluded that fertilisation has been defective, as the absence of the seed in a date is in most cases due to the ovule not being fertilised. In cases in which seedless dates are got, if hand pollination has been employed, the method of performing it, the stages of development of both the male and female flowers, the rainfall, etc., at the time of pollination, should all be carefully looked into. If the trees were pollinated by natural agencies, the number of male trees around, their distances from the female plants, the direction of the wind and the rainfall at the flowering period, etc., should all be carefully considered. Notes on such cases would be very acceptable to the Agricultural Department

ILLUSTRATION No. 33.

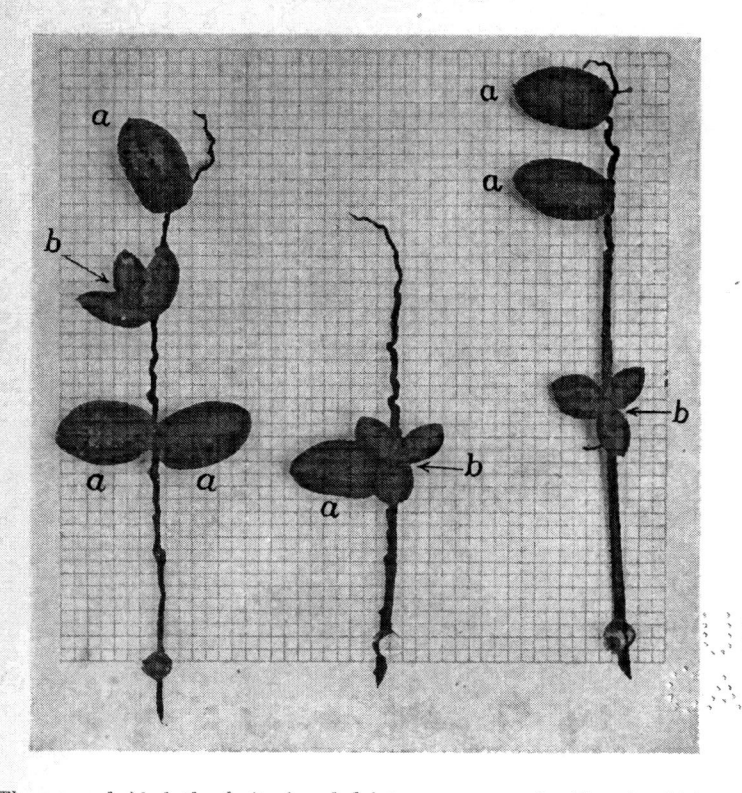

The paper behind the fruits is ruled into squares, each side of which is half a centimetre in length.

(*a*) Almost full grown normal seed-bearing fruits; the two other carpels of the flower in each case have been shed long previously.

(*b*) Cases where all three carpels of the flower are still developing. They are *Khassi* (unfertilised and seedless) fruits. Where the carpels are fertilised, two of the three carpels are shed from each flower when they are the size of peas or less.

(*See page* 98.)

71. After the fruits have become sufficiently developed
Reducing the number of bunches of fruits to 8 or 12 per tree. to show what sort of bunches may be expected, about 8 to 12 of the best bunches should be selected to remain on each adult tree and the remainder should be all cut down. If the bunches are poor, and the tree is vigorous, a greater number are left on the tree.

72. If more fruits are left than the tree can develop properly, the size of the fruits may be considerably
Too many fruits on a date tree. diminished, and in excessive cases a large number shrivel and do not come to proper maturity. In Multan and Muzaffargarh districts I have seen a good many trees on which more fruits had been allowed to remain than they were able to mature properly. With those people who do not understand date culture properly, there is always a tendency to avoid reducing the number of date bunches where the trees are overladen, but there is no more advantage in leaving too many bunches of fruits on a date tree than there is of leaving too many maize plants in a maize field. Also when a tree has been allowed to carry an over-load of fruits in one year, it usually bears a very poor crop in the next.

73. The chief enemies complained of to me are human
Protection of fruits from enemies. thieves, parrots, and other birds, wasps, and monkeys in some parts of the Province. A chaukidar (watchman) usually looks after the trees from the time the fruits have developed sufficiently to attract enemies, until they are harvested. The following is recorded in the *Multan Gazetteer*, 1901-2, regarding the watchman :—" He receives about Rs. 4 per month and a small number of dates, and he attends, taking one month and one locality with another, some 300 trees." He sees that no human thieves steal the fruits, and he keeps off birds by shouting, slinging stones, etc. To help to scare away birds he frequently hangs bells and other contrivances for making a noise on the trees, and shakes these occasionally by means of strings. In date-growing countries the bunches of fruits are often encased in rough mats made of palm leaves, to stop birds from destroying the fruits. The mat

is usually wrapped round the bunch, is sewn together at the top and left open at the bottom, making a protecting case of the appearance of a huge cow bell (*see* illustration No. 34 opposite). The matting should be made as open as is consistent with its purpose, as it prevents a good deal of sunlight from getting at the cluster of fruits, and probably retards ripening. Another method is to hang a number of small branches of some very thorny plant round each cluster of fruits. This is very effective in preventing birds getting at them and is more open than the basket usually is but is difficult for the fruit picker to manipulate. A good thick layer of thorns round a fruit cluster would probably also give monkeys some trouble in getting at the fruit bunches. Rings of thorns round the stems of the trees, where the trees are not too close together, might also hinder monkeys from getting at the fruits. Fortunately, however, there are no complaints of depredations by monkeys in the areas of the Punjab which grow most dates. If the fruit bunches are encased in coarse muslin bags, birds and some insects will be kept off, but wasps, which are among the most insistent depredators, cut their way through these and suck the sugary juice from the dates. Net-wire or other special net bags such as are sometimes used to protect grape and other fruit bunches, may be used to protect the date fruits against attacks by these insects.

74. In the date-growing places in the Punjab, most of the fruits are usually harvested between the 20th of July and the 20th of August. A few both earlier and later fruits have been seen. July and August may, however, be taken as the harvesting season. All the dates on a cluster do not ripen simultaneously. If a variety is a fairly good one, the people in these districts usually pick the dates off the cluster as soon as their ends show a small soft translucent spot. The ripening is then completed by spreading the fruits on mats in the sun (*see* frontispiece). Dates are rarely completely ripened on the trees in the Punjab. Those fruits, which have their skins broken or which are in a bad condition, should be carefully removed from the cluster when

Harvesting and ripening of the fruits.

ILLUSTRATION No. 34.

Date trees at Leiah, Muzaffargarh District, showing fruit bunches protected by cowbell-
shaped mats.

(See para. 73, page 99.)

ripening. If these are not removed, the whole cluster becomes tainted. If the variety is not very good, the cluster is cut from the tree when about 50 per cent. of the fruits on it are ready and the fruits are then spread in the sun. Any dates which do not ripen while spread in the sun are fed to goats, etc.

75. As has been stated already (*see* page 44, para. 20), fruits are apt to ferment and fall off the tree before they are ripe if the atmosphere in the ripening period is wet. Great damage may be done in this way to the crop by wet weather at the ripening time. The fear that the crop might be spoiled by rain or damaged by enemies, accounts for the Punjab custom of harvesting the fruits as soon as a small spot on the end becomes soft ; and of finishing the ripening process on mats in the sun, rather than attempt ripening the fruits completely on the tree as is usually done in countries where the date-harvesting season is practically rainless.

Wet atmosphere in the ripening time.

76. Different varieties of dates differ very much in the length of time they keep fresh without being preserved. The large purple date known as the "Ghatti" found growing at Muzaffargarh, has usually begun to ferment in about 24 hours after it has been plucked, if it has been taken from the tree at the stage of ripeness at which other dates are harvested. When harvested at this stage of ripeness, most varieties of dates only keep fresh for a few days after being plucked from the trees unless they are further ripened and partly dried or otherwise preserved. Preservation of dates by drying depends upon the fact that the organisms concerned in fermentation cannot live and perform their work in a sugary solution above a certain concentration. Therefore the juice of those dates that keep longest fresh is usually less watery than those that go rancid sooner. The further ripening and preservation by drying is, as already mentioned, usually done by spreading the fruits thinly on a mat in the sun. The object to aim at is to dry off just as much of the water from the fruit as will leave the juice as concentrated as will preserve the fruit for the length of time required. More water than this should

Preservation and packing of date fruits in the Punjab and elsewhere.

not be dried off as weight is lost, the fruits have a less plump and attractive appearance, and the flavour is impaired. Different varieties of date fruits will require to be exposed to the sun for different lengths of time to bring them to the necessary stage of dryness ; and if the sky is cloudy or the atmosphere is more or less humid, the length of time of exposure required to dry a particular variety sufficiently will also vary. In Muzaffargarh, in good weather some varieties require to be spread in the sun about one week in order to reduce them to the proper stage of dryness ; others require only three or four days. Plucked at the stage at which they are here, one-third, or over, of the weight of the fruit is generally lost during the drying process. Much, however, also depends on the quality of the date. Date cultivators very soon get to know approximately how long a particular variety of date fruit will require to be exposed to dry it to the proper stage, and they become very accurate in their estimations of how dry the fruits must be in order to preserve them sufficiently for their particular purposes. All decaying fruits must be carefully removed from the others during drying, as they taint the whole lot if not removed. The fruits require the closest attention while being preserved if the best results are to be got. After this treatment they are usually placed on the market or stored for private use. The local date fruits which find their way into the market are practically all sold in bulk without any packing. Those that are retained by the growers for their own use later are usually packed in unglazed earthen jars (*chātties*) which when filled are closed at the top to prevent the entrance of a moth, the eggs of which give rise to wormlike larvæ in the fruits later (*see* page 139, para. 96). The closing is sometimes done by a piece of cloth tied over the top of the jar or by its lid being cemented on to it, with a paste of flour or mud, etc. These unglazed earthen jars absorb a good deal of sap from the fruits during storage. This should be allowed for when the fruits are being prepared for these vessels. Dates keep very well for six months to a year or more, when packed in this way, provided that insects have not laid eggs in the fruits before they were packed. If that has happened, insect larvæ may appear among the fruits in autumn or winter. The purple date known as " Ghatti " cannot be preserved by drying to the above stage and is usually either sold and consumed fresh, or preserved by being split open and dried in the sun till hard. The seeds may or may not be removed in the process. In the Punjab inferior fruits of other varieties are sometimes treated similarly.   Date fruits treated in this way are known as " Chirvi " or " Shingistan. " Sometimes also date fruits—especially inferior ones—are plucked from the tree before they begin to soften, are boiled in water to which has been added a little oil or ghee (boiled butter) or milk, and sometimes a little salt. They are then dried hard and stored. Such fruits are called " Bhugrian." They can be kept for years in this state and are used at festivals.

Most of the world's date fruits that find their way into large markets, are either plucked from the trees when they show a tanslucent soft spot, or when they are more fully ripened ; get what drying they require to make them keep properly by being spread in the sun and are then packed for market without further treatment. The world's finest fruits are used for confectionery purposes. Such fruits are usually packed in very thin wooden or cardboard boxes holding ½lb. or less each. The boxes always have some attractive shape and wrapper. They usually hold one layer of fruits in depth and two rows in width ; the dates in these two rows being ranged on either side of a date flower branch to look as if they were growing from it. Those found packed in this way generally keep in good condition through the winter following their harvest, if free of insects' eggs when packed. Where they are desired to keep for several years, each small box is sometimes encased in a hermetically sealed tin case.

A large quantity of fruits of superior quality from date-growing countries are used for dessert purposes. These are usually found packed in layers in cardboard boxes containing 1—3 lbs. of fruits. In all cardboard boxes a lining of butter paper should be placed between the fruits and the cardboard, otherwise the dates may taste of the cardboard after a certain time. Such small packets are usually further packed in large wooden cases for shipment.

The world's dates of lower quality are usually sold retail unpacked. They are transported to the markets in bulk in large boxes ; in mats of date leaves, in skins, etc. (*see* page 142, para. 97). A large number of other methods of preserving and packing dates are practised by date-growers and traders in various parts of the world, but the preparations are chiefly for home consumption, and are met with in the markets on a comparatively small scale. Perhaps some of the Baluchistan methods are the most famous of these. I give below a few notes about some of them.* These dates are preserved in date syrup in unglazed red clay vessels called " Humbs." Three sizes of humbs are used ; the largest resembles a large pitcher in shape. It is difficult to transport with safety and is only kept for home use. The middle sized and the smallest " Humbs " are more vase-shaped (*see* illustration No. 35 opposite). As a rule dates to be preserved in this way are harvested when fully ripe, but in some cases the immature fruit is gathered and put in the sun for four to eight days and then preserved. In Kech the process of extracting the juice to be used as the syrup is as follows :—A space of ground is cleared about four by two feet, hollowed towards the centre, and carefully plastered. In the centre an earthen basin is fixed. Baskets of dates are laid over this space and the juice is pressed out of the fruits by placing one or more heavy date tree trunks over the baskets. The juice collects in the basin. The " humbs " are then filled with unpressed fruits and a sufficient amount of the syrup is added to cover them. The syrup is so thick that its upper layer soon crystallises and forms a sugary plug to the humb. They are stored or come into the market in this state.

In Panjgur the famous Muzāti date is preserved in this way in the syrup made from a variety of date known as the Kahsuba.

---

* *Note*—Practically all the subject-matter for the descriptions of these Baluchistan methods of curing dates has been taken from the *Baluchistan Gazetteer*, Volumes VII and VIII, published by *Times* Press, Bombay, 1907.

ILLUSTRATION No. 35.

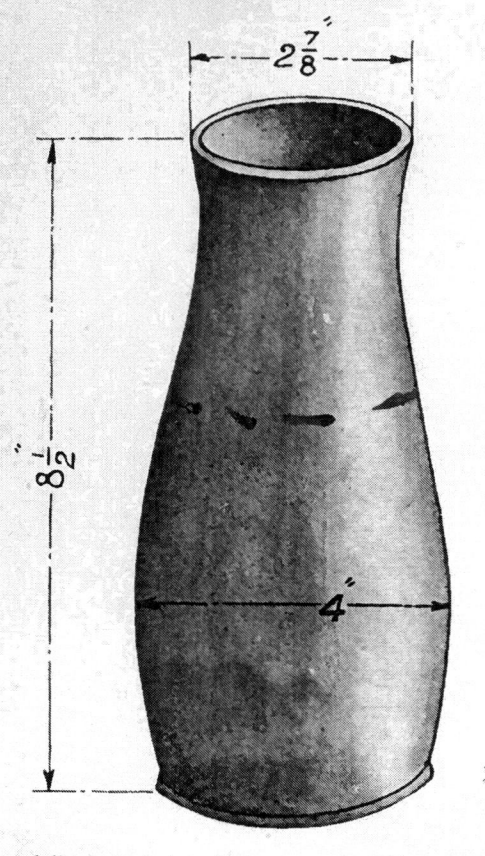

"Small humb" in which date fruits are preserved in Baluchistan.

(*See page* 104.)

Major T. H. Keys, Assistant Political Agent, Baluchistan, very kindly sent me several humbs of fruits in June 1913, and they were delicious to taste.

A special preparation made in Baluchistan is a date paste known as "Dastlaghāsh." The fruit is skinned and the perianth* and seed are removed. A mass of the preparation is then kneaded into a paste and stored in dried sheep-skins or bags made of date palm leaflets. In Kech "Dastlaghāsh" is prepared from the date varieties known as "Haleni" and "Dandāri"; in Panjgur from "Muzāti."

In Kech another special preparation known as "Tallo" is made from the varieties "Haleni" and "Begam-jangi." The dates are cut lengthwise in two pieces and then preserved in jars.

In Panjgur the Muzāti date is cut in two halves at right angles to the long axis and then threaded on a string. Each string when full weighs about 1 lb. Such dates are known as "Lar."

Another preparation made in Panjgur is known as "chup tagen kulont." It is made from the "Sabzo" variety by cutting the fruits into small pieces and preserving them in juice in a jar. It is not made for sale.

The immature fruits of Haleni and Muzāti are boiled and dried in the sun. They are then known as "Harag." In Kech, harag prepared from Muzāti dates is pounded very fine and mixed with fried sesame (*Sesamum orientale*) and called "Kunchitoharag."

Mr. Gaskin, Assistant for Commerce and Trade, Baghdad, in a note kindly forwarded to me on 22nd October, 1912, states: "A considerable quantity of boiled dates are annually shipped from the British Coast, Katif, and Basra to India where they are considered a luxury, and are used by the Hindus at their festivals. The Indian date-growers could perhaps with much advantage treat their surplus in the same manner, and cut out the imports from Arabia. The dates are boiled when they

---

* The perianth is composed of the scales shown in illustration No. 18, page 12d.

are yellow before they become ripe, and fetch a higher price than
the ripe dates. One advantage is that the grower can get rid
of his inferior dates and recoup himself early in the season."

In the past season, the date fruits from the Arabian plantations in the Punjab were plucked when a spot on the end of the
fruit turned soft and were dried in the sun sufficiently to preserve
them. Some of them were packed in cardboard boxes holding
about one lb.; others in coarse earthenware jars, glazed inside and
out, and holding about $2\frac{1}{2}$ lbs. (*see* illustration No. 36 opposite).
The empty cardboard boxes with their butter paper lining,
printing charges, etc., cost Rs. 38 per 1,000 and were $7\frac{3}{4} \times 3\frac{1}{2} \times 1\frac{1}{2}$
inches in size. The jars were made in Multan and cost Rs. 8
per 100 at the pottery. If large quantities of the boxes and jars
are ordered they would probably be got much cheaper. The
dates were of a quality well suited for dessert purposes and the
demand for them was many times the supply available. Those
of them that I see being used for dessert purposes now (May 1916)
are in excellent condition (For quality of these fruits as compared
with local fruits, *see* page 113, para. 85, and for prices obtained
for them, *see* page 115, para. 86). Shopkeepers sometimes
complain that insect larvæ appear in Persian Gulf date fruits
in winter or spring and ruin the fruits for table purposes. Insect
larvæ have also been found in Punjab date fruits in winter. A
number of the insects have been sent to the Entomological section.
They will be identified there and their life history will be worked
out. Experiments are being conducted to discover when the
eggs are laid in the fruits, and steps will be taken either to guard
against the eggs being laid, or to sterilise them when they are
there (*see* also page 139, para. 96).

At present the date-growers in the Punjab cannot hope to
carry on a large and successful trade in dates nicely packed for
the higher prices in the market, as even if samples of the fruits
were accepted in the market as suitable, date-growers could not
collect any considerable quantity of exactly the same quality
of fruits, owing to the pernicious habit that the people have of
rearing most of their trees from seeds (*see* page 108, para. 80).

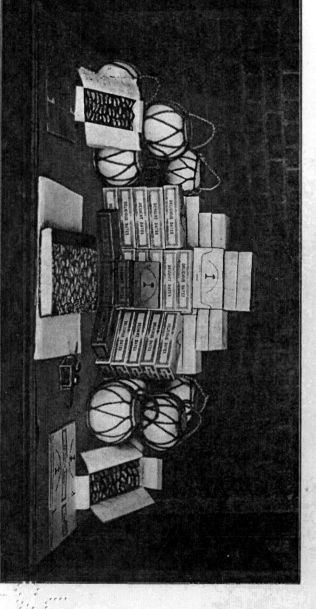

Punjab-Arabian Date-fruits packed for dessert purposes.

(See page 106.)

CHAPTER V.

Extent of date-growing in the principal date-growing localities of the province, date fruits from local and imported trees and profits to be expected from date farming.

Where dates are grown in the Punjab. 77. In the Punjab dates are grown most extensively in the riverain tracts and along canal banks in the Multan, Muzaffargarh, Dera Ghazi Khan, and Jhang districts. In Lahore and Shahpur districts dates are also grown, and indeed the date tree is found growing in the riverain tracts, on canal banks, or around wells in almost every district in the plains of the Punjab as far up as Rawalpindi.

Number of date trees and revenue from them in Multan, Muzaffargarh, Dera Ghazi Khan, and Jhang districts. 78. The following information is to hand regarding the number of trees and the Government revenue derived from them, in Multan, Muzaffargarh, Dera Ghazi Khan, and Jhang districts.

TABLE XIX.

Reference.	Number of female trees.	Revenue.	Revenue per tree per annum.
		Rs.	Rs. A. P.
Multan Gazetteer (1901-02)	315,055	24,521	0 1 0
Muzaffargarh Assessment Report, by P. Hari Kishen Kaul.	838,999	38,999	0 0 9
Dera Ghazi Khan (from information received from Tahsildar, Dera Ghazi Khan) 1911.	126,384	7,899*	0 1 0*
Jhang (information received from D. C. Jhang)..	127,394	5,624	0 0 9 (Jhang Tahsil) Rs. 0-1-11 (Shorkot Tahsil).
TOTAL ..	1,407,832	77,053	

* *Note.*—A fixed revenue per tree is levied on many of the date trees in Dera Ghazi Khan district, but the revenue from a number of trees is collected on the system of part profits of the fruit crop and may vary annually. The figures given to me are therefore evidently an estimate for the whole.

79. In our researches in date culture in the Punjab we have, as one would expect from previous remarks, come across a very large number of varieties of fruits. These are sometimes known by distinct names and sometimes several varieties, which nearly resemble each other, are grouped under one name. By far the greater number of date trees, grown by the people of the Punjab, bear dates of very poor quality. The groves which contain the best dates are at Alipur North in Muzaffargarh district ; at Shershah, Mailsi, and Multan, in the Multan district ; and near the old city of Dera Ghazi Khan in Dera Ghazi Khan district. A few isolated trees bearing dates above the average quality are to be found at various other places in the province. Even in the best plantations it is very difficult, however, to collect any considerable quantity of date fruits of exactly the same quality owing to most of the trees having been reared from seeds. A very large percentage of the trees bearing the best fruits are unfortunately past the age when they give off suckers, and therefore no suckers are available now to reproduce these trees.

Punjab varieties of dates.

80. That by far the greater number of date trees growing even on the western side of the Punjab bear dates of an extremely poor quality does not appear to be the fault of the soil or the climate, as there are numbers of trees in the province which bear dates of comparatively good quality growing side by side with trees bearing inferior dates : also where off-shoots from female trees bearing good fruits have been removed and planted in districts suitable for date-growing, they have produced good fruits there. The reason that so many inferior trees are growing in the Punjab, therefore, appears to be that the majority of them have been grown from seeds (*see* also paras. 61 and 62, pages 94 and 95).

Why many of the dates growing in the western side of the Punjab are so very inferior.

As it is very easy to scatter a large number of seeds where a date plant is required, and as seedlings are extremely hardy and a few plants usually struggle up and establish themselves without receiving any attention, this habit of replacing date trees by seedlings instead of by off-shoots is probably partly due to its being a very much easier method of propagation than by giving to off-shoots the large amount of water and attention required to pull them through the precarious period of the first two years after planting. It is probably also due in part to the cultivator being ignorant of the facts that off-shoots give fruits of the same quality as the parent, while seedlings may form either male or female trees, and that nearly all the female seedlings give inferior fruits (*see* para. 27, page 66). I believe that in most cases trees simply arise from seeds dropped from neighbouring trees; by people passing along, etc., and that as a rule the propagation of date trees gets no attention whatever.

81. When I began my enquiries into the possibility of improvement of date culture in the Punjab in 1909 and suggested to date-growers that suckers of good varieties should be imported from Basra, they expressed serious doubts as to whether the trees to be imported would bear the same character of fruits here that they do in Basra. It was pointed out to them that some fairly good dates are already grown in the Punjab and that no evidence to hand either from the Punjab or from other parts of the world indicated that the quality of the fruits produced here from Arabian trees would be as inferior as from the trees at present grown. Dr. Bonavia's work was also appealed to. At page 29 of his book "The Date Palm in India," he says: "In the Horticultural Gardens at Lucknow there are 252 seedlings from imported seeds from 13 to 16 years old and one hundred and twelve palms from imported off-sets from 12 to 13 years old. Both the lots are fruiting. There are many varieties, and the fruit of the best of them has been differently styled good, very good, and delicious." At page 41 of the same book the following statement is recorded as being an excerpt from a report on these dates by Mr. Reid, the Superintendent of the Lucknow Garden :—" One peculiarity of the date trees in the garden is that no two trees give precisely the same kind of fruit. Some are apparently worthless varieties, others indifferent, some good and

The question whether Arabian trees imported into the Punjab would bear fruits here of a better quality than those of the local trees.

a few excellent." Personally I should have been surprised if the plantation had not been in a state very like this, and there is no doubt in my mind that all the trees with worthless fruits were seedlings, and that most of those that gave good and excellent results were from off-shoots. I think that if the author of the statement referred to had had a proper record of the history of each tree, he would have found this to be so, and that if he had looked carefully into the matter, all trees from off-shoots of the same variety were producing fruits of the same quality. A good clear record of this sort would have settled the doubts raised by the people as to whether imported trees from Basra would bear a good quality of fruits here. No such record seemed to exist, however, and we were left with a lesson on the importance of keeping accurate and minute records of such experiments. All information to my hand seemed to indicate that excellent fruits could be got in the Punjab from trees grown from off-shoots of trees that gave excellent fruits in Basra, but I recognised that people would only be absolutely convinced on this point when they could actually pluck fruits from known Arabian trees grown in the Punjab.

A number of Arabian trees were therefore imported in 1910 and planted in Multan and Muzaffargarh. These have already borne fruits and this question has now been very satisfactorily settled (*see* para. 85, page 113).

82. If any cultivator wishes early satisfaction regarding the

How to discover early whether a variety of date palm is suited to a particular locality.

quality of the fruits that a particular variety of date palm will produce in his particular conditions of soil and climate, what months it will ripen its fruits in, etc., he should procure and plant on his land a few young date trees of that variety which have just become old enough to bear fruits. If he will treat them well as regards water, etc., they will probably yield fruits in their second year after planting. As will be seen from para. 84, page 111, we got fruits from a few strong Arabian suckers in the second year after planting, but this result is much more likely to be got if young trees which have just begun to bear fruits are used instead of younger ones. In either case it is very important that the plants shall be planted in good soil, and be well treated.

83. In the summer of 1910 suckers of the (a) Halawee, (b) Khadrawee, (c) Sayer, (d) Zaydi, and (e) Deree varieties, were asked for from Basra through His Britannic Majesty's Consul there, and in early September of the same year 972 plants were received in reply. A Basra Arab working-overseer sanctioned by Government for three years' service in the Punjab to assist with the planting and looking after the trees accompanied the consignment. Consignments were also received from Basra through the same agency in 1911 and 1912.

Varieties of dates imported into the Punjab from Basra and their distribution.

Plantations, of considerable size, of these trees are now to be seen in the garden of the Central Jail, Multan ; in the Taleri Bagh, Muzaffargarh ; and at Leiah, Muzaffargarh district ; while smaller ones are to be seen in the compound of the Memorial Hall, Muzaffargarh ; at Rakh Chhabri, Dera Ghazi Khan district ; and at Lyallpur. In addition to this some 1,764 plants were given or sold to various canal officers ; to Bahawalpur State ; to the North-West Frontier Province ; and to private growers in and outside the Punjab. The trees in Multan, Muzaffargarh, and Dera Ghazi Khan plantations, with certain reservations, were given respectively to the Multan Jail authorities and to the different district boards concerned. The Agricultural Department planted the trees and gave instructions as to the requirements and general care of the plants. From planting time up to date officers and staff of the Botanical Section of the Agricultural Department have inspected the plantations as often as other duties would permit and have on such occasions demonstrated what the plantations required.

Number of trees planted in 1910 in the Taleri Bagh, Muzaffargarh and Multan Central Jail which have come into flower up to the present time (end of 1915 season) and the fruits yielded by them.

84. The number of trees planted in 1910 which have come into flower up to date, are as follows :—

THE DATE PALM.

TABLE XX.

Situation of the plantation.	Number of trees planted 1910 and now growing (1915).	Number of trees which produced flowers in			
		1912.	1913.	1914.	1915.
Taleri Bagh, Muzaffargarh	249	3	20	115	104
Central Jail, Multan	188	5	42	90	92
TOTAL ..	437	8	62	205	196

Taking the average of these figures, we find that less than 2 per cent. of the trees referred to flowered in 1912; 14 per cent. approximately in 1913; 47 per cent. approximately in 1914; and 45 per cent. approximately in 1915. Only two or three bunches carrying a few fruits were borne by the trees in 1912 (*see* illustration No. 37 opposite). In the following years as the trees became stronger, they gradually bore heavier crops. A number of very small trees came into flower in 1914 but bore practically no fruits. They did not re-flower in 1915. Last year (1915) the Central Jail plantation yielded 201 lbs. of fresh fruits, from which 120 lbs. of cured fruits were obtained. The Taleri Bagh plantation yielded 720 lbs. of fresh fruits from which about 430 lbs. of cured fruits were got. This works out at an average of 1·30 lbs. of cured fruits per tree which actually bore fruits for the Multan plantation and 4·13 lbs. of cured fruits per tree which bore fruits in the Taleri Bagh. The strongest of the trees bore up to nearly 30 lbs. of cured dates, the weakest of them only a few fruits.* (For prices got for these fruits, *see* para. 86, page 115.) The Central Jail fruits were not of as good quality as those from the Taleri Bagh, and had to be dried further in order to preserve them, although the trees in both gardens were of the same varieties, and from the same consignment from Basra. The permanent water-level is about 7 feet or less below the soil surface in the Taleri Bagh and at a depth of over 20 feet in the Central Jail garden. The greater

---

* Unfortunately sufficient responsible staff to guard the crop of date fruits properly have not been available, and although all concerned have done their very best to prevent pilfering of the fruits from the trees, there can be no doubt that this has occurred. The amounts of fruits weighed out therefore understate the actual crop borne.

ILLUSTRATION No. 37.

Young Arabian date tree bearing its first crop of fruits at Lyallpur in
July 1912.   The plant was planted as an offshoot in September 1910.

(*See para.* 84, *page* 111.)

Arabian date plantation in the Taleri Bagh, Muzaffargarh ; planted September 1910 ; photographed July 1915, before the fruits were ready for harvesting.

The tree near the man is one of the biggest in the plantation and yielded about 60 lbs. of fresh fruits in 1915.

Owing to the very great demand for suckers from the Arabian trees, a larger number of suckers have been allowed to grow from the bases of these trees than is advisable where large crops of fruits are desired.

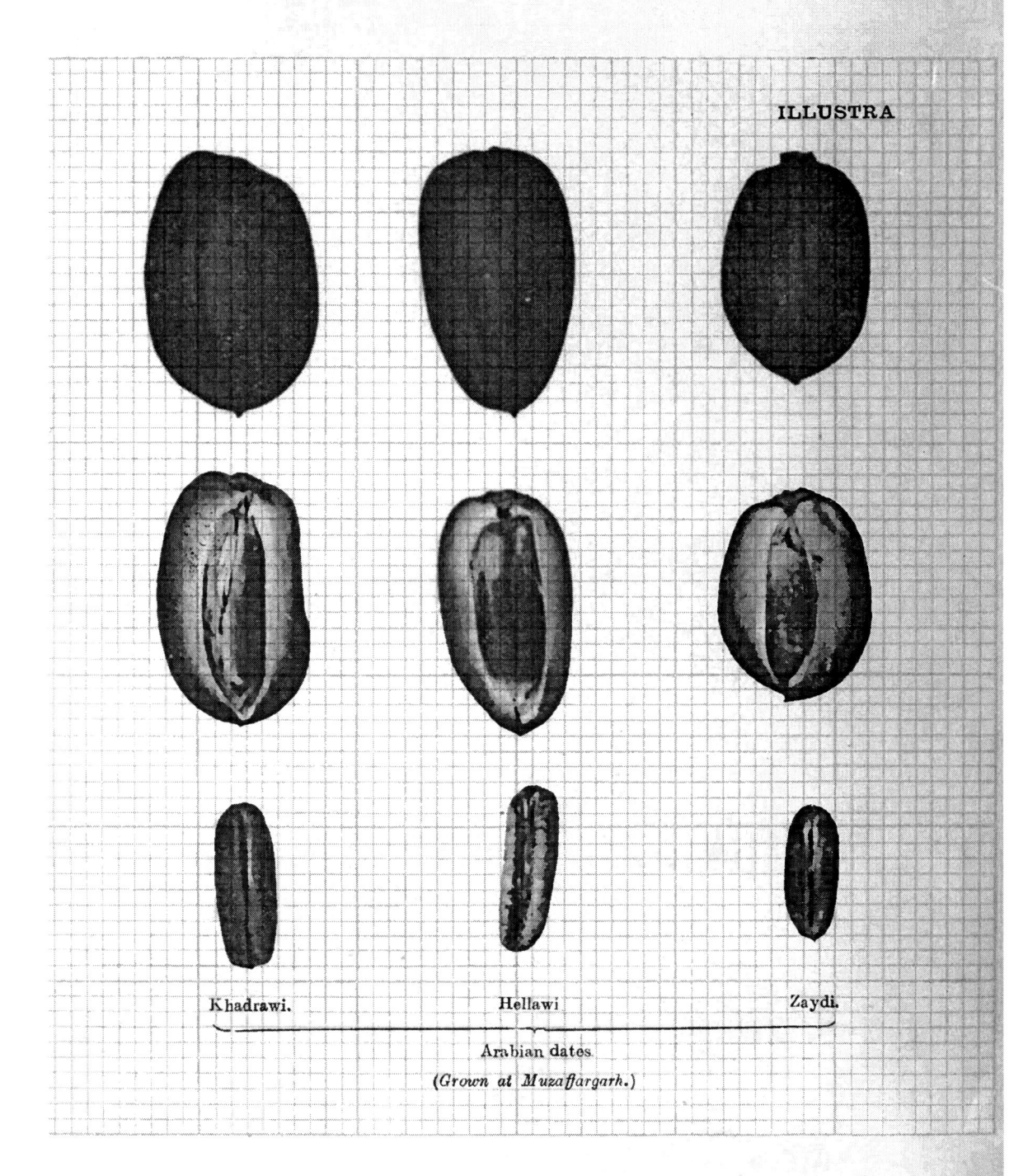

Khadrawi.　　　　Hellawi　　　　Zaydi.

Arabian dates.
(*Grown at Muzaffargarh.*)

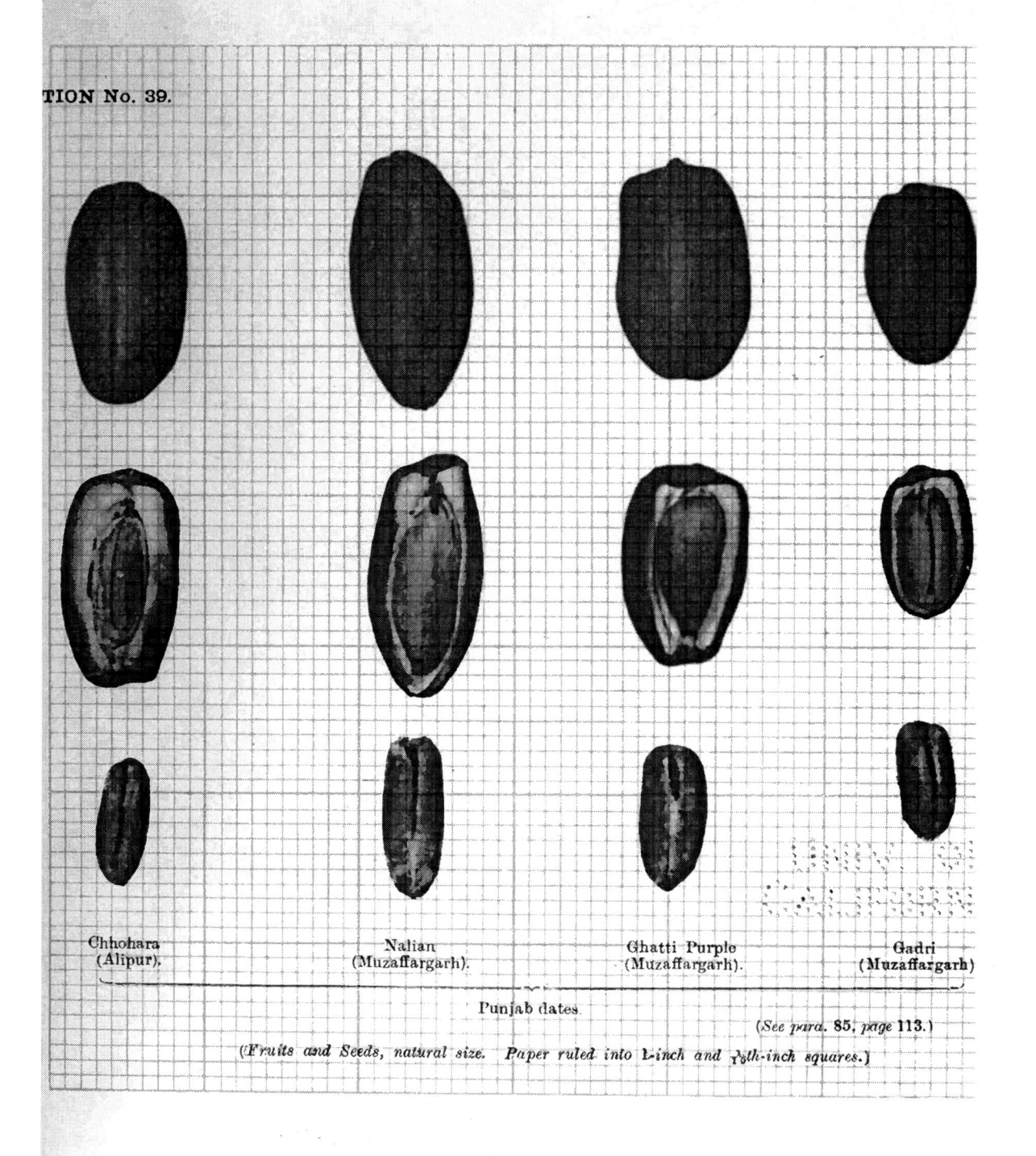

Chhohara
(Alipur).

Nalian
(Muzaffargarh).

Ghatti Purple
(Muzaffargarh).

Gadri
(Muzaffargarh)

Punjab dates.

(*See para.* 85, *page* 113.)

(*Fruits and Seeds, natural size. Paper ruled into 1-inch and 1/10th-inch squares.*)

amount of water available to the Taleri Bagh trees seems to be responsible for the differences in both quality and quantity of the fruits. In the Multan Jail garden, it was also noticed that the fruits were larger and of better quality on trees near water channels, but in situations where there is a plentiful water-supply, these young trees are of course bigger and more robust than those of the same age in less fortunate situations. The case is, however, one which shows the very great importance of a plentiful water-supply to young plantations.

85. The comparative sizes and shapes of the fruits and seeds produced at Muzaffargarh in 1915 by three different varieties of date trees imported from Basra in 1910 and from four varieties of local trees in the same district can be seen from illustration No. 39, pages 112c and 112d respectively. The Khadrawi, Hellawi, and Zaydi are the Basra varieties and the Alipur Chhohara, Khaji Nalian, Ghatti, and Gadri are local. The fruits were average samples of those produced by these trees in the gardens last year.

Comparison of fruits from imported trees growing at Muzaffargarh and from local trees growing in the district.

A further comparison of these fruits can be made from Table No. XXI below.

TABLE XXI.

Showing the number of date fruits per lb. approximately; the weight of seeds got from these and the percentage of cellulose (fibre) in the pulp in the case of 7 varieties of dates grown in Muzaffargarh District.

Variety of date		No. of date fruits in 1 lb. approximately.	Exact weight of the fruits.	Total weight of seeds from the fruits.	Percentage of cellulose (fibre) in the fruits after removal of the seeds.
			lbs.	oz.	
From off-shoots imported from Basra in September 1910.	Khadrawi	35	1.022	1·42	1·93
	Hellawi ...	41	1·015	1·71	1·76
	Zaydi	47	1 0008	1·65	1·75
From adult local trees.	Alipur Chhohara	61	1·016	2·4	2·13
	Khaji Nalian ...	51	1·01	3·04	2·73
	Ghatti ...	62	1·004	3·258	3·02
	Gadri ...	118	1·006	4·96	3·72

NOTE.—*The figures in the column "percentage of cellulose in the fruits" were got for me by the Agricultural Chemist, Punjab, from fruits which I supplied to him from the samples out of which I got the data for the other columns in the above statement.*

All the date fruits were collected from the trees on 8th August 1915. When plucked from the trees, the dates were just at that point of ripeness when they were ready to start softening but had not yet any soft spots. They were weighed and examined on 9th August for all the data in Table XXI except for the percentage of cellulose. The Agricultural Chemist who kindly provided the figures for this column informs me that "all the dates were analysed when they were soft—that is, when the fermentation process of ripening was apparently complete."

The number in the second column against each variety is the least number of fruits which would turn the scales against 1 lb. weight, *i.e.*, 1 lb. exactly would have required a fraction of a fruit less in each case. From this column it appears that 35 fruits of Khadrawi weighed practically as much as 61 fruits of Alipur Chhohara or 118 fruits of Khaji Gadri, etc. The third column shows the exact weight of the fruits in each case. The fourth column gives the weight of seeds got from the number of fruits against each variety, *i.e.*, 1 lb. approximately. It will be seen from the above that the imported Arabian trees are producing fruits which are larger ; have a less proportion of seeds in them, and less fibre. They also taste better and are on the whole far superior to the local fruits. The imported trees are still very young, being only planted in September, 1910, and there is the possibility of their fruits improving in quality as the trees become stronger.

Of the fruits from the local trees, the Alipur Chhohara are the best. Unfortunately there are very few trees yielding this quality of fruits in the Punjab. These are chiefly at Alipur North, Muzaffargarh District. The fruits of these trees are now packed like our Arabian fruits in small cardboard boxes for dessert purposes and have been selling at about Re. 0-8-0 per lb. Since our date improvement work began in the Punjab in 1909, all available off-shoots of these trees have been planted out, but there is still less than 100 trees of that variety growing. Therefore these fruits are in no way representative of the general quality of fruits produced in the Punjab. There appears to be no record of their origin, or how they came to Alipur. The Khaji Nalian fruits were gathered from trees growing at Muzaffargarh, but there appear also to be very few trees producing fruits which could be described as of this variety.

Khaji Ghatti is a purple date ; and although a considerable number of date trees exist which bear fruits that come under this name, they do not form an important part of the date crop of the Punjab. The fruits can only be kept for a lengthened time if dried hard. They are usually split to facilitate drying and are sold under the name of " Chirvi " or " Shingistan " (*see* para. 76, page 101). They are not of good quality. A very large proportion of their weight is lost in drying them hard, and even when dried they sell at about 1 to 1½ annas per lb. If they are to be used fresh, they must be eaten within 24 hours of the time they are plucked from the tree, otherwise they ferment too far and become bad. Khaji Gadri is the sort of fruit that forms the bulk of the Punjab date crop and it is with this that the fruits from the imported trees should be compared when considering the advantages of the introduction of improved varieties into the Punjab. The date trees of the province with few exceptions having been all raised from seeds, the number of varieties of dates is innumerable, but the above gives some idea of the general quality of the fruits produced at present.

86. The prices of these local fruits vary a little from year to year, but from information which I have *Prices of date fruits in the Punjab.* received from time to time the most inferior date fruits can usually be bought in the local market at Re. 1 or less per maund (82 lbs.) and the greater part of the crop can be bought at Rs. 2 to Rs. 3 per maund, while the best classes of dates generally sell at Rs. 8-10 per maund. Sometimes the few specially good fruits can hardly be bought at any price.

I have found fruits of the variety known as Deree imported into the Punjab, from Basra in the Persian Gulf. These are

Note 1 anna = 1 penny.
Re. 1 (1 rupee) = 16 pence.

generally sold unpacked in the bazars and railway stations at about 3 to 4 seers (6 *to* 8 *lbs. approx.*) per rupee. Muskat dates simply packed in cardboard boxes each containing about 1 lb. of dates are annually sold at 8 annas approximately per box in Lahore ; also Algerian dates, first packed in small wooden sided boxes each containing about ½ lb. of dates and then encased in air-tight tin cases are sold in the Punjab at 9 annas per box.

The first-class fruits of the 1915 crop from the Persian Gulf trees growing at Muzaffargarh and Multan Central Jail were sold at annas 6 per lb. packed for dessert purposes in small cardboard boxes or jars, and most glowing tributes to the quality of the fruits were received from those to whom the fruits were sent. Indeed the limited quantity which we had, could have been sold several times over at Re. 0-10-0 per lb.

87. The crop of fruits got per adult tree from the local Punjabi trees has been variously estimated at from 10 seers (20½ lbs.) to 250 seers (512½ lbs.) and average yields in various places have been calculated at anything from 20 seers (41 lbs.) to 60 seers (123 lbs.) or more. Owners of the more important date gardens usually lease their trees annually to a second party early in the fruiting season. This second party known as a " baikhar " arranges for the guarding of the fruits while on the trees ; the harvesting and marketing of the fruits ; and takes all risks of making a profit on the sum which in the early part of the season he agreed to give the owner for the season's produce. For reasons given in para. 25, page 64, the owners of these larger gardens are generally unable to give accurate information regarding the crops got from the trees and both the " baikhar " and the smaller owners who harvest their fruits themselves, do not care to give the information required. Again, the crop of fruits per tree varies greatly not only with the variety of tree, but with the age of the tree, the quality of the land, the amount of water-supply, the climate of the locality, etc., therefore, a fair estimate of the average yield is very difficult to get. Regarding the crops of dates per

Crops of dates per adult tree.

tree in the Punjab, the *Multan Gazetteer* dated 1901-02 informs us as follows :—

"It is difficult to say what the average produce of a full grown tree may be. At the recent settlement the produce recovered by the owner, or baikhar after deducting payment in kind and miscellaneous losses was assumed to be 30 seers (61½ lb.) of green dates in Kabirwala, and 20 seers (41 lb.) in other tahsils." From the rather meagre information, which we have been able to collect so far, the above seems to be as near an estimate as we will get until the Government plantations at Multan, Muzaffargarh, and elsewhere are in full bearing.

88. When a young plantation is laid down as advised in para. 39, page 77, the trees, channels, etc., need not take up more ground than a strip 4 feet in width for each line of trees, although they are more often allowed to take up a strip of 5 feet in width. If they are restricted to a width of 4 feet and the lines of trees are 16·4 feet apart therefore only 4/16·4 or ¼ approximately of the land will be occupied by the date plants and the remaining ¾ should be available for the cultivation of other crops (*see* para. 46, page 83). Even more of the land can be utilised in this way if cabbage or other suitable plants are planted along the inner edges of the channels between the trees. These crops may bring a considerable return from the land right from the time that the plantation is laid down. Until the trees become established, however, a disadvantage—when the plantation is on a large scale—is that bullocks cannot be used to plough and work the land between the rows of trees without risk of knocking the trees about and thus harming them. When the date plants become established this danger ceases. Regarding the time which will elapse before the trees will bear fruits it will be seen from para. 84, page 111, that a few trees in our plantations at Multan and Muzaffargarh came into flower and bore a few fruits in the second year after planting, and that the number increased until in the past year (the fifth year after planting) 45 per cent. of the trees bore fruits. In the same paragraph it is

Gross income from date plantations.

also shown that the trees which bore fruits bore an average of
1·30 lb. of cured fruits per tree in the Multan garden and an
average of 4·13 lb. per tree in that of Muzaffargarh.

We expect the number of trees which bear fruits and the
amounts of fruits borne per tree to increase rapidly now until
the trees bear a full crop. Regarding adult plantations, it has
been already indicated that local Punjabi date trees generally get
no cultivation whatsoever except the removal of as many of the
old leaves as enable the people to get at the fruits or satisfy the
cultivators' wants. I, therefore, think that if date trees received
fair attention, we would be well within the mark if we assume
that the crop of green fruits per tree in these districts would be
20 to 30 seers, *i.e.*, 12 to 18 seers of cured fruits *vide* para. 84,
page 111.

If 139 good palms are planted per acre (trees 19 feet apart
in the rows, and the rows 16·4 feet apart *see* para. 39, page 77)
they are hand pollinated, 12 seers of cured fruits are got per tree,
and the value of the fruits is 1 anna per lb. (*see* para. 97, page 142),
then allowing 4 male trees per acre, the gross income for fruits
would be Rs. 207-9-0 (£13-16-9) and if 18 seers were got per tree,
the gross income would be Rs. 311-5-0 (£20-15-1). We have
already seen in para. 86, page 115, that Muscat dates simply
packed in 1 lb. cardboard boxes are selling in the Punjab at
annas 8 per lb. ; that we could have sold all our 1915 crop of
fruits from the imported Arabian trees at Re. 0-10-0 per lb., and
that Algerian dates packed in ½ lb. packets in a way that will
preserve them for more than a year, are selling here at Re. 1-2-0
per lb. Papers at my hand show that in America in 1912, some
dates grown in Indo-California were sold at Rs. 2-10-6 per lb.
and that they sold at Rs. 3-2-0 per lb. there in 1913. These
prices are for dates packed to have a more or less nice appearance
on the dinner table, or to preserve them for a lengthened period,
etc. ; but although they give some indication of the possibilities
of date culture, an extensive market could not be got for such
commodities at once. I, therefore, do not wish to take too much

notice of these prices. Dates do not require to be re-sown every year like most farm crops ; they do not usually require much attention as regards water after the trees are established, if the water-level is well within 20 feet of the soil surface ; they require no or little attention during the greater part of the year, and the fruits require little preparation for the market. In considering the gross income which may be got from a plantation, that from bye-products (*see* paras. 89, 90, and 91, pages 119 to 122) and from the auxiliary crops already referred to should also be taken into account. With Basra date fruits of fourth or fifth quality actually selling in the unpacked condition in the market here at 3 to 4 seers (6 or 8 lb. approx.) per rupee (16 pence) our estimate of a gross income of Rs. 207-9-0 or Rs. 311-5-0 per acre for fruits alone seems most moderate, and if this is so, dates properly farmed ought to be an extremely remunerative crop when grown in suitable districts.

89. Date-growers in Arabia estimate that they receive about 5 annas (5 pence) per tree for the sale of date palm leaves, fibre from the bases of the leaves, stalks of date inflorescence, etc. (Gaskin's note dated 22nd October 1912). This works out to Rs. 43-7-0 (£2-17-11) per acre of 139 palms. The different parts of the date palm are put to a great many uses. The stems are hollowed out to form water channels. They are also used as beams for the roofs of houses ; to pivot the gearing of Persian wheels on, etc. The fibre at the base of the leaf stalk (Kabal) is used for making ropes, nets, and such things. The flattened bases of the leaf stalks are used as floats for fishing nets, etc. From the main axes of the leaves (lakre) crates for fruits, poultry, etc. ; cages for small birds, fencing for fowl runs, chairs, stools, sleeping couches, and so on are made. The leaflets are woven into mats, baskets, etc. The finest matting is made from the tender leaflets of the young terminal bud (gācha). Date leaflets are sometimes partly retted and beaten, and the fibre (sclerenchymatous strands) so extracted from them is made into ropes, etc. When fodder is very scarce, the leaflets are fed to buffaloes.

Date palm, bye-products, their value and uses.

The inflorescences from which the fruits have been removed, are used as brooms. Fibre from the spathe (sippe) is used for making ropes. The dried spathes, leaves, etc., are used as fuel. Articles made from parts of the date palm do not rot readily in water, therefore, date ropes, etc., are much used in connection with water lifts and such things. Samples of mats and baskets from date leaflets and ropes made from date fibre are shown in illustration No. 40 opposite. Those interested in such things, however, should purchase small samples of these from Muzaffargarh or Dera Ghazi Khan. The cost will be practically nothing, and the articles will give a better idea of their suitability for the purposes for which they are made than any description could convey.

90. I have not seen any one in the Punjab tapping date

Date toddy and sugar-making from the sap of the palm.

trees and making wine or sugar from the sap so collected, but I have seen this done elsewhere. Indeed wine (palm toddy) extracting is practised to some extent in almost all countries where dates are cultivated. For wine or sugar-making, a V-shaped notch is cut in the stem near the base of the gācha (young terminal bud) and the juice is collected in pots. The empty pots are usually smoked to delay fermentation and the juice is removed from the pot after collecting it for about a day. If the sap is to be used as wine, it is drunk before it ferments too far, and is liked best when it is quite fresh from the tree. It usually sells for about one anna per quart. If sugar is to be made, the juice is simply boiled down at once to form gur (unpurified sugar) and is mostly sold and used in that form. Tapping the trees for these purposes prevents the trees from fruiting and is a very severe strain on the plant. If roughly done it may kill the tree altogether. Where tapping is much practised, however, the people become adepts at it, and trees showing the scars of 20 years or more of successive tapping can be seen. Owing to want of staff we have not been able to look into these points in the Punjab, but it is hoped that they, with others awaiting investigation, may be taken up soon. Meantime those interested in sugar-making from

Samples of a few articles made from parts of the date palm by Ch. Khem Chandra, Alipur, North, Muzaffargarh District.

(See page 120.)

palm sap may refer to Mr. H. E. Annett's most interesting experiments on the wild date palm (*Phœnix sylvestris*) and other plants in his " Investigations into the Date Sugar Industry in Bengal " (*see* Memoirs of the Department of Agriculture in India, Chemical Series, Vol. II, No. 6, March, 1913). It should be remembered that it is the *wild* date palm (*Phœnix sylvestris*) that he has carried out his investigations on,—not the date palm (*Phœnix dactylifera*) cultivated for its fruits, and which we have here. The two plants are so nearly related, however, that botanists have not yet recorded a very clear difference between them. For the convenience of those interested, a few remarks may be quoted here from Mr. Annett's work. Mr. Annett reckons that a plantation farmed for sugar made from the palm sap comes into bearing five to six years after planting and that it goes on bearing for fully 25 years (Annett, page 380) ; that the average yield of juice per tree per season in Bengal is 170 lb. (Annett, page 351) ; that $22\frac{1}{2}$ lb. of gur are got from that amount of juice (Annett, page 351) ; and that the gur sells at Rs. 2-8-0 per maund (82 lb.) (Annett, page 379). This would give about Re. 0-11-0 gross income per tree. He reckons the tapping season as extending from the second week of November to first week of March (Annett, page 324) ; and that two tappers and one assistant coolie would manage the work connected with gur-making from 350 trees (Annett, page 379). A tree is tapped something like 40 to 50 times during the tapping season. To get at the net profits, the wages of these men for the $2\frac{1}{2}$ months of the tapping season, the cost of fuel for boiling the gur, and other expenses to be incurred would have to be deducted.

We have seen that *Phœnix dactylifera* here will yield at least 12 seers ($24\frac{3}{5}$ lb.) of fruits, value Re. 0-1-0 per lb., *i.e.*, a gross income of Re. 1-8 approx. per tree, and that the expenses connected with fruit-farming are much less than those which must be connected with gur-making, therefore gur-making could not be considered, where good fruits can be grown, if each tree did not yield several multiples of the weight of gur which *Phœnix sylvestris* does in Bengal.

It is possible that gur might be made from some of the many
male date trees which are growing in the Punjab, but the comparatively high price of labour here (6 to 8 annas per coolie per
day), and the cost of fuel would probably make gur-making even
from these a poorly paid business. The severe damage done to
the trees by the tapping should be remembered when considering
the question.   An actual test would set the whole matter at rest.

91. In date growing countries various wines are made
by fermenting the fruit of the date and then
distilling the products. They are generally
made from inferior fruits. Sometimes a mixture
of date and other sugary and starchy fruits or
plant products are used in their manufacture. In other cases
drinks of the nature of beer are made by merely fermenting
these materials. The variations in the methods of manufacture and of the materials employed are many.

Beverages of the
nature of wine or
beer made from
date fruits.

ILLUSTRATION No. 41.

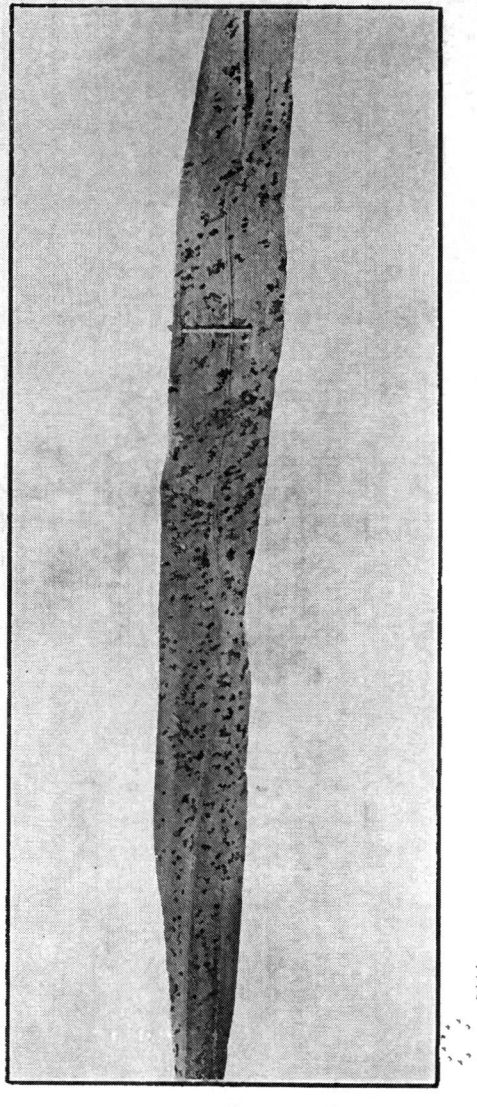

Leaflet of date palm half natural size showing Palm Leaf Pustule
(Graphiola phœnicis Pait.)

(*See para.* 92, *page* 123.)

ILLUSTRATION No. 42.

Graphiola phœnicis × 35 diams.

a Hyphæ.
b Hard black wall of sporocarp.
c Leaf.

Nat. Size.

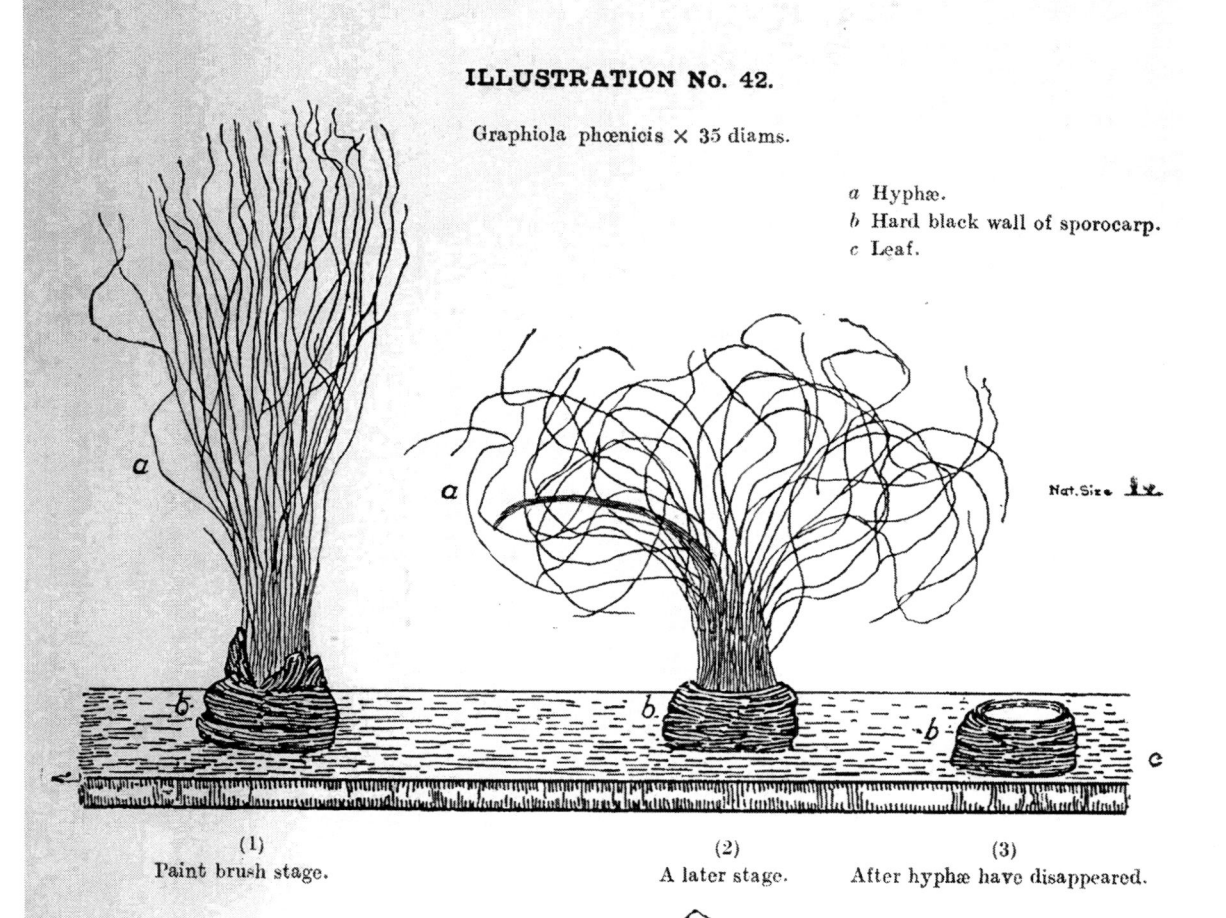

(1)	(2)	(3)
Paint brush stage.	A later stage.	After hyphæ have disappeared.

(4)

Piece of hypha with spores attached × 430 diams.

(*See page* 123.)

CHAPTER VI.

DISEASES OF THE DATE PALM.

Palm leaf Pustule.   (Graphiola phœnicis Pait.)

See illustrations Nos. 41 and 42 on pages 122*a* and 122*b*.

92. This is a fungoid pest and is reported from North America, parts of South America, Ceylon, Algeria, Egypt, other parts of India and elsewhere. It is to be found among the local date trees wherever they grow in the Punjab. In some cases where the trees had a large number of old leaves on them, I have seen it quite bad. In most of these cases the younger leaves are usually practically free of it. It has not yet been a cause of trouble among our imported date trees and little attention has been paid to it.

The disease is often seen as small hard black-pustules scattered over both the lower and upper surfaces of the leaflets (*see* illustration No. 42, Fig. 3). They are often about $\frac{1}{2}$ millimeter in diameter; about $\frac{1}{3}$ of that in height, and the top has a depressed yellowish centre.

The mycelium (body of the fungus) is composed of hyphæ (thread-like filaments) which are hidden in the tissues of the leaf, and absorb nourishment from the leaf cells. The black pustules are developed from the mycelium. They burst the outer layers of the leaf cells and appear on the surface of the leaf. These pustules are the sporocarps (structures in which the spores are developed) of the fungus.

Inside the sporocarp is the spore forming tissue which gives rise to vast numbers of pale yellow roundish spores about ·003 mm. in diameter and which eventually lie loose in the pustule. These minute spores, in suitable conditions are capable of germination and reproducing the disease. From the centre of the pustule also, long yellow hyphæ are developed which protrude from the pustule at first like hairs from a tiny paint brush and later become more spreading (*see* illustration No. 42, Figs. 1-2). Large numbers of the spores adhere to the sides of these long hyphæ (*see* illustration No. 42, Fig. 4), and are carried with them out of the sporocarp to the open air, where wind, insects, etc., may convey them to other leaves or plants, there to germinate and start a new centre of the disease. The hard outer black wall of the sporocarp protects the developing spores inside, and is left standing on the leaf after the long brush-like hyphæ and spores have disappeared (*see* illustration No. 42, Fig. 3). A microscope magnifying over 60 diameters is required to distinguish the spores and a magnification of over 300 diameters is required to see them well. The long hyphæ protruding from the sporocarp when they are present, and the sporocarp itself, are seen by the naked eye but are better examined with a pocket lens.

As old leaves very naturally become worst affected the trees

Remedial measures. should be kept properly pruned (*see* illustration No. 29, page 86*a*). Spraying with a solution of permanganate of potash or with Bordeaux mixture are recommended by those who have found it necessary to control the disease. Bordeaux mixture gives excellent results against many fungoid diseases.

The mixture consists of copper sulphate ($CuSO_4$) and quick-

Bordeaux mixture. lime (CaO).

The quantities generally used are 6 seers of copper sulphate and 4 seers of quicklime in 50 gallons ($12\frac{1}{2}$ kerosene tinfuls) of water.

The copper sulphate should be as good and pure as possible; copper sulphate containing a large amount of iron or of zinc sulphate should not be used.

The lime should also be as pure as possible and should be freshly burnt.

Prepare the mixture as follows :—

Powder the copper sulphate and then dissolve it in a little hot water in an earthenware or a wooden vessel. When quite cold add 28-36 gallons (7 to 9 kerosene tinfuls) of cold water to the solution.

Next slowly and thoroughly slake the quicklime in another vessel by first adding to it about a pint of water and repeatedly adding that amount of water as the previously applied liquid is used up by the lime. Continue until about a kerosene tinful of water has been added and the whole lime is dissolved into a cream. The lime must be stirred well during this slaking process. When quite cold stir the lime water again and filter it through a coarse sacking into the vessel containing the copper sulphate, stirring the copper sulphate all the time. Add water to the mixture to make the whole lot up to about 50 gallons (12½ kerosene tinfuls) and apply within 6-8 hours after its preparation as the ingredients are not easily kept in suspension in the liquid longer than that, and the mixture is not so adherent to the plants.

The above proportions of lime and copper sulphate must be adhered to carefully as these proportions are required to neutralise each other. The copper sulphate by itself is injurious to plants therefore none of it should exist in the free state in the prepared wash. This is sometimes the case when old or clayey quicklime is used.

To test whether the mixture is properly made, dip a clear steel knife blade into the solution. If a brown deposit appears on it, it indicates that free copper sulphate exists in the wash, therefore a little more lime should be added to it. When a great excess of lime is used the wash is almost useless. A wash as near the neutral point as possible should be prepared.

The exact amount of water mentioned above is not essential but that is the amount found useful when the mixture is used as a general fungicide in various parts of the world.

The wash should be applied with a spraying machine in all cases.

The red weevil or Indian Palm weevil.

(Rhynchophorus ferrugineus.)

93. As far back as any one can remember both adult and

First sign of the disease among date trees in the Punjab.

young country date palms in the Punjab have occasionally been seen to die from some disease which caused their tops to wither up (*see* illustration No. 43 opposite), and in the case of adult palms, the stem to sometimes bend or break over in a characteristic manner (*see* illustration No. 44, page 126*b*).

Before the trees break over, a dirty resinous juice which has leaked from the tree is sometimes to be seen on the stem. On the imported Arabian date palms the disease was first noticed at Muzaffargarh in 1913.

In the case of small palms the tops of which could be closely examined by one standing near them the first indication of the coming death of the plant was the appearance near the terminal bud of a considerable quantity of chewed fibrous material evidently thrown out from the interior of the stem near the growing point through a burrow 1 inch approximately in diameter, made by some animal. In some young trees the stems of which were not over 2-4 feet high, similar burrows were found almost at ground-level. Usually such plants then gradually dry up and die some weeks or months later, depending on the severity of the attack and on whether it is on a vital spot. Sometimes apparently healthy trees suddenly collapse. Attacked trees seldom recover if untreated.

A number of both desi and imported Arabian date palms similarly affected have been examined, and in all cases insects in the form of either grubs (the worm-like stage) and pupæ (the dormant stage) or as imagos (the adult insect stage), or in two or all of these stages, have been found together inside these trees.

In very developed cases the inside of the stem was frequently completely eaten out and contained a lot of decaying rubbish

ILLUSTRATION No. 43.

Showing two date trees at Multan, killed by the red weevil (*Rhynchophorus ferrugineus*).

(*See page* 126, *para.* 93.)

ILLUSTRATION No. 44.

Showing date tree attacked by the red weevil in the Am-o-khas garden, Multan. In this case the stem has bent sharply over at a point a little below the top so that the head hangs down. The centre of the stem from the bend upwards is completely eaten out and filled with rotten matter. The leaves have all withered and fallen off.

(*See page* 126.)

THE RED WEEVIL OR INDIAN PALM WEEVIL. (Rhynchophorus ferrugineus Olive.)

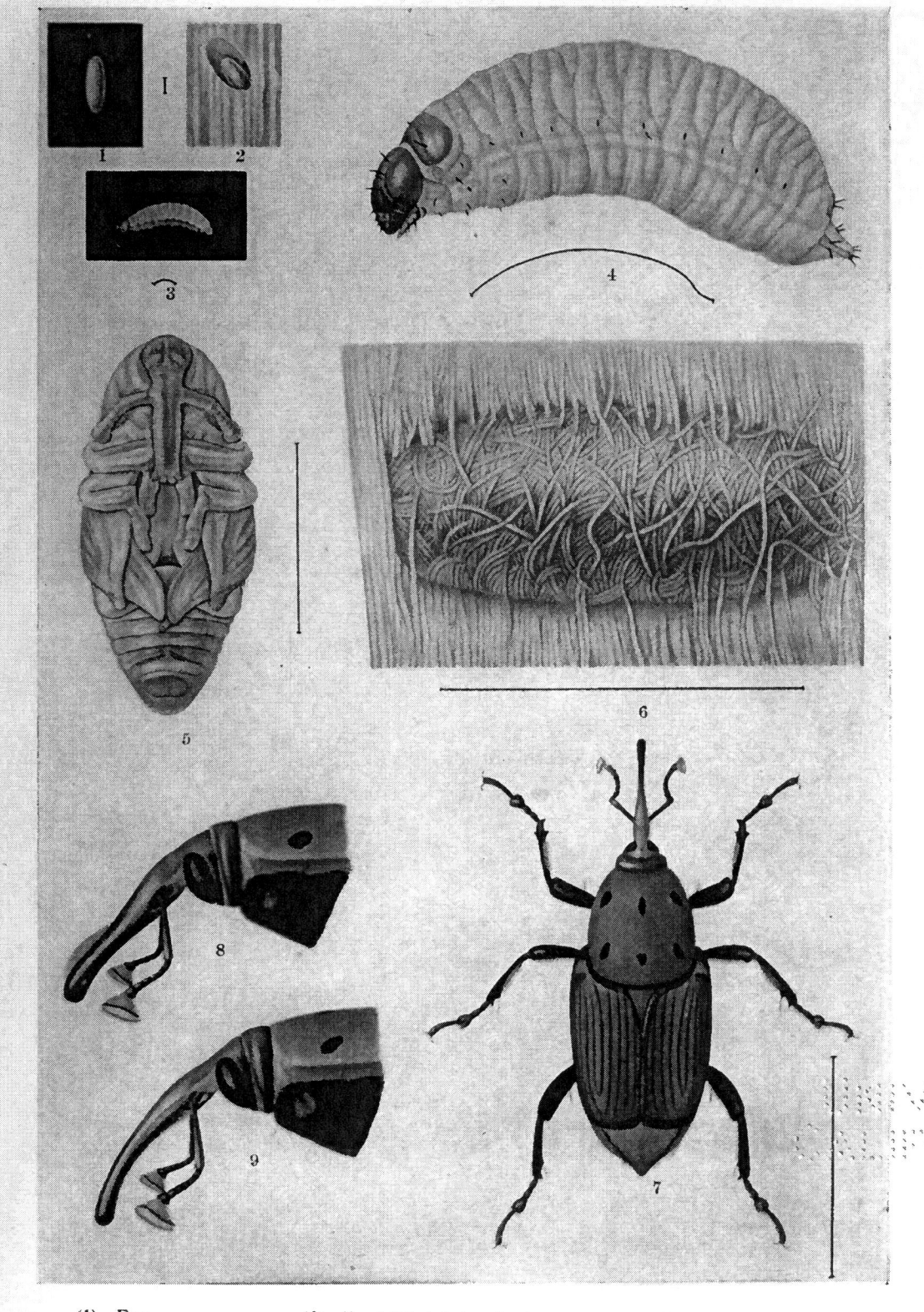

(1) Egg. (2) Egg laid in hole in palm tissue. (3) Newly hatched larva.
(4) Full grown larva. (5) Pupa. (6) Cocoon.
(7) Adult weevil. (8) Side view of head of male weevil enlarged.
(9) ,, ,, female ,,

The natural sizes of the stages shown in figs. 1—7 are indicated by the hair-lines alongside each figure.

at the points of attack. In bad cases where the tree stems were only 3 or 4 feet in height, the grubs and pupæ were found even at the base of the stem. Writers elsewhere record that the grubs may be found at any point in the stem of an affected tree.

These insects have been identified for us by the Assistant Professor of Entomology to the Agricultural Department, Punjab, as the Indian Palm Weevil or Red Weevil (*Rhynchophorus ferrugineus*, Olive). Descriptions of the weevil, accounts of its life history, methods of preventing its attacks and remedial measures will be found in (*a*) Memoirs of the Department of Agriculture in India, Entomological Series, Volume II, No. 10, December, 1911, under Life-Histories of Indian Insects—III, by C. C. Ghosh, and (*b*) Indian Insect Pests, by Lefroy, page 209. The material for the following brief account of the pest is practically all taken from these works and the coloured illustration No. 45, page 126*c*, is from (*a*) above mentioned.

Identification of the pest and literature concerning it.

It has been already noticed in the following places :— Saharanpur, Lucknow, Buxar, Bankipur, Gaya, Pusa, Darjeeling, Dikang Valley, Suleman Range, Shillong, Sylhet, Assam, Moulmein, Calcutta, Singbhum, Madras, Bangalore, Wynaad, Andaman Islands, Ceylon, and we have now found it in Multan, Muzaffargarh, and Dera Ghazi Khan Districts of the Punjab. Doubtlessly it will be found also in adjacent date-growing districts of the Punjab.

Distribution and breeding season.

The weevil appears to breed throughout the year. There is no regularity in the occurrence of the broods and adult weevils. Pupæ and larvæ in different stages of growth may be found together at the same time.

The Indian Palm Weevil is a big red brown flattened insect with or without a few black spots on the thoracic region (region between the head and abdomen) and with a long slightly curved snout. The snout of the male is provided with a brush of hairs above, and is

The imago (adult insect).

stouter than that of the female (*see* illustration No. 45, Fig. 8).

The snout of the female is more slender and has no tuft of hairs on it (*see* illustration No. 45, Fig. 9). The elbowed antennæ are inserted near the base of the snout. The terminal joint of each antenna is thick, truncated and spongy. The elytra (hard wing cases) are ribbed longitudinally and they do not entirely cover the end of the body (*see* illustration No. 45, Fig. 7).

The insects fly at night with a loud droning sound and fall with a thud. They hide from the light and when disturbed fold up their legs and pretend to be dead.

The larva is at first straw-coloured but in the course of a few hours its head and a small patch just behind its head become brown. The body remains pale yellow and is soft, fleshy and wrinkled transversely. The margins of the anal segment are slightly curved upwards forming a small concavity above. There are no legs of any kind. It is stated that full-grown larvæ in the insectary measured 6·0 to 6·5 cms. in length and 2·0 cms. in thickness, but that larvæ have been found 7·5 cms. long on trees outside the insectary. The larva is usually curved a little lengthwise so that its under-side is concave and its back is convex. This is especially marked when its body is contracted (*see* illustration No. 45, Figs. 3 and 4).

The larva (worm-like stage).

The eggs are creamy white; their surface smooth and somewhat shiny. They are about 2½ mm. long by about 1¼ mm. across and are cylindrical elongate-oval (*see* illustration No. 45, Fig. 1).

The eggs.

Apparently much has yet to be learnt about the habits, etc., of this insect in its natural state but in the literature above referred to it is recorded that in the insectary,—at Pusa I presume—the weevils fed and laid their eggs in soft interior pieces of stem of the palm Phœnix sylvestris, Roxb. and of "Tal" (Borassus flabellifer, Linn.) which were supplied to them. The weevils gnawed a hole 3 to 5 mm. in depth in a piece of

Some observations made in the Insectary on the habits and life-cycle of the pest.

these and then usually deposited a single egg in it. Sometimes 2 or 3 eggs were found near each other in a separate hole. One female in captivity laid 276 eggs in 49 days and another laid 127 eggs in 46 days. Eggs laid in March hatched out about 4 days after being laid. The larvæ spun their cocoons 24 to 61 days after hatching. The insect remained in the cocoon stage for periods of from 18 to 34 days, and the whole time taken from the laying of the egg till the appearance of the imago was 48 to 82 days. The imago lived for 50 to 90 days and required a constant supply of food. The pest appears to pass the whole of its life on the food plant; eggs are laid, the grubs (larvæ) feed and pupate (form cocoons) in the plant.

It is not exactly known how and where the eggs are laid in nature, but it seems that they are not laid deep in the plant tissues. It also seems that the part chosen for oviposition will be moist and provide more or less soft pithy tissues for the young grubs. The beetles themselves also want such tissue to feed upon. This would explain why the top regions of the stems of adult trees are apparently first attacked.

Mode of affecting trees.

Dr. Barber, Government Botanist, Madras, appears to think that the weevil enters the inflorescence where the spathe opens, and lays eggs there. It is believed that the weevils do not require any special crack or cut for laying their eggs in, as they can easily creep down the leaf-sheath and reach the soft base of the top of the shoot, then gnaw a hole there and thrust in the egg. It is thought most probable that eggs are deposited in this manner in the comparatively soft tissues near the tops of the trees and that the larvæ bore down the stem. The exposure of soft tissues by wounds, etc., is supposed to specially expose trees to attacks however. Another insect pest—the Rhinoceros beetle—referred to on page 135, is said to bore a hole often over 1 inch in diameter into the base of the central bud of date trees in some parts of India and the red weevil is said to often make use of this hole to get at the soft heart of the tree. Many trees are supposed to be attacked by the red weevil in this way in these localities.

The damage done to date trees by red weevil is done by the grubs only. After hatching, the grub begins to feed on the plant tissues and forms a tunnel in them. This tunnel increases in diameter as the grub grows. The grub prefers the inside of the stem where the tissues are softer and where it can keep away from the light. Therefore the stem from outside may appear unaffected although the tree is badly attacked. A cross section of a date palm stem shows it to be made up of a large number of fibrous strands lying side by side and more or less firmly bound together by other and usually softer tissues. Some of these fibres can be followed into the old leaf scars of the tree trunk, and others into the green leaves which crown the tree (see illustration No. 7, page 6a). The function of the strands connected with the green leaves is to conduct the food material from the soil to the leaves and the elaborated foods from the leaves back to the various parts of the plant. The leaves of a palm may therefore look healthy after the plants are badly affected if a sufficient number of the strands of tissues which feed these leaves remain uncut by the insect. Consequently also we sometimes see the sudden collapse of apparently healthy trees when at length these fibres are cut. At points where the insects have bored to the outside of the stem, a thick resinous juice has been found to ooze out and harden on drying.

The damage caused by the imago (adult weevil) is insignificant. When the adult weevils emerge from the cocoons they may fly to other trees and infect these. Apparently they are capable of flying great distances. They are recorded to have been seen on the wing in the insectary for 2-3 minutes at a time.

It has been advised by some writers that the leaves should
Preventive and remedial measures. not be pruned from the trees, but that they should be allowed to dry and fall off themselves. In my opinion that advice should not be followed in the case of date trees in the Punjab as (a) if there is any leaf disease such as the scale insect referred to on page 137 on the palms, the old leaves often become very badly infected and these spread the disease to the fresh young leaves coming out of the bud.

(*b*) After the palm leaves have passed the fresh green stage and are no longer capable of carrying on their functions of assimilation, transpiration, etc., with vigor, they are an encumbrance to the plant and the thorny mass of these old leaves forms a serious obstacle to attending properly to the fruit bunches.

(*c*) The leaving of the old leaves on the plant does not prevent the attack of the pest, as trees left absolutely unpruned are attacked. I recently cut down such a tree very badly affected at Mahmud Kot in Muzaffargarh district and could find many others among the unpruned male palms there. Unless the people want the leaves for any purpose the male plants in the Punjab are frequently left unpruned, as pollination is left entirely to the wind, and the people have usually no need to get at the male flower bunches.

The weevil is attracted by the tissues exposed when leaves are pruned from a tree and is suspected of laying its eggs in these tissues; but as the number of leaves removed from a tree in a year is very small it would be quite practicable to tar the cut surfaces left exposed, or treat them with other material which would keep the insects from attacking these parts. The cost of the tar required would be insignificant. All other wounds and places where soft tissue is exposed, should be tarred. When a tree slightly attacked is noticed, attempts should be made immediately to open the affected part as far as possible without unduly harming the tree, so as to get at, and kill the grubs; the wound then to be treated as above. If left untreated an attacked tree will certainly be severely harmed and will probably die. Cut stumps or useless parts of date trees left lying about should be destroyed. Palm stumps and soft palm tissues are said to be used in the West Indies to attract and trap a similar weevil there, the stumps, etc., being visited in the morning and the weevils collected and killed. It is [recommended that where the Rhinoceros beetle is found, the red weevil should be prevented from getting into the hole bored by the former beetle, by plugging these holes with dry grass or some such stuff after the Rhinoceros beetle has been extracted from them, and that the beetle may be extracted by probing the hole with an iron wire hooked or barbed at the end. A little tar on the top of the plug is also recommended.

In past years, however, I found that syringing 3 per cent. sanitary fluid, or an emulsion composed of 2 lb. Toria (*Brassica campestris var. toria*, Duthie) oil, $\frac{1}{2}$ oz. of asafœtida, and 2 gallons of water into the holes in the trees occupied by the red weevil gave good results, and the idea of getting insecticides to reach the insects when they have penetrated deep into the tree trunk has been further elaborated. In the most recent and most severe attack on our young Arabian trees, eighty palms approximately were more or less severely attacked by red weevil within a month of the removal of suckers from them. Insect burrows, 6 to 8 inches in length, were in many cases found in the stem at the bases of the green functional leaves, running parallel to the line of insertion of the leaf-base on the stem, and near enough the stem surface to be exposed along the whole length of the burrow by removing the leaf-base from the stem. Other burrows were found to penetrate into the hearts of young suckers that had been still left on the tree. Others again had gone deep into the tree trunk. Where burrows came near the surface of the stem, their presence was usually indicated by a copious flow of dirty juice from the stem at that point. Many nearly full-grown larvæ were taken out of the burrows while endeavours were made to get at those in the deeper burrows by probing with wires, injecting various insecticides into the burrows, etc. Later we cleared the débris from the insect burrows as far as possible, filled them with concentrated insecticide—undiluted sanitary fluid in some cases, crude oil emulsion or lead arsenate in others—made a large mud-basin round the base of each affected tree (*see* Illustration No. 46, page 118*a*), and filled the basins with water twice daily. The walls of the basins were made higher than the affected parts of the trees and the water was filled to over the levels of these parts. Large numbers of larvæ which had come out of the affected trees were found dead in the water within three or four days after this treatment started, and none came out after about a week of it. Of the 80 trees approximately affected, only three trees have died. The others appear to be cured of the disease and will apparently live, but as the attack did not occur till after this edition went first to press the effects of it on the fruit-bearing capacity of the trees will only be seen later. A more detailed account of the case will be given in due course. Meantime I may mention that we are indebted to Mr. J. Hallahan, Engineer to the District Board, Muzaffargarh, and to the Entomological Section, Lyallpur, for help in connection with the suppression of the outbreak.

When date trees are tall and the attack—as usually happens —occurs near the top of the stem the mud-basin method of bringing the liquid in contact with the insect would not be practicable. I hope, however, to devise suitable methods of dealing with such cases. Several ideas are being worked out and the results of these will be reported later.

It is most important for the checking of the disease in date-growing localities that all trees showing the symptoms already described should be treated or cut down, and burnt, or the pests in them otherwise rendered harmless immediately.

When affected trees have been cut down submerging the trunks in water is recommended to rid them of red weevil. This would be useful in the case of slightly affected trees, the trunks of which could be used for building or other purposes. One some-times sees the stems of date palms intended for such pur-poses, submerged in village ponds, etc., in the South-Western Punjab. From our experience already gained I am inclined to think that submerging for a week would be sufficient to disinfect a stem. I hope that some tests will be made soon which will give us further information wanted on this method and on others. It is, however, most important to remember that while a simple coating of tar on a wound will effectually prevent red weevil from attacking that wound, the pest is most destructive and difficult to deal with once it gets into a tree.

The disease has not yet been seen among the Arabian trees at Lyallpur, Rakhchhabri, and Charata in Dera Ghazi Khan; nor in the Central Jail, Multan, plantations. In 1914 in a plantation of 250 trees approximately in Muzaffargarh, some seven trees were attacked. All received some treatment. One of these died. In 1915 in the same plantation some 16 trees were affected. In many of the cases it was the suckers at the bases of the trees that were attacked. This was to be expected as the tissues of suckers are particularly soft and juicy. All these affected plants were treated by syringing an emulsion of oil of Toria (*Brassica campestris var. toria*, Duthie) and asafœtida into the holes made in the trees by the pest, and stopping the mouth of the holes by fibre dipped in tar. Some of the more weakly suckers died but no mother tree succumbed. In the case of the recent severe attack referred to above suckers had been removed in September from 180 trees and the wounds on the mother trees had not been tarred nor apparently properly earthed up. As about 80 of the plants, *i.e.*, 44 per cent. of them were at once attacked the case was most serious.

Proportion of cases of attack by red weevil.

So far as we can find from records, this is the first time on which a considerable number of suckers have been removed from date trees in the Punjab, and the effects of red weevil on the parent trees noted, but even if the percentage of trees attacked by red weevil were to be far less than in the case quoted when wounds caused by the removal of suckers are left exposed and untreated, it will still be of vital importance to date-growers to tar all such wounds immediately the suckers are removed. It cannot be too strongly emphasised that while this simple and inexpensive procedure will prevent red weevils from attacking these wounds, it is extremely difficult to prevent the insect from materially harming the tree for years, or killing it altogether once it gets in. It may also be noticed here that so far there seems to be no evidence to prove that the Rhinoceros beetle is connected with this attack.

ILLUSTRATION No. 46.

Photograph of Arabian date trees attacked by Red weevil, in the Taleri Bagh, Muzaffargarh showing mud basins which were filled with water during the treatment of the pest.
(*See* Preventive and Remedial Measures, *para.* 93, *page* 132.)

THE RHINOCEROS BEETLE OR BLACK PALM BEETLE. (Oryctes rhinoceros.)

(1) Eggs: that on left newly laid: that on right about to hatch.   (2) Young larva, natural size.

(3) Full grown larva.   (4) Pupa.   (5) Beetle.

(6) Beetle, side view of head of mlae enlarged.   (7) Beetle, side view of head of female enlarged.

The natural sizes of the stages shown in figs. 3—5 are indicated by the hair-lines alongside each figure.

Rhinoceros Beetle or Black Palm Beetle (*Oryctes rhinoceros*).

94. The pest is reported from Ceylon, Madras, Malabar, Bombay, Kanara, Bandra, Bengal, Tenasserim, Maliwon, Siam, Annam, Singapore, Pahang, Sumatra, Java, Celebes, Ceram, Amboyna, Philippine Islands, Formosa, Korea, and Hongkong.

It is said to do a great deal of damage to the toddy palm (*Phœnix sylvestris*) in Bombay, Madras and elsewhere in India. It has not yet been found in the Punjab, as far as I know, but as the work of observation on the diseases of the date palm is only starting here and the attacks of the red weevil (*see* page 126) are frequently associated with this pest elsewhere, it is possible that they are so in the Punjab, although this has not yet been proved. The few remarks made here regarding it are therefore made to help the people to recognise it and report to us if it should be found.

It is a dark brown beetle about 4 cms. long and having a prominent structure on its head resembling the horn of a rhinoceros, therefore the name (*see* illustration No. 47, page 134*b*). The elytra (hard wing cases) are marked by lines of closely placed annular punctures, one of these lines being close to where the two elytra meet on the insect's back, and three pairs of other lines rather wide apart. The tibia (longest segment of leg visible as the beetle walks) in each of the front pair of legs has four teeth along one side, the uppermost one of these being small. On the other side of the tibia and at its lower end, there is also a short and conspicuous tooth. The tibiæ of the middle pair of legs are much shorter than those of the hind ones.

The beetles are reported to appear after winter and the majority of them about May ; the greatest damage being reported about the time of the rains.

The usual mode of attack on palm trees is for the imago (mature beetle) to bore a hole 1 inch or more in diameter through the opening leaf-bud or stalks of the leaves into the succulent top of the stem. They are believed to feed on the soft tissues inside. When the insect bores down into the leaf-bud, it eats away many of the soft leaflets in the process, and when the bud opens the lateral rows of leaflets appear more or less raggedly eaten away from the main axes of the leaves. This appearance is usually found in the date trees in the South-West of the Punjab in which the " red weevils " have been found (see illustration No. 48 opposite).

It is stated that a quantity of chewed-up fibre is often found thrown out from the hole made by a Rhinoceros beetle. Quantities of such fibre are also commonly seen in summer on date trees affected with red weevil in the Punjab.

The beetles usually so damage the growing part of the tree that the tree ultimately dies. When rain falls, the water also lodges in the holes and sets up decay.

The beetles fly at night and hide in holes by day. They are attracted by light. The egg when laid is white, smooth, oval in outline, and $2 \times 3\frac{1}{2}$ mm. approximately, but becomes yellowish, rounder, and bigger before hatching. See Fig. 1 illustration No. 67, page 134b.

The young larva (worm-like stage) is about 6 mm. long with a flattened lower surface, pale yellow or greyish body, a row of yellowish dots along each side and numerous pale yellow hairs, yellowish brown head, and 3 pairs of pale yellow legs near the front of the body. See Fig. 2, illustration No. 47.

The full-grown larva is a big fleshy grub about 100 mm. (4 inches approximately) long when extended and about 25 mm. (1 inch approximately) across. It is thicker at the posterior end and lies doubled up ventrally. See Fig. 3, illustration No. 47.

The pupa (dormant stage) is about 45 mm. long and 20 mm. across. The legs and wing cases are distinctly marked on the ventral surface and so also is a protuberance on the head which represents the horn. See Fig. 4, illustration No. 47. The eggs, larvæ, and pupæ are usually found in dung heaps and decaying vegetable matter. Only the imago (mature beetles) are said to cause damage to living palm trees.

ILLUSTRATION No. 48.

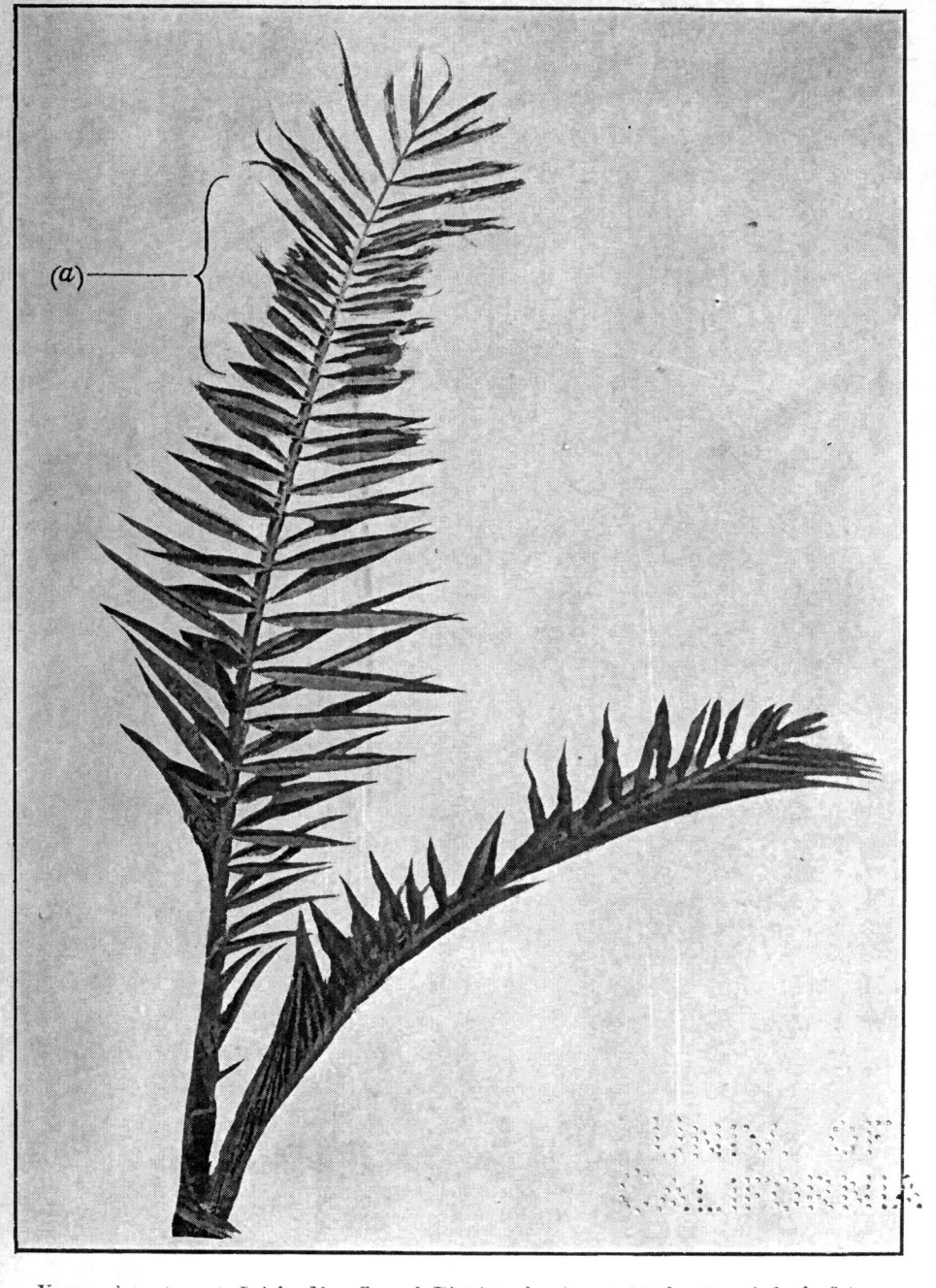

Young date tree at Leiah, Muzaffargarh District, showing at (a) the tips of the leaflets on both sides of the leaf axis eaten away. The leaflets came out of the bud in this state

(*See page* 136.)

Piece of leaf of Punjab-Arabian date palm about half natural size infested with scale insects. The insects are very tiny and appear like a white mealy substance on the leaf.

($\frac{11}{12}$th Natural size.)

(See page 137.)

ILLUSTRATION No. 50.

Scale Insects × 14 diams. on Date Palm leaflet.

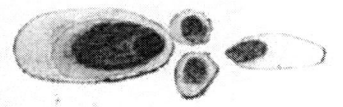

Nat. Size.

The darker body of the insect is seen through the thin, hard outer scale covering.

(*See page* 137.)

For more detailed information regarding this pest, *see*
(*a*) Memoirs of the Department of Agriculture in India, Entomological Series, Volume II, No. 10, Life-Histories of Insect
Pests, III, December, 1911, by C. C. Ghosh.

(*b*) Indian Insect Life by Lefroy, and

(*c*) Fauna of India, Vol.—Coleoptera Lamell, Part I,
from which the subject-matter for the above note has been taken.
The coloured illustration No. 47 at page 134*b* has also been
kindly supplied by the Imperial Entomologist to the Government
of India and is from (*a*) above mentioned.

I have already found two specimens of a beetle identified
for us by the Imperial Entomologist as Oryctes nasicornis. One
of these two was found in Dalhousie in early July, 1915, and the
other in Lyallpur a few weeks later. This beetle has a horn on
its head and might be mistaken by many people for Oryctes
rhinoceros. There are other beetles also which might be confused
with it; therefore likely specimens should be sent to the
Agricultural Department for identification.

Scale Insects (Coccideæ).

95. Scale Insects (*see* illustrations Nos. 49 and 50, pages
136*b* and 136*c*) are usually to be found in local date trees in the
date-growing districts of the province. They are most commonly
found on the leaflets and on the main axes of the leaves, in
the angles at the bases of the leaflets. When few, they are
usually restricted to the leaflets on the shady side of the trees,
or such places. They have attacked the imported trees much
more vigorously than the local ones; indeed they have hindered
the growth of the imported trees a good deal in some cases.
At Lyallpur, at Multan, or Muzaffargarh, in some years they
have even attacked the ripening fruit bunches spoiling the
appearance of the fruits. In no case has any of our imported
trees been killed by the pest however. It appears to waken
up with the rains, increase towards winter, remain evident on
the trees all winter, and then decrease as the temperature
increases till the rains come.

The insects are very minute and covered with a thin greyish scale. Full-grown insects are more or less oval in outline; usually 1 to 1½ mm. in length and approximately half as much in breadth. The body of the insect is seen through the covering scale as a darker spot often with a pinkish border. The whole thing is very flat and appears very closely adherent to the plant. In that stage the insect appears incapable of moving about.

Specimens of these insects have been sent to Pusa for identification but information on the point is not yet to hand.

Pending further information, we may remark here, however, that the *young* of coccidæ can generally walk actively and may go for some distance in search of a fresh food plant, thus spreading the disease. The female eventually settles down, buries a long beak in the tissues, and sucks the plant juices. The male, after passing through a period of rest, emerges as a very tiny two-winged fly, searches for a female, mates and dies; later the female produces eggs and dies (*see* Indian Insect Pests by Lefroy, page 243, and similar works).

Old leaves become most affected, therefore the plants should Remedial measures. be kept properly pruned, and diseased leaves thus removed should be burned. In some of the most attacked of our trees, we have pruned away practically all the leaves except those in the opening central bud. The remaining leaves are then easily treated with an insecticide. This drastic pruning may retard the growth of the tree a little but does not permanently harm it. Repeated spraying with almost any insecticide has a harmful effect on the leaves. The growth of the plant is therefore retarded even if the trees are sprayed without being pruned, and a larger quantity of insecticide is required. Where the attack is slight, however, only the old leaves should be removed and an insecticide should be sprayed on the plants.

The insecticide which has given us the best results is that recommended by Lefroy in Indian Insect Pests, page 284, No. 5.

It is called "Rosin Compound" and the directions for its preparation are as follows :—

"Powder 2 pounds of rosin and 1 pound of washing soda (sodium carbonate) crystals. Place these in a kerosene tin with enough water to cover them, and boil. Continue boiling till both are dissolved and then slowly add cold water to the steadily boiling fluid. Water is to be added a little at a time for fear of chilling the liquid, and the mass should gradually be brought up to 2 gallons. The liquid changes as the boiling proceeds, becoming thick and soapy ; after boiling for half an hour or longer the liquid becomes clear, thin, of a deep brown colour. Continue boiling pouring a few drops of the mixture into cold water at intervals ; at first the wash on mixing with cold water forms a slightly opaque fluid, but after some minutes further boiling, it forms a clear amber liquid on being mixed with cold water.

"This is the test of the liquid being finished and it should on cooling remain clear. To this stock solution 6 gallons of water may be added to make the strong wash ; 10 gallons to make the normal wash. One pound of rosin is used for every 4 to 6 gallons of wash required, and half as much soda. The wash keeps indefinitely if properly prepared, and it is best to keep the stock solution and dilute it as required."

The *fruit bunches* should not be sprayed with washes which will give them a bad taste, and poisonous washes must, of course, never be sprayed on the fruits.

INSECTS FOUND IN STORED DATE FRUITS.

96. In the winter and spring, the caterpillar of a moth
Tineid Moth. is sometimes found in date fruits in the Punjab. The caterpillar reaches a length of ½ inch approximately and a diameter of about ⅛ inch. It lives on the fleshy tissues of the fruits. The presence of the caterpillar, the excrement, and débris make an attacked fruit quite unfit for table purposes. Date-growers state that the attacks are most serious

in winters following wet fruit harvesting seasons. There was certainly a lot of damage done to stored date fruits by these insects in the winter following the wet harvesting season of 1914 and apparently none—at least in the fruits that I have had stored and examined, or in others that I have heard about—after the dry harvesting season of 1915. Specimens of the insects and attacked fruits have been sent to the Assistant Professor of Entomology, Lyallpur. That officer has not yet worked out the case completely but has given me the following note *protem.*

"The pest is a small Tineid Moth.

Life-history.—The eggs are laid singly on the outside of the fruit ; each egg is small and flattened. The caterpillar is of a dirty white colour with a palish tinge. As soon as it hatches out, it bores into the fruit and feeds on the soft pulp. It passes its whole life in the fruit and fills it with excrement. When the caterpillar is full fed it prepares a thin cocoon of silk and excrement and pupates inside it."

Experiments are in progress to discover just when the eggs are laid on the fruits and measures will be taken either to prevent the eggs being laid there or to sterilise them after they are laid ; whichever is most practicable.

A small more or less copper coloured beetle about $\frac{1}{12}$th inches long was found in date fruits stored at Lyallpur in 1914 and was sent to the Assistant Professor of Entomology. He informs me that it is Lesioderma testaceum, Duft, the beetle which bores into cigars. He writes as follows :—

Cigar boring beetle. (Lesioderma testaceum, Duft.)

"Its life-history is being studied and the following is a brief though incomplete account of it.

Life-history.—The female beetle gnaws a hole through the external skin of the fruit and deposits an egg in the soft pulp. Then the external hole is covered over. The eggs are laid singly by the beetle and are small and shiny. They hatch out in six days ; when the grub emerges it eats its way through the pulp, reaches the seed and tunnels into it. The whole of the fruit is filled with excrement. The pupa (dormant form) is situated inside the fruit in a thin silken case. The mature beetles, when they emerge, are quite active and feed on the external tissues of the fruit."

This beetle apparently gets into the fruits in the store room and where it is found precautions will have to be taken to store the fruits in such a way that it will not get at them.

CHAPTER VII.

Imports and Exports of Date Fruits and Prospects of Date Farming in the Punjab Plains.

97. Tables Nos. XXII, XXIII, XXIV, and XXV which

Quantities and value of date fruits imported into and exported from British India by sea during the five years ending March 31st, 1915.

follow, show the places from which date fruits were imported by sea into British India during the five years ending 31st March, 1915, the quantities imported from each place, the values of the consignments, and the total monthly quantities and values of those dates.

TABLE XXII.

Places from which dates were imported by sea into British India during the five years ending 31st March, 1915, quantities imported annually from each place, and values of the consignments.

Imported from	QUANTITY.					VALUE.				
	1910-11.	1911-12.	1912-13.	1913-14.	1914-15.	1910-11.	1911-12.	1912-13.	1913-14.	1914-15.
	Cwt.	Cwt.	Cwt.	Cwt.	Cwt.	£	£	£	£	£
United Kingdom	1	9,211	3	11	9	4	4,171	4	14	11
Aden and dependencies	22	*Nil.*	3,204	2	1	12	*Nil.*	1,696	1	1
Ceylon	376	195	262	177	188	148	81	121	81	83
Bahrein Islands	37,703	23,035	25,234	20,794	27,841	17,964	9,919	11,462	10,388	12,357
Straits Settlements (including Labuan).	533	222	302	238	86	295	119	128	124	33
Other British Possessions	7	6	10	11	2	2	4	6	7	2
TOTAL BRITISH EMPIRE	38,642	32,669	29,015	21,233	28,127	18,425	14,294	13,417	10,615	12,487
Turkey, Asiatic	507,455	*Nil.*	*Nil.*	*Nil.*	*Nil.*	201,093	*Nil.*	*Nil.*	*Nil.*	*Nil.*
Levant and Black Sea	*Nil.*	*Nil.*	27,176	1,262	*Nil.*	*Nil.*	*Nil.*	9,968	430	*Nil.*
Red Sea	*Nil.*	27	6	492	870	*Nil.*	14	2	131	376
Persian Gulf (Ports of the Gulf which were before the war Turkish).	*Nil.*	552,320	427,157	548,849	372,557	*Nil.*	204,225	155,088	218,468	146,453
Muskat Territory and Trucial Oman.	271,799	242,717	238,896	207,398	212,045	144,069	127,809	116,139	113,734	120,736
Other Native States in Arabia	75	15,749	30,802	32,822	23,951	38	6,778	12,177	13,335	9,743
Persia	92,052	119,693	122,966	105,069	146,761	43,000	48,513	51,038	44,029	63,534
Egypt	*Nil.*	*Nil.*	3	1,312	7	*Nil.*	*Nil.*	1	669	7
Other Foreign Countries	*Nil.*	*Nil.*	45	*Nil.*	*Nil.*	*Nil.*	*Nil.*	22	*Nil.*	*Nil.*
TOTAL FOREIGN COUNTRIES	871,381	930,506	847,051	897,204	756,191	388,300	387,429	344,435	390,796	340,849

Data obtained from the Director-General, Commercial Intelligence Department, India.

TABLE XXIII.

Monthly quantities of date fruits imported by sea into British India during the five years ending 31st March, 1915.

Month.	QUANTITY.				
	1910-11.	1911-12.	1912-13.	1913-14.	1914-15.
	Cwt.	Cwt.	Cwt.	Cwt.	Cwt.
April	15,290	28,077	18,343	13,035	11,298
May	8,920	14,984	3,803	5,753	6,301
June	6,580	8,680	9,102	10,197	7,719
July	5,808	10,632	6,281	13,391	10,125
August	54,685	33,574	45,915	29,156	52,175
September	80,590	62,888	75,184	83,398	37,175
October	138,543	107,101	195,938	177,427	111,187
November	199,427	219,642	239,353	237,132	131,296
December	199,473	219,491	141,795	152,293	129,527
January	96,166	158,481	88,970	96,383	161,258
February	53,303	68,090	33,904	50,751	77,231
March	51,238	31,535	17,478	49,521	66,026

Data obtained from the Director-General, Commercial Intelligence Department, India.

TABLE XXIV.

The monthly values of date fruits imported by sea into British India during the five years ending 31st March, 1916.

Month.	VALUE.				
	1910-11.	1911-12.	1912-13.	1913-14.	1914-15.
	Rs.	Rs.	Rs.	Rs.	Rs.
April	94,776	2,04,307	1,17,854	94,837	73,689
May	57,251	1,00,758	27,593	42,436	46,016
June	40,396	58,291	54,056	80,230	49,249
July	40,540	68,079	41,632	1,21,640	72,515
August	4,05,214	2,30,320	3,20,606	2,30,980	4,50,964
September	6,07,083	4,60,441	5,05,027	6,31,952	2,77,791
October	9,39,381	7,14,043	12,12,000	12,04,235	7,35,177
November	12,96,866	13,56,777	14,09,985	13,92,545	8,79,093
December	12,57,836	13,40,556	8,17,111	9,45,510	8,62,835
January	6,34,445	9,21,453	5,47,800	6,21,641	9,66,070
February	3,68,248	3,86,053	1,99,394	3,34,002	4,87,023
March	3,66,338	1,84,772	1,28,225	3,21,154	3,99,614

Data obtained from the Director-General, Commercial Intelligence Department, India.

TABLE XXV.

Annual quantities of date-fruits imported by sea into British India during the 5 years ending 31st March 1915, their ports of landing, total values and mean values per pound.

Year.	Total quantity imported in cwts.	Ports of landing.	Amount landed in cwts.	Value in £ sterling.	Total value in £ sterling.	Mean value per pound in pence and decimal fractions of a penny.
1910-11	910,023	Calcutta	25,537	13,416	407,225	0·96
		Bombay	635,628	297,632		
		Karachi	237,082	92,324		
		Madras	10,976	3,563		
		Rangoon	800	290		
1911-12	963,175	Calcutta	15,260	7,867	401,723	0·89
		Bombay	661,983	289,237		
		Karachi	244,635	90,619		
		Madras	40,586	13,748		
		Rangoon	711	252		
1912-13	876,066	Calcutta	22,451	11,481	358,752	0·87
		Bombay	586,915	249,340		
		Karachi	227,944	85,286		
		Madras	38,261	12,476		
		Rangoon	495	169		
1913-14	918,437	Calcutta	19,537	9,967	401,411	0·93
		Bombay	646,196	298,906		
		Karachi	212,675	79,170		
		Madras	39,134	12,830		
		Rangoon	895	538		
1914-15	784,318	Calcutta	3,861	1,976	353,336	0·96
		Bombay	559,261	267,007		
		Karachi	194,955	74,541		
		Madras	26,227	9,799		
		Rangoon	14	13		

Data obtained from the Director-General of the Commercial Intelligence Department, India.

From the data in Tables XXII to XXV, there are apparently 40,000 to 45,000 tons approximately of date-fruits annually imported into India by sea in addition to those grown in India and imported by land routes. The dates imported by sea arrive all the year round but October, November, and December are the chief months of import. The bulk of the fruits come from Persia including the Persian Gulf, Arabia, and Asiatic Turkey. Very few fruits come to India from Egypt and North Africa. Over $\frac{2}{3}$rds of the imports are landed at Bombay; about $\frac{1}{4}$ at Karachi and the remainder at the other Indian ports.

In reply to my enquiries, the Director-General of the Commercial Intelligence Department, India, writes :—" According to the provisions of the Indian Sea Customs Act the value of goods imported or exported represent (1) the wholesale cash price, less trade discount for which goods of the like kind and quality are sold or are capable of being sold at the time and place of importation or exportation as the case may be without any abatement or deduction whatever (except in the case of goods imported) of the amount of duties payable on the importation thereof ; or (2) where such price is not ascertainable, the cost at which goods of the like kind and quality could be delivered at such places without any abatement or deduction except as aforesaid."

The prices of dates vary of course according to the quality of the fruits, but they vary much more according to the way they are packed and the purposes for which they are to be used (see page 115, para. 86). The dates imported into India are all of fairly good quality. They are classified under the following three heads in the import tariff schedule : (1) dates, dry, in bags ; (2) dates, wet, in bags, baskets and bundles, and (3) dates, wet ; in pots, boxes and crates. Therefore there is no detailed information in the trade returns as to the amounts which are packed in small fancy boxes for dessert or sweetmeat purposes. I am told, however, that the amount packed for these purposes is negligible so the prices quoted in these returns will represent approximately the wholesale prices of dates which have been simply filled into large boxes, baskets, bags, etc., and imported in that state.

The following statement shows the average prices per cwt. of the different kinds of dates in each of the principal ports during the year October, 1914, to September, 1915.

TABLE XXVI.

	Calcutta.	Bombay.	Karachi.	Madras.	Rangoon.
	Rs. A. P.	Rs. A. P.	Rs. A. P.	Rs. A. P.	
Dates, dry, in bags ..	14 6 4	9 2 5	7 1 10	9 10 3	No quota-tions.
Dates, wet, in bags, baskets and bundles.	10 8 6	7 0 6	5 0 7	6 15 7	No quota-tions.
Dates, wet, in pots, boxes, tins, and crates.	16 9 6	5 15 4*	No quota-tions.	No quota-tions.	No quota-tions.

Data from Commercial Intelligence Department, India.

* *Note.*—The rates were nominal for the first eleven months of the period owing to the unsettled conditions arising from the war. Rs. 10 to Rs. 12 is the usual average rate per cwt.

These figures indicate that it is more profitable to preserve the dates by drying off only as much moisture as will keep them from fermenting, than to dry them hard, as much weight is lost in the latter process apparently without a corresponding rise in market price to compensate for that. The prices against the dates in boxes, tins, etc., bear out the statement that the quantity of fruits imported packed for dessert or sweetmeat purposes, is negligible. The returns for the 5 years ending 31st March 1915, show that the annual value of dates imported by sea into India is from over £350,000 to over £400,000, and that the average wholesale price per lb. is slightly less than one penny (*see* Table XXV). From the dates grown in India or imported into it by land or sea, there were apparently, from over 1,300 to over 1,900 tons of fruits exported annually in the past 5 years (*see* Table XXVII, page 148), and their value was from over £14,000 to over £20,000 (*see* Table XXVIII, page 149).

TABLE XXVII.

Places to which dates were exported by sea from British India during the 5 years ending 31st March 1915, quantities exported annually to each place and values of the consignments.

Exported to	QUANTITY (Cwt.)					VALUE (£)				
	1910-11	1911-12	1912-13	1913-14	1914-15	1910-11	1911-12	1912-13	1913-14	1914-15
United Kingdom	Nil.	Nil.	Nil.	Nil.	248	Nil.	Nil.	Nil.	Nil.	149
Aden and Dependencies	1,358	Nil.	1,400	86	Nil.	554	Nil.	731	60	Nil.
Bahrein Islands	Nil.	411.	487	2,990	Nil.	Nil.	208	162	926	Nil.
Ceylon	8,207	8,643	8,794	8,037	7,138	3,983	4,484	4,340	3,954	3,965
Straits Settlements (including Labuan)	20,317	20,113	10,788	19,600	13,416	9,553	10,227	5,524	11,912	6,932
Hongkong	7	34	Nil.	2	Nil.	5	18	Nil.	2	Nil.
Zanzibar and Pemba	1,547	2,229	3,331	1,443	1,429	874	1,223	1,500	916	809
East African Protectorate	814	243	716	608	1,058	503	130	430	326	566
Other British Possessions	146	156	205	70	171	90	61	127	40	105
TOTAL BRITISH EMPIRE	32,396	31,829	25,721	32,836	23,460	15,592	16,351	12,814	18,136	12,526
Muscat Territory and Trucial Oman	1,207	54	2,443	2	40	421	24	689	1	26
Persia	Nil.	Nil.	Nil.	Nil.	Nil.	Nil.	Nil.	Nil.	Nil.	Nil.
Siam	1,933	1,601	1,574	1,859	1,056	833	838	820	1,022	563
Portuguese East Africa	477	384	404	418	279	195	138	220	223	102
Italian East Africa (Somaliland) and Eritrea	1,600	2,323	772	464	2	784	1,040	388	253	2
Java	Nil.	Nil.	Nil.	Nil.	844	Nil.	Nil.	Nil.	Nil.	379
Madagaskar	35	59	88	214	71	14	25	41	112	34
German East Africa	1,056	842	1,320	1,087	986	554	426	746	635	517
Other Foreign Countries	11	198	221	16	228	8	104	109	11	110
TOTAL FOREIGN COUNTRIES	6,319	5,461	6,822	4,060	3,506	2,809	2,595	3,013	2,257	1,733

Data obtained from the Director-General, Commercial Intelligence Department, India.

Table XXVIII.

Annual quantities of date-fruits exported by sea from British India during the 5 years ending 31st March 1915, their ports of export, total value and mean value per pound.

Year.	Total quantity exported in cwt.	Ports of export.	Amount exported in cwts.	Value in £ sterling.	Total value in £ sterling.	Mean value per lb. in pence and decimal fractions of a pence.
1910-11	38,715	Calcutta .. Bombay .. Karachi .. Madras .. Rangoon ..	9 37,451 1,243 12 Nil.	5 17,973 418 5 Nil.	18,401	1·02
1911-12	37,290	Calcutta .. Bombay .. Karachi .. Madras .. Rangoon ..	Nil. 36,746 484 60 Nil.	Nil. 18,861 162 23 Nil.	19,046	1·09
1912-13	32,532	Calcutta .. Bombay .. Karachi .. Madras .. Rangoon ..	49 31,825 597 61 Nil.	25 15,556 219 27 Nil.	15,827	1·04
1913-14	36,896	Calcutta .. Bombay .. Karachi .. Madras .. Rangoon ..	14 33,405 3,312 11 154	11 19,207 1,035 5 135	20,393	1·14
1914-15	26,966	Calcutta .. Bombay .. Karachi .. Madras .. Rangoon ..	850 25,851 94 Nil. 171	385 13,752 42 Nil. 80	14,259	1·13

Data obtained from the Director-General, Commercial Intelligence Department, India.

Most of the dates were apparently exported in these years from Bombay, and the chief places to which the fruits were exported, seem to be Ceylon, Straits Settlements, Zanzibar, Siam, Italian East Africa, and German East Africa. It should be noted that the wholesale value of the dates imported into India works out to 0·87 to 0·96 pence per lb., while that of those exported works out to 1·02 to 1·14 pence per lb. The values are those given at the Indian ports in both cases; therefore, the chances are that the Indian importers simply re-exported the fruits at the higher price to cover custom dues, profits, etc. It seems rather curious, however, that considerable quantities of date-fruits have in some of these years been exported to such places as the Bahrein Islands, Muscat, and Oman. No satisfactory explanation of this is to hand but it seems possible that this may represent consignments returned to the owners in these places as unsatisfactory or for other reasons.

For the convenience of those who may wish to communicate with people in India already engaged in the date import trade, I append a list of importers of date-fruits into India (*see* page 154).

98. From what has been said above of our experience of date cultivation in the Punjab in the past 5 years and what we have seen on our tours in date-growing districts, it is quite evident that the date palm will grow luxuriantly over the whole of the plains if ordinary attention is given to it. It is also evident that high humidity combined with actual rainfall in the fruit-ripening season are the factors which limit the areas suitable for date-fruit farming in the province. Some idea of the maximum rainfall and humidity under which the fruits can be farmed, can be gathered from what has been written in this note, but a closer study of the case is required before more detailed statements are made. We know, however, that considerable crops of dates are annually got from date trees in Multan, Muzaffargarh, Dera Ghazi Khan and Jhang Districts, and it is clear that much can be done to improve date culture in these parts of the province at least. As already mentioned most of the plants grown in these districts as well as in other parts of the Punjab appear to have grown from seedlings, and the fruits produced by the vast majority of these are of very inferior quality. Only a few trees in the province produce fruits of good quality. Rs. 2-8-0 per maund is apparently a very fair price for the whole crop in the four districts mentioned. Taking 14,07,832 trees (*see* page 107) and 12 seers (24⅔ lbs.) of cured fruits per tree—the lowest estimate—the total value of the crop there would be Rs. 10,55,874, and if 18 seers ($36\frac{9}{10}$ lbs.) of cured

Prospects of date culture in the Punjab plains.

fruits are got the crop value would be Rs. 15,83,811. From the Journal of the Khedevial Agricultural Society, Volume 3, No. 6, page 263, November and December, 1901, I find data showing that the average quantity of dates exported from Egypt during a period of 15 years was 645 tons valued at £18 per ton or about 2 pence per lb. Taking into consideration the prices that dates are sold at, to the working class of people in the Punjab (*see* page 115, para. 86), the wholesale rates of dates imported into India (*see* page 142, para. 97), and the prices actually received by us for date-fruits grown on the trees imported into the Punjab from Basra, I do not think I am extravagant if I value those at 1 anna per lb. If this is so then by merely growing these varieties in place of the seedling females already grown, giving them no more cultivation or attention than is at present given to the local trees and getting only 12 seers ($24\frac{3}{5}$ lb.) of fruits per tree, the value of the crop would be raised to Rs. 21,64,541 and of 18 seers ($36\frac{9}{10}$ lb.) were got the value of the crop would be Rs. 32,46,812. In the date groves that I have examined there are over 50 per cent. male trees, and all information to hand seems to indicate that this may be taken as representing the state of affairs throughout the districts. Assuming this to be so then if cultivators would hand-pollinate their trees and thus require only 2 to 3 per cent. of male trees, they could replace the remaining 47 to 48 per cent. of males by good fruit-producing females and have practically double the harvest of fruits, *i.e.*, over Rs. 43,00,000 to Rs. 66,00,000 worth or about four times the value of the present crop from the same land and with the same water-supply. The only extra expenses to the grower would be that of hand-pollination which is practically nothing, and the guarding, collection and curing of the extra fruits. Practically the whole of the difference between Rs. 10,55,874 and Rs. 43,00,000 or between Rs. 15,83,811 and Rs. 66,00,000 would therefore go into the pockets of the date-growers. This difference of Rs. 30,00,000 to over Rs. 50,00,000 per annum could obviously be far exceeded as the trees would give much more than 12 to 18 seers of fruits each if they were fairly looked after. For these figures it is assumed that no more trees are to be grown than there are growing at present, but any one who has seen the large tracts of waste land lying along the sides of the rivers in these four districts will readily understand that the above estimate would fade into insignificance if only a small proportion of these wastes were planted with good date palms. Hundreds of square miles of lands which are at present yielding practically nothing would then become among the most remunerative in India (*see* page 117, para. 88), and the people would be supplied with a most sustaining food easily transported and capable of being preserved by the most simple means for many months. In districts the climates of which are suitable for date-growing and where the subsoil water or irrigation arrangements, etc., are suitable, those farmers who have no right to the waste lands referred to, can share in the benefits of date-farming by planting date trees along the borders of their fields, roadsides, water channels, etc. Then there is the possibility that we may be able to improve date culture in the districts mentioned or extend it to other districts by introducing varieties of dates which will ripen before or after the rainy season or by other means under consideration.

Fruits grown from good trees in the Punjab have been sold for far more than 1 anna per lb. (*see* page 115, para. 86), and it seems to me that any one who cares to take a little trouble to farm his plantation and cure his fruits properly could make very much more profit out of them for many years to come than is shown from my calculations based on that price.

99. Perhaps some one will suggest, however, that if date-farming became extensive in the Punjab, the market would be glutted with the fruits. I do not think so. In date-growing countries, dates often form more than half the food of the people. They are delicious to taste and would be preferred to many common foods by both rich and poor in any country. As already stated they are a most sustaining food. I have been in company with men who have walked 20 to 30 miles per day for hundreds of miles on end, with nothing to eat but an occasional handful of date

Over-production of dates.

and a little native bread. This was the fare of these men for many months each year, and they were as fit on it as any one could be on the most carefully selected food. Unlike most fruits, dates are, as already stated, so easily and simply preserved for many months that the question of an immediate market is not of vital importance. It seems to me that what is required to prevent a glut in their case is (*a*) their qualities as a food should be widely known, and (*b*) there shall be suitable facilities for their transport to markets. The great advances that have been made of late years in facilities for travel, transport of goods, and inter-communication among different peoples have already made date-fruits known practically all over the world ; therefore, there would be no difficulty in selling dates in any market. As regards (*b*) we have the Punjab rivers and a most excellent system of railways throughout the whole of India now, opening up to us a market of over 300,000,000 people in India alone. All the dates that are grown in the Punjab at present are simply swallowed up as soon as they are ripe by the people near where the dates are grown, and I have met people in the eastern side of the province who did not know that dates could be grown in the Punjab. Also Punjab date-fruits are only seen for a very short time after they are harvested. I feel sure that the population of the Punjab alone could consume many multiples of the quantities already consumed. In years of short crops or of famine owing to want of rain, dates would be at their best and would be very acceptable indeed. The extraordinarily high temperature, the extremely dry atmosphere and the plentiful supply of soil water required to grow dates successfully, is a combination extremely difficult to find and limits date cultivation to a very few places on the face of the earth.

D. MILNE,
Economic Botanist, Punjab, Lyallpur.

LIST OF IMPORTERS OF DATE-FRUITS
INTO INDIA.

KARACHI.

Salleh Mahomed Oomer Dossul, Napier Road.
Lalji Lakhmidass, Bombay Bazar.
Ruttonsi Purshotam, Bombay Bazar.
Haji Thawar Tharia, Kharadhar.
Rahmitoola Lutifali, Kharadhar.
Ramzan Hashim, Bombay Bazar.
Dharamdas Thawardas, Bombay Bazar.
Dhamanlal Gordhandas, Bombay Bazar.
Kushaldas Mangatram, Joria Bazar.
Jasam Majid, Kharadhar.
Haji Jetha Gokul, Khori Garden.
Harzuk bin Mahomed Marzuk, Kharadhar
Ismail Aziz, Kharadhar.
Naroomal Mewaram, Kharadhar.
Lekhraj Tikamdas, Kharadhar.
Raghunath Kalianji, Khori Garden.
Teka Moolchand, Mithadhar.
Moosajee Jafferjee, Napier Road.
Sunderdas Valabdas, Rampart Row.
Husseni Allidad, Kharadhar.

BOMBAY

Vassanji Nursee, Kharak Bazar, Mandvi.
Khetsi Ludha, Kharak Bazar, Mandvi
Chotalal Vadilal, Kharak Bazar, Mandvi.
Damodar Dharamsey, Kharak Bazar, Mandvi.
Allibhoy Chagla, Kharak Bazar, Mandvi.
Tricumji Damji, Kharak Bazar, Mandvi.
Allarakhia Abdulla, Kharak Bazar, Mandvi.
Lilladher Purshotam, Kharak Bazar, Mandvi.
Devji Cooverji, Kharak Bazar, Mandvi.
Mohanlal Bhawan, Kharak Bazar, Mandvi.

MADRAS PRESIDENCY.

Venktesh Naik, Coondapur.
Bande Narayana Pai, Coondapur

DATE-FRUITS.

MADRAS PRESIDENCY—(contd.)

Mowjee Vallabhdas, Hangarkatta.
T. Nagappa Kini, Hangarkatta.
Vaman Futher Kini, Malpe.
Hassan Abba, Mangalore.
Mahomed Moidin *alias* Mayappa, Mangalore.
Abdul Rahim Kutty Haji, Cannanore.
Manakat Moidin Cooty Haji, Cannanore.
Madathil Mamed, Cannanore.
Thackarakal Manoth Moidin Kutty, Tellicherry.
Adiyilagath Abdu, Tellicherry.
P. Abdul Rahiman Cootty, Badgara.
P. A. Koyaman Kutty Haji, Badgara.
P. Mahomed Haji, Badgara.
Palliparambath Mamed, Badgara.
A. Kaladum, Badgara.
A. Ibrayan Kunhi, Badgara.
Haji Karim Haji Mamed, Calicut.
Aderji Mancherji & Co., Calicut.
M. Ithan Coya, Calicut.
V. Ali Barami, Calicut.
Purushothem Goerdhan, Calicut.
Pithamber Sunderji, Calicut.
Hassan Kassan, Ponnani.
Haji Habib Haji Purmohamed, Ponnani.
P. M. Mohamed, of Kalvathy, British Cochin, Cochin.
Lalji Tejpal, Mathancherry, Native Cochin, Cochin.
Viljee Senejee, Mathancherry, Native Cochin, Cochin.
Danjee Laladhar, Mathancherry, Native Cochin, Cochin.
Hussan Cassim, Mathancherry, Native Cochin, Cochin.

BENGAL.

Gopal Dass Virjee, 50, Ezra Street, Calcutta.
Hajee Tar Mohamed Ayoob, 13, Amratolla Street, Calcutta.
Meghjee Ratanjee & Co., 28, Amratolla Street, Calcutta.
Dalsookhraj Khub Chand, 17, Amratolla Street, Calcutta.
Ratonjee Jivan Das, 19, Mullick Street, Calcutta.
Madhusudan Dey & Sons, 2-10, Bonfield's Lane, Calcutta.
Tribhuvan Heera Chand & Co., 9, Amratolla Street, Calcutta.
Kanai Lall Johur Mull, 4, Amratolla Street, Calcutta.

CPSIA information can be obtained at www.ICGtesting.com
Printed in the USA
LVOW090715080313

323337LV00009B/127/P